INTERNATIONAL YEARBOOK COMMUNICATION DESIGN 2012/2013

[Editor PETER ZEC]

VOL **2**

INTERNATIONAL YEARBOOK COMMUNICATION DESIGN 2012/2013

[Editor PETER ZEC]

reddot design award
communication design 2012

VOL **2**

MULTIMEDIA SPECIAL

DIGITAL PRESENTATIONS ON DVD
EDITORIAL, TYPOGRAPHY, EVENT DESIGN,
GAMES & ELECTRONIC ART, INTERFACES & APPS,
TV, FILM & CINEMA, CORPORATE FILMS,
SOUND DESIGN

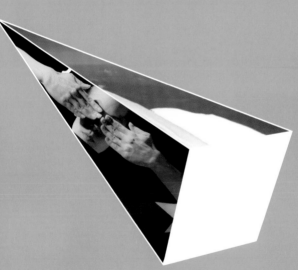

6823

entries in total participated in the
"red dot award: communication design 2012".

THE AWARD
BY THE NUMBERS

511

works were honoured with a red dot distinction by this year's jury.

0.9

per cent of all entries were awarded the "red dot: best of the best".

15

outstanding works were conferred the "red dot: grand prix".

2.36

minutes takes the corporate film for which three young designers won the endowed "red dot: junior prize".

1

st and most awarded client in this year's competition was: Mercedes-Benz.

601

bisang was awarded the honorary title "red dot: agency of the year 2012".

1

st time: the winners' exhibition in the Alte Münze Berlin is featured by guided tours & talks.

1412

seats are available in the glamorous Konzerthaus Berlin for the winners and guests of the red dot gala.

1153

certificates were printed for all winners of the "red dot award: communication design 2012".

Mercedes-Benz

Das Beste oder nichts.

red dot:
client of the year

THE BEST OR NOTHING.
Mercedes-Benz

Far more than a campaign slogan, this statement has been a permanent fixture of the Daimler corporation since its founding. Coined by founder Gottlieb Daimler, "The best or nothing" acts as an incentive and a benchmark at the same time. Many technical innovations that are taken for granted in automobiles today have their origin in Stuttgart, among them the safety cell, the anti-lock braking system, the airbag, the electronic stability programme and the drowsiness detection system "Attention Assist".

Again and again, Daimler managed to set new standards. The accomplished and confident brand presence is reflected not only in the technology and the product design, but also in the communication design. In 2010, Mercedes-Benz revamped its corporate design, namely by merging the visual and verbal elements of the brand – the star and the word "Mercedes-Benz". The star now has a three-dimensional and chrome-coloured appearance. And both of these elements are complemented with the slogan "The best or nothing".

In the year 2011, Mercedes-Benz celebrated the 125th birthday of the automobile. With the anniversary campaign "Inventors of the automobile. Since 1886!" Mercedes-Benz proclaimed its position as a premium brand. In this year's "red dot award: communication design", no less than ten awards were given to the brand with the three-pointed star, and a total of eleven awards to the Daimler corporation.

As no other competition participant was more successful, Mercedes-Benz was granted the honorary title "red dot: client of the year 2012". Anders Sundt Jensen has been at Daimler for more than 20 years and is, since November 2008, Head of Brand Communications Mercedes-Benz Cars. In an interview with red dot, he spoke about the communication of the premium brand.

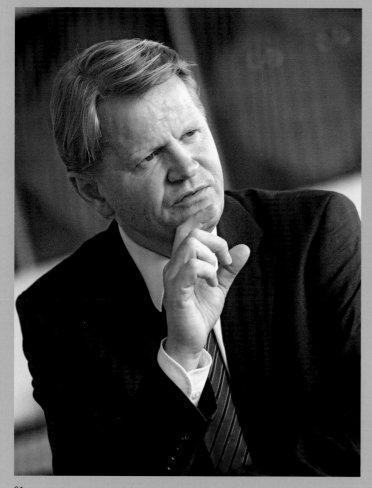

01

02/03

MERCEDES-BENZ
UNDER A GOOD STAR

01   **Anders Sundt Jensen**
      Head of Brand Communications
      Mercedes-Benz Cars

02   **Mercedes Next!**
/03 [Trade Fair Exhibition at the IAA 2011]

04   **smart eball**
      [Game Event]

Mr. Jensen, what distinguishes the Mercedes-Benz brand from other premium brands in the automobile sector?
We have a distinct history, as a brand, that sets us apart from the competition. However, at the same time we take care to continue developing the brand on an ongoing basis. And, at all times, our ability to inspire awe and fascination is the core of our focus.

What values do you attach to this ability to inspire awe?
Basically, we want to expand our role as a driver of innovation in the automobile industry, because, as the inventor of the automobile, Mercedes-Benz has always been a significant force in the development of the automobile. This is also reflected in our management philosophy that prioritises the brand values perfection, fascination and responsibility.

What role does the "Made in Germany" label play, which is as old as the automobile? How "German" is the Mercedes-Benz brand outside of Germany?
The perception of our brand is not uniform throughout the world. In Asia, Mercedes-Benz is strongly associated with its geographic origin, yet in a very positive sense. In other markets, we're perceived more as a global premium brand. There, the emphasis in our communications on the German origin of the brand is rather subdued.

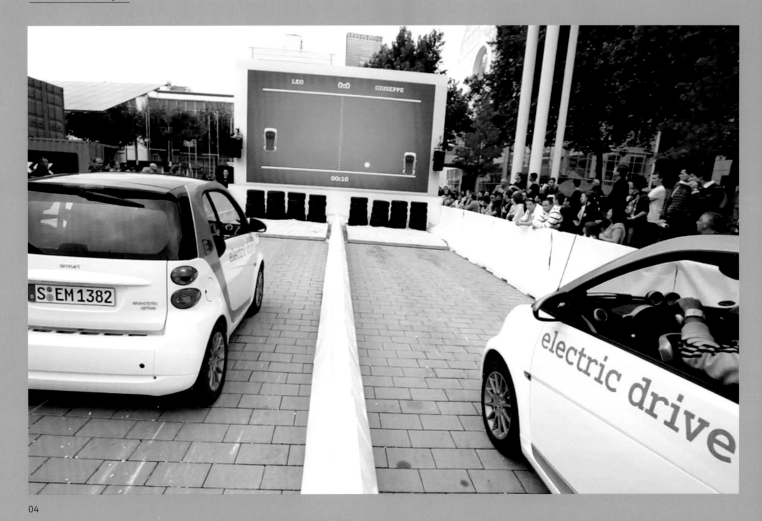

04

The orientation towards brands appears to be increasingly important in a globalised world. Is there anything that needs special consideration in the management of global brands?
Global brand management is not a 100-metre sprint but a never-ending marathon. To look at only the current situation would be myopic. However, this year our focus is to continue our effort to open up towards younger target groups.

Where do you see opportunities and risks for the Mercedes-Benz brand with regard to younger target groups?
Reaching out to new target groups is of immense value to us. The young people that we can "wow" for the Mercedes-Benz brand today are tomorrow's clients. However, at the same time we have to continue communicating with and retaining our long-standing clientele. Developing the brand, authentically, in that state of tension, bears certain risks. Yet these are risks we are well prepared to face.

Today, Mercedes-Benz calls into play a wide array of media in order to allow clients to engage in the brand experience. How has the mix of analogue and digital media changed under your management?
In the past years, digital media have gained enormously in significance in brand and product communications. Today, the Internet and new media are, aside from the dealerships, the most important source of information for our clients and those wishing to find out more about Mercedes-Benz.

In that sense, we view digital communication as an essential complement and expansion of the classic communication mix consisting of print and film. In particular when reaching out to and capturing modern and younger target groups, the web is the contact medium number one. Social media platforms are our main media channel for marketing and communication. And, here we are currently moving from monologue to dialogue, in other words, from of a traditional web presence to open, dialogue-oriented offers. For this reason, we've adapted our events on the web and in the new media to the media use behaviour of these target groups.

The agency Scholz & Volkmer was awarded with a red dot for its relaunch of Mercedes-Benz.com. The brand's Internet platform is designed to function as an online "brand magazine". Where do you think the emphasis lies? In "content is king" or "the medium is the message"?
There's no question about it – in "content is king". Here as well, our mission is to give clients "the best or nothing". Given the virtually infinite offer on the World Wide Web, our offers have to convince content-wise and be relevant to the target group. Only in this way will users come back again and again and stay in touch. Of course, this requires an immense public relations effort. However, we believe that this will pay off in the long term. At present we have more than eight million Facebook fans – that speaks for itself.

DIE STIRN BIETEN

Look to the side without looking to the side.
Blind Spot Assist from Mercedes-Benz.

Mercedes-Benz
The best or nothing.

ALLES FLIESST. *Die optische Verbindung zwischen den Radläufen*
ist strömungstechnisch das Optimum. Dass etwas so Nützliches gleichzeitig auch
so KRAFTVOLL *und so* DYNAMISCH *gestaltet sein kann, diesen*
Beweis kann man gar nicht oft genug so schön vor Augen geführt bekommen.

Look to the side without looking to the side.
Blind Spot Assist from Mercedes-Benz.

Mercedes-Benz
The best or nothing.

05   06

As the inventor of the automobile, Mercedes-Benz stands like no other brand for a time-honed tradition. Is this an advantage or a disadvantage as regards new media?

None of that. A strong tradition is neither an advantage nor a disadvantage. The digital channels give us access to target groups that we would have no way of reaching otherwise. The digital world also offers a wide range of possibilities for explaining things in detail. Our new Tech-Center, for example, makes extensive use of this to explain Mercedes-Benz technologies. It always boils down to (primarily) recognising the preferences of users and to getting them on the same page as regards the content we wish to communicate.

When clients use digital media, they leave traces on the Internet. So, what is happening behind the pretty user screens of Mercedes-Benz online? What findings have emerged from your evaluations of how users use those screens?

What we are most interested in is what contents are accepted by our users and which ones are not. Because knowing that allows us to continuously optimise our offer. That's not to say that we haven't had our share of surprises; in particular in the early days of new media we had to invest quite a bit, time- and budget-wise, in the learning curve.

To what extent do you allow consumers to participate in an open dialogue? And how difficult is it to strike a balance between transparency and openness on the one hand and leadership and direction of the brand on the other hand?

We've been very active for quite a few years in social networks, such as Facebook and Google+, and are using these platforms to inform, very early on, about new products and other offers such as events. Our goal here is to establish an open dialogue with our target groups. The new digital media have certainly brought about change in marketing and communications in the last years. At a cultural and structural level, we've had to adapt to the growing significance of real time, in other words, to think more in terms of interaction and to engage in dialogue. We had to learn to deal with open communication. However, the loss of control is more than compensated for by the gain in credibility. At Mercedes-Benz, we were active early on in the new media and social networks and have integrated these into our marketing and campaign planning. And today, they are an integral component of all our communications activities.

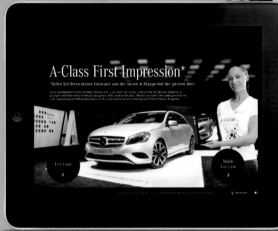

07/08/09

For your marketing and communications needs,
you engage the services of a great number of agencies.
How do you deal with the many different personalities
and characters?
Well, you know our brand claim "The best or nothing".
This also applies to how we deal with our partner agencies.
And, let me tell you, we have very, very good agencies
with whom we work.

Where do you see the biggest challenges
for creative and media agencies?
We're convinced that campaigns should have even more
of a cross-media approach. It's immensely important to
speak with those responsible for purchasing the media
and ads very early on in the campaign development about
how to reach the target group as efficiently as possible.
This is also important because you can't always expect
a one-to-one transfer when switching content from
conventional channels to digital media. You have to stick
to an underlying concept, but the content has to be adapted to each medium. At the same time, you have to make
sure that the consumers are given elements that they can
recognise and that they're already familiar with, be it in
the form of colours, shapes or sounds. To realise this without a loss in effectiveness and efficiency is only possible
if there's a strong and close collaboration between the
agencies. This will be one of the upcoming challenges for
the agencies and us.

Is there an area where the creatives
could improve, in your opinion?
They could be more efficient in contributing to selling
our cars in saturated markets. This can only happen
by delivering the right stimuli at the right time, and by
having the passion for it.

Mr. Jensen, thank you very much for the
conversation and congratulations to the distinction
"red dot: client of the year 2012".

05   **Dimensionen / Dimensions**
     [Magazine, Special Publication]

06   **Look Twice**
     [Illustration, Poster, Print Ad]

07   **A-Class First Impression**
     [Web Special]

08   **Mercedes-Benz.com**
     [Website]

09   **AVANT/GARDE DIARIES**
     [Microsite]

Packaging Design

red dot: grand prix

grafik:plastic

[Glasses/Sunglasses Case]

The "grafik:plastic" glasses brand opens up a new approach concerning user experience and client interaction. Created as part of a promotion campaign, the packaging design systematically integrates clients into itself. Profile photos of prospective customers are used and applied to paper holders that fit right into the semi-translucent plastic case when folded. This not only evokes the impression that this person is wearing these glasses, but simultaneously also demonstrates to each new customer how glasses effectively change a face. Customers are thus invited to become part of the collection of hundreds of faces that make up the campaign already. Other components in the package are paper bags that also feature faces, cases for the exchangeable temples that can be used with the glasses frames and a white cleaner fabric that reads "I can see clearly now". The backside of the profile photographs features a user manual written in four languages, the company history, quality claim and the hint that the glasses case can also be used for other purposes such as a pen case or for jewellery.

Statement by the jury

»The packaging design impresses with the outstanding idea of how it presents the glasses. The faces help make immediately clear how the glasses will look when being worn, thus allowing prospective wearers to connect with the brand. The entire appearance follows a simple and humorous approach that immediately attracts attention.«

client
GRAFIK FACTORY,
Seoul

design
GRAFIK FACTORY,
Seoul
Jong Yeol Baik

→ designer portrait: p. 413

kiyutaro weather station
[Packaging]

Different kinds of weather can cause different taste sensations; this assumption provides the backdrop against which the packaging design of the food label kiyutaro was designed. The way the spicy taste of wasabi brings tears to the eyes is similar to rain falling on people's faces on a rainy day; the aroma of curry is associated with the wind on a beautiful moonlit night; and the sweet taste of caramel is connected with sunshine. Accordingly, the white cardboard packaging features distinctive typographical labels that identify the different meteorologically inspired product names such as "Thunder storm" or "Sunny day", complemented by drawn illustrations showing reduced and charming motifs. The idea here is that these illustrations integrate the product itself, a popular Taiwanese root snack, in its actual shape as sunbeams, raindrops or thunder, by presenting it visually on the packaging. Thus, in an original way, consumers are offered new experiences of taste that congenially correspond to different weather conditions.

Statement by the jury

»This packaging design surprises with a sophisticated concept for a common Taiwanese product. The idea of having different motifs reflect the moods evoked by different types of weather and thus to identify the different flavours of the snacks is highly humorous and has been realised in a convincingly simple and cheerful manner.«

client
kiyutaro,
Kaohsiung City

design
Victor Branding Design Corp.,
Taichung

head of marketing
Fred Wang,
B. B. Shee

creative direction
Chung Yuan Kuo

art direction
Bee Liu

graphic design
Johnny Hsu

text
Lynn Lin

→ designer portrait: p. 441

red dot: best of the best

milk talk

[Body Wash Packaging]

With the product series "milk talk" the Asian beauty and cosmetic brand Etude
aims to provide its customers with a joyful shower time through a humorous design.
The bottles of these wash lotions are made of a material with a soft texture that
has a highly pleasant feel, echoing the product name and evoking associations of
milk. The moisturising body soaps are scented with real strawberry, apple or banana,
which is not only indicated in the colour of the bottles but also in the illustrations in
combination with the names. The fruits are furthermore reflected in the supplemented
sponge tops, which were designed according to the different scents of the body soaps.
On the one hand, they aim to allow the target group of 16 to 22 year old girls to identify
themselves with their individual scent, and on the other hand they help space in
bathrooms to be used more efficiently.

Statement by the jury

»This packaging design is more than just a container for a shower lotion with a fresh
and young design. It provides added value with the sponge that is at the same time
a toy but also highly useful. With its colour choice and the cheerful illustrations,
the entire design is highly self-explanatory, allowing the target group to positively
identify with it.«

client
Etude Co., LTD,
Seoul

design
Design Team Etude Co., LTD,
Seoul

head of marketing
Jung Jae Won,
Yu Cha Young

product design
Sul Se Mi

graphic design
Kim Min Hee,
Choi Ji Yee

project management
Jung Mi Jung

strategic planning
Yu Yeon Jeong

→ designer portrait: p. 410

Hands Up Deodorant Depilatory

[Packaging]

The Hands Up series is a product range for girls in Asia, who tend to be shy about using deodorants and depilatory products. The unique product packaging achieves a witty brand identity. Arm-shaped embossing is added to the packages, urging users to put up their hands with confidence. Complemented by a smiling face as the key visual, the containers look like people putting up their hands out of joy and excitement at a concert. The paper boxes and spray cans encourage in a humorous way to interact with the arm-shaped embossing.

client
Etude Co., LTD,
Seoul

design
Design Team Etude Co., LTD,
Seoul

head of marketing
Jung Jae Won,
Yu Cha Young

art direction
Jung Mi Jung

design concept
Sul Se Mi,
Yu Yeon Jeong

product design
Sul Se Mi,
Lee Mi Jin

graphic design
Kim Min Hee,
Kim Ji Eun (purun image)

strategic planning
Yu Yeon Jeong

→ designer portrait: p. 410

Missing You Honey Bee Hand Cream

[Packaging]

The hand cream series Missing You Honey Bee from the Asian cosmetic brand Etude is the main product of a campaign for the protection of honey bees. The charmingly designed containers represent little insects and are made of a material that is easy to recycle. The honeycomb-shaped outer box is made of recycled newspaper and printed with soy-based ink. The hand creams are made of 90 per cent natural ingredients, free of parabens and colourants. Part of the profits are donated to the international organisation WSBF (World Save Bee Fund).

client
Etude Co., LTD,
Seoul

design
Design Team Etude Co., LTD,
Seoul

head of marketing
Jung Jae Won

creative direction
Jung Mi Jung,
Yu Cha Young

product design
Sul Se Mi

graphic design
Sul Se Mi,
Kim Bo Ram (purun image)

concept
Jung Kyung A

product planning
Yu Yeon Jeong

→ designer portrait: p. 410

heidelberger
naturkosmetik

[Packaging]

heidelberger naturkosmetik
is a new brand of high-quality
natural cosmetics for kids.
The certified products contain
natural ingredients from controlled organic cultivation. With
funny ideas and stories about
Karo the Cat and an innovative
packaging solution, the cosmetics line aims to convey the fun
aspects of natural body care
to its young target group.
The design concept also allows
for a valuable educational alternative use of the packaging:
children may play with the boxes,
using them to build towers and
bridges of a knight's castle.

client
Tinti GmbH & Co. KG,
Heidelberg

head of marketing
Simone Ristock

design
Heidi Fleig-Golks,
grafik und form,
Weinheim

concept
Heidi Fleig-Golks

graphic design/illustration
Heidi Fleig-Golks

text
Steffen Herbold

public relations
Philipp Dieterich

→ designer portrait: p. 411

Kokorico

[Packaging]

Jean Paul Gaultier's new male fragrance is an expression of confident, urban masculinity. The onomatopoeic name, Kokorico, inspired by the cocky outcry of the rooster, embodies the spirit of the fragrance. The highlight of the packaging design is the duality of the flacon: head-on, it shows a man's face, in profile, and from the side, the silhouette of a torso. This sense of surprise and sensuality is further dramatised with a bold, red and black colour palette.

client
Beauté Prestige International, Paris

design
Interbrand Paris

HUMIECKI & GRAEF

[Packaging,
Limited Porcelain Edition]

client
HUMIECKI & GRAEF GmbH,
Zurich

head of marketing
Andreas Oettmeier

design
BEL EPOK GmbH,
Cologne

creative direction/concept
Sebastian Fischenich

project management
Stephanie Herse

illustration
Wouter Dolk

production
Erhard Kämmer,
Porzellanmanufaktur
Kämmer

→ designer portrait: p. 408

The limited porcelain edition of the luxury perfume brand HUMIECKI & GRAEF comprises four fragrances, with an exclusive production of only 130 flacons each. The challenge was to develop a rectangular porcelain flacon, which formally recalls the design of the brand's basic products. With a specially developed blowing technique, the flacons were glazed from the inside to make them suitable for perfume oils and alcohol. The decorative floral motifs were designed in collaboration with the Dutch artist Wouter Dolk and applied with a traditional hand-painting technique. The protective outer packaging is made of high-quality paper board; the flacon rests like a relic on a linen bed within.

VETIA FLORIS

[Packaging]

client
Skin Concept AG,
Affoltern am Albis

design
ALL – A'Court Law Ltd,
London

→ designer portrait: p. 432

Rare and hardy alpine flowers that grow in cool, high-altitude air inspired the Swiss cosmetics manufacturer to create the skin care series Vetia Floris. The packaging reflects the luxury feel, while the colours were selected not only according to their symbolic meaning: gold, the colour of power, pride and luxury, emphasises that gold is also used as a natural ingredient in the products. White, as the colour of purity, perfection and the divine, illustrates that white flowers are part of the formulation. Black, as a basic colour, stands for prosperity, elegance, power and modernity. The packaging concept includes glass jar, flacon, inside box, leaflet and spatula.

Pola B.A

[Packaging]

This exclusive cosmetics series
by Pola was created to fulfil
desires, its quality conveying
a feeling of luxury to customers.
The elegant silhouette of the
containers is impressively
emphasised by elegantly curved
lines – reminiscent of the arched
roofs of Japanese shrines and
castles. The bronze-coloured,
shiny surface evokes a pleasantly
tactile sensation. The packaging
design aims to create a product
identity, which appeals to
the emotions of women who hold
these cosmetic containers in
their hands.

client
Pola, Inc.,
Tokyo

design
Pola Chemical Industries, Inc.,
Tokyo

creative direction
Takeshi Usui

art direction
Takashi Matsui

design team
Kentaro Ito,
Yushi Watanabe

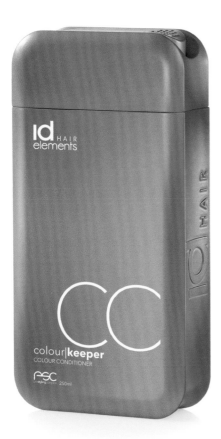

IdHAIR Hair Care Product Line

[Plastic Bottles]

Objectivity, precision and new operating functions are what distinguish these bottles, which convey the effectiveness of the hair care products and the classification of the product line in a highly coherent manner. The integrative design includes common cap elements, such as hinged lids and standard pumps, and clearly defines their function through the semantics of the control areas. The embossed logo on the side creates high product recognition and guarantees that the bottle rests comfortably and safely in the hand.

client
IdHAIR Company A/S,
Lystrup

design
Rolf Hering,
Hering's Büro,
Kronach

project management
Dr. Matthias Rebhan,
Rebhan GmbH & Co. KG FPS
Kunststoff-Verpackungen

→ designer portrait: p. 417

Esthaar

[Packaging]

Esthaar is a natural hair care series with an energising system whose active ingredients are extracted from herbal sprouts. The asymmetric shape lends the shampoo bottle a natural appeal, while the pump cap, reminiscent of a pebble stone, has a highly pleasing feel. The logo at the top end of the bottle represents the brand identity and, furthermore, creates a non-slip surface. The self-contained packaging design moreover impresses through its delicate, natural colours with pearl effect.

client
Aekyung Industry,
Seoul

design
Aekyung Industry,
Seoul

Innisfree Forest for Men

[Packaging]

Innisfree is a Korean natural cosmetics brand with plant-based active ingredients extracted from the untouched nature of Jeju Island. The Forest for Men collection promises a relaxing effect. The packaging design is an expression of the life force and the majestic aesthetics of the Jeju Gotjawal forest. The design language of the labels features masculine lines. The containers rest comfortably in the hand and are made of a recyclable material produced using a low-carbon manufacturing process. The two series differ in regard to their basic colour.

client
AMOREPACIFIC Corporation, Seoul

design
AMOREPACIFIC Corporation, Seoul
Innisfree Design Team, Seoul
Jihye Park, Yeonji Kong
Duffy & Partners, Minneapolis

Theodent
Toothpaste

[Packaging]

design
Theodent,
New Orleans

creative direction
Arman Sadeghpour

graphic design
Rencher Lann

strategic planning
Tetsuo Nakamoto,
Joseph Fuselier

project management
Jantzen Hubbard

photography
Theresa Cassagne,
Anthony Verde

tube engineers
Jeffrey Hayet,
Michael Furey

box printing
Karen Del Bianco

→ designer portrait: p. 438

The packaging design for Theodent, a revolutionary new toothpaste line, purports an extract from the cocoa bean as a non-toxic alternative to traditional toxic fluoride therapies. This toothpaste is for the discerning customer with its proprietary and patented active ingredient "Rennou". With a new look for the oral care market, it recalls the aesthetics of the finest chocolate packaging. The nostalgic logotype is surrounded by classic filigree and an embossed emblem of a cacao pod. The copper foil provides a beautiful contrast against the chocolate-brown and crème-white tubes. The cap shines elegantly in a brilliant copper surface. The innovative shape of the honed tip dispenses the toothpaste in a perfectly dosed flat ribbon, to match the rectangular shape of a toothbrush head. Theodent aims to be the new gold standard in oral care.

LEDERHAAS
Collection Box 1800

[Soap Wrappers, Cardboard Box]

client
LEDERHAAS Cosmetics e.U.,
Vienna

design
LEDERHAAS Cosmetics e.U.,
Vienna

creative direction
Wolfgang Lederhaas,
LEDERHAAS Cosmetics e.U.

art direction/logo lettering
Roland Hörmann,
phospho type foundry

concept
Wolfgang Lederhaas,
LEDERHAAS Cosmetics e.U.

graphic design
Roland Hörmann,
phospho type foundry;
Albert Scoma

printing
Wilhelm Beyer,
pri-ma.net print-management

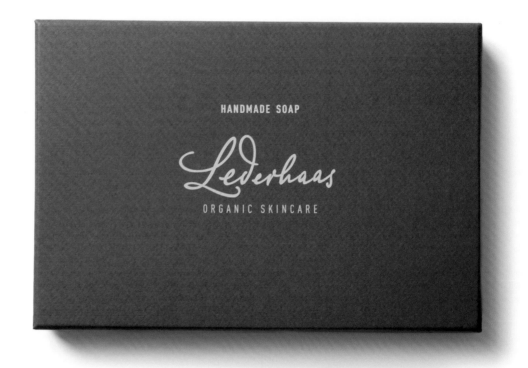

The inspiration for the "Collection Box 1800" of handmade organic soaps was drawn from six romantic novels and short stories from around 1800. The logo was developed from the handwriting of the poet Novalis, which lends the cardboard box its romantic signature and underlines the artisanal character of the company. The elaborate box manufactured from natural materials plays with the contrast of a dark mineral-like outside and a bright white inside, which – after folding back the white parchment sheet – reveals organic natural colours.

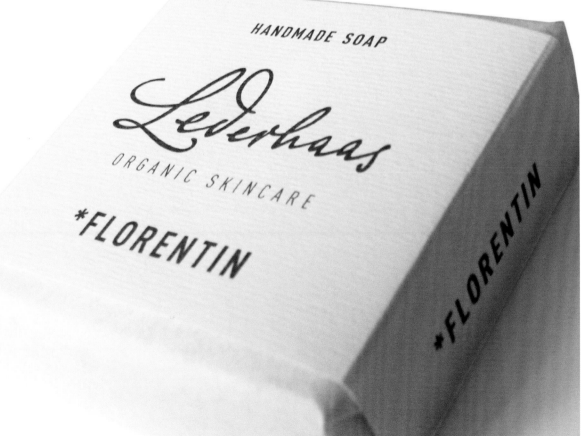

Oona –
the first Swiss caviar

[Packaging]

This caviar from Siberian
sturgeons raised in alpine water
in Switzerland is highly original.
It comes packed in an aesthetically appealing ice cube, which
conveys quality, indulgence and
purity. The handcrafted transparent glass cube in the form of
an ice cube symbolises the origin
of water. The caviar rests in
the centre of the cube, shaped
like a ball, as reflection of a
perfect pearl of caviar. Form and
aesthetics encourage the use
of the ice cube as a stylish
decorative objective, once the
caviar inside has been consumed.

client
Tropenhaus Frutigen AG,
Frutigen

design
ARD DESIGN SWITZERLAND –
Zurich AG, Zurich

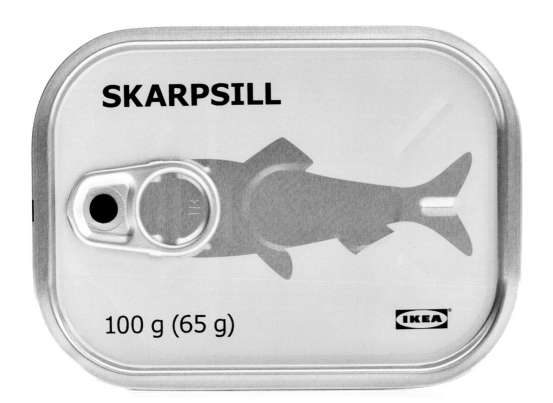

IKEA SKARPSILL

[Food Packaging]

IKEA's private food label offers Swedish quality products for reasonable prices and is sold everywhere in the world. The challenge for the design of this tin of herrings was to present the food, despite its Swedish product name, in a self-explanatory and appetising way. The use of IKEA's house font Verdana in a set style and size creates a high level of recognition. The purist graphics convey the content in a humorous way, and form a visual entity with the opening tab, creating a piece of packaging that is easily understood by consumers all over the world.

client
IKEA FOOD SERVICES AB, Helsingborg

design
Stockholm Design Lab, Stockholm
Björn Kusoffsky, Nina Granath

project management
Camilla Nilsson

Tzukuan
Seafood Pastry
[Packaging]

Taiwanese fishing culture inspired the packaging design of
these seafood pastries. Each
box shows a fish, with different
flavours marked by different
colours. With a string, two or
three packages can be packed
together as a gift set. This recalls
the traditional way fishermen
packed their dry fish to share
with friends and family in ancient
times. In this way, they shared
not only the fish but also their
happiness – an idea that the
packaging promotes in a symbolic
way.

client
Tzukuan Fisheries Association,
Kaohsiung City

design
Bosin Design,
Kaohsiung City

Olami

[Packaging]

Olami, a hand-made mini salami from the Eifel region, presents itself in a rustic wooden box with burnt-in logotype and mechanical copper clasp. The tear-open paper sleeve features a reduced layout with hand-drawn pig illustrations and an elegant, simple typography. Subdued, bold colours on a coarse natural paper reflect the characteristics of the naturally produced product. All elements of the packaging are consistently balanced and lend the product a young, modern and high-quality appeal.

client
Olami UG,
Cologne

design
großgestalten
kommunikationsdesign,
Cologne
Tobias Groß,
Dominik Kirgus

illustration
André Gottschalk

John & John

[Packaging Concept]

John & John Crisps are "hand cooked style" crisps made in Great Britain. The high quality of the product is reflected in the independent packaging concept, which stands out from competitors by its clear graphics. Unlike common designs for the German market, the packaging does completely without food images. Different flavours are communicated by different relief stamping motifs, numbers, individual colour codes and the signs of the international maritime signal flags. The British origin is conveyed through the brand name and the designation of the flavour varieties in English. The open design allows for future extensions of the product line.

client
Market Grounds GmbH & Co. KG, Hamburg

design
Peter Schmidt Group, Hamburg

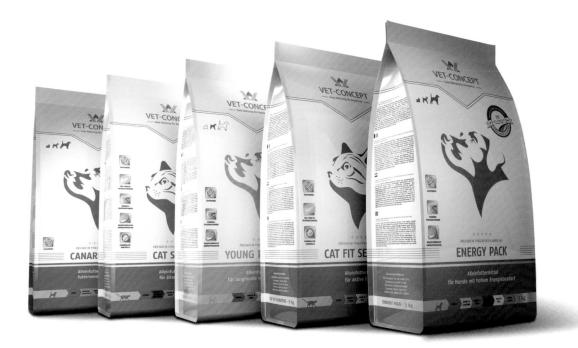

Vet-Concept

[Packaging]

The packaging is characterised by clear and understated graphics. The key visual, positioned in the centre of the package, lends the brand a unique look. In addition to the white base colour, which conveys the medical aspect, the packaging uses a wide colour spectrum that allows easy identification of the different types of feed. Each packaging features a three-part navigation system: 11 icons on the left side of the front, symbolising the main contents of the feed, a banderole with a line of arrows, showing its characteristics and effects, as well as a symbol indicating the respective animal size.

client
Vet-Concept GmbH & Co. KG,
Föhren

design
Werbeagentur Zweipunktnull
GmbH, Föhren

creative direction
Reiner Rempis

art direction/graphic design
Christian Krein,
Uli Deus

text
Frank Jöricke

Alprausch

[Chewing Gum Packaging]

Alprausch is well known for reinterpreting Swiss national pride with a wink of the eye. This idea is reflected in the packaging of the herbal chewing gums, which is reminiscent of a piece of wood. Matt, wood-brown colours are combined with delicate structural embossing, which strengthens the illusion of wood when touched. An eye-catcher is the strikingly glossy double-embossed edelweiss pin. In contrast to this, the texts are embossed in reverse, which lends the packaging a pleasantly tactile feel. The distinctive appearance is complemented by the printing of the inside of the envelope.

client
roelli roelli confectionery

design
rlc | packaging group

concept
roelli roelli confectionery

graphic design
Schwarzhochzwei GmbH

structural design/production
rlc | packaging group

Mother's Little Helpers

[Chewing Gum Tins]

"Mother's Little Helpers" were popular tranquilisers among housewives in the 1960s. This chewing gum with the same name ironically recalls their fame. The packaging design of the small handbag-sized tins plays, somewhat tongue-in-cheek, with the therapeutic promise – the chewing gum itself, of course, contains purely natural ingredients. With psychedelic retro-motifs and symbols of femininity, each tin shows the pseudo medical conditions associated with each of the four different flavours. The colours match those of the original tranquilisers.

client
The Deli Garage,
Hamburg

design
Kolle Rebbe / KOREFE,
Hamburg

creative direction
Katrin Oeding,
Antje Hedde

art direction/graphic design
Christine Knies

text
Lorenz Ritter,
Gereon Klug,
Moritz Heitmüller,
Elena Bartrina y Manns

project management
Inga Eickholt

illustration
MASA

photography
Roland Liedke

47

A letter
from homeland

[Packaging]

With the nostalgic appeal of
a letter, this rice packaging
reflects the sentimental value of
food from one's home country.
The vacuum-sealed Taiwanese
rice is sold in a little burlap bag,
which emphasises the origin of
the rice in the form of an envelope. The print of the sender's
name states the Taiwanese
producer. The stamp motif shows
a rice field set in an idyllic landscape and appeals to the emotional connection with the home
country. Moreover, the packaging
is suitable as a gift, which can
be labelled individually.

client
Green In Hand Food Bank Co.,
Ltd., Taipei

design
Green In Hand Food Bank Co.,
Ltd., Taipei

creative direction
Yun-Yi Cheng

art direction
Chien-Te Lee

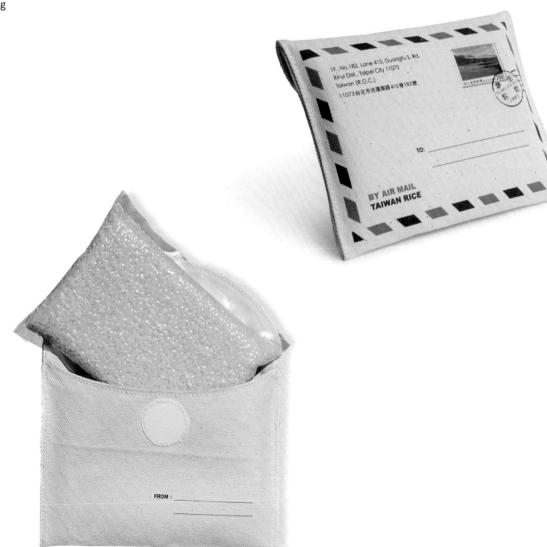

Caffè Gemelli – L'espresso di elevata qualità

[Packaging]

As the name suggests, twin brothers are behind the coffee brand Caffè Gemelli, which is accordingly available in two varieties, Alessandro and Giuseppe. The two brothers differ a lot in character and so do the two coffee varieties. This difference is also reflected by the simplicity of the packaging design which, with its urban look, clearly distinguishes itself from other brands. With a wink of the eye, it conveys the cheekiness of the twin brothers and, at the same time, lends the products an appearance of sophisticated professionalism.

client
Gemeos,
Kronstorf

design
Studio Novo,
Communication &
Product Design e.U.,
Vienna

→ designer portrait: p. 436

Everygarden
Superfood

[Packaging]

Rich in nutrients, Everygarden
Superfood is a food supplement
for busy people. The packaging
in the form of a box with two
compartments lends the product
the appeal of a gift set. In addition,
five small boxes inside the main
box improve its utility. Different
colours are used to highlight
the five main nutrients in each
compartment – red wine, broccoli,
garlic, tomato and paradise nut.
The easy-open system and the
angle construction of the cover
support its usability.

client
CJ Cheiljedang,
Seoul

design
CJ Cheiljedang,
Seoul
Moon Chan Bae,
You Jung Jang

creative direction
Ji Seon Kim

art direction
Kang Kook Lee

Pfeffersack & Soehne

[Packaging]

The aesthetically packed spices by Pfeffersack & Soehne achieve perfect flavour preservation. Hand-made ceramic pots from the Westerwald protect the spices from light and provide a favourable climate. Portuguese cork oak gives the container an airtight seal when closed. The discreet design has a timeless appeal, yet is humorously reminiscent of the old days, when Hanseatic spice traders were mocked "Pfeffersaecke" – (money)pepper bags. From filling to labelling and distribution, every stage of the production process is carried out with the care of an artisan manufacturer.

client
Pfeffersack & Soehne,
Koblenz

design
Pfeffersack & Soehne,
Koblenz
Raphael Fritz,
Christian Ganser,
Stefan Ternes,
Thomas Winkler

Formosa Ecology
Tea Gift Set

client
Pin Shiang Tea Co., Ltd.,
Nantou County

design
Victor Branding Design Corp.,
Taichung

head of marketing
Fred Wang,
B.B. Shee

creative direction
Chung Yuan Kuo

art direction
Bee Liu

graphic design
Rita Chang

text
Lynn Lin

→ designer portrait: p. 441

The packaging design of this fine Taiwanese tea collection not only invites to enjoy a cup of tea, it furthermore communicates the necessity for the protection of certain species. The front of each tea package shows an endangered animal, most of which are endemic to Taiwan. The charming illustrations have an emotional appeal and call for responsibility towards nature. In this context, the design also points out the importance of sustainable tea production and motivates customers to buy the gift box containing three varieties of tea.

Bravo Oolong Tea

[Packaging]

The growing season and the
production methods influence
the aroma and flavour of tea.
This is why the packaging of
this Taiwanese tea collection
distinguishes different tea varieties with different colours. Each
colour represents the growing
area, the season and the flavour.
The winter tea is marked by dark
amber colours representing its
rich aroma, while the spring tea
has a cheerful and bright colour
that signifies its sweet fragrance
and the spring awakening. The
tea comes in light-proof individual
cup portions.

client
Green In Hand Food Bank Co.,
Ltd., Taipei

design
Green In Hand Food Bank Co.,
Ltd., Taipei

creative direction
Yun-Yi Cheng

art direction
Chien-Te Lee

Dr. Groß

[Food Packaging]

After more than 50 years, the traditional company Biologische Präparate Dr. Groß GmbH (company producing biological compounds) launches a redesign of its products and packaging. The new design aims in particular at emphasising sustainability. All packaging follows a clear design layout that leaves sufficient scope for individual solutions: as for example the product-specific typography and instructions for use on the back. A simple, high-impact packaging has thus been created that quickly draws attention to the product benefits, sets it apart from competing products, and increases brand recognition.

client
Biologische Präparate Dr. Groß GmbH, Königsdorf

design
New Cat Orange, Wiesbaden

creative direction/art direction
HP Becker

text
Cordula Becker

Zweifel Popcorn

[Packaging Redesign]

The redesign of the packaging
for the popcorn varieties of
the ZWEIFEL brand was inspired
by the product's original American-
Western style. The vertical
stripes on the packaging symbolise the characteristic American
popcorn bucket, used as a
container when buying popcorn
in the cinema. This distinctive
stripe design is interrupted
visually by an emblem indicating
the product name and flavour.
Product illustrations and a colour
code additionally help to dif-
ferentiate between the different
flavours.

client
Zweifel Pomy-Chips AG,
Zurich

design
ARD DESIGN SWITZERLAND –
Zurich AG, Zurich

A garden with God's blessing – Camellia Nectar

[Packaging]

This Taiwanese camellia honey was collected at the beginning of the summer 2012 after the blooming season in late spring – an exquisite combination of nectar from the camellia and schima superba blossoms. A heart-shaped paper leporello on the lid of the bulbous honey glass unfolds into the shape of a decorative camellia blossom. Some of its white pages offer space for personal messages, while the outer blossom leaves feature a beautifully cut out flower pattern. This design also decorates the protective cardboard box.

client
Green In Hand Food Bank Co., Ltd., Taipei

design
Green In Hand Food Bank Co., Ltd., Taipei

creative direction
Yun-Yi Cheng

art direction
Kuo-Hui Lien

Hortus Honey

[Packaging]

The Hortus Botanicus Amsterdam is one of the few botanic gardens with its own bees. The bees produce their honey with the nectar of a unique collection of rare flowers, resulting in a refined taste and unique texture. The packaging design of the limited edition product reflects the premium character. To show the colour, transparency and texture of the honey, a drop-shaped cutout from the gift box reveals part of the glass. The ball-shaped bottle is also reminiscent of a honey drop.

client
Hortus Botanicus Amsterdam

design
PH Ontwerp,
Hilversum
Marcel Verhaaf,
Hilversum

The Deli Garage
Spachtelmasse
The Deli Garage Filler
[Packaging]

The packaging design for the spreads of "The Deli Garage" is inspired by the brand name and focuses on the topic of construction work. The chocolate spread is marketed humorously as "filler compound": the five cartoon workmen on the can make these spreads attractive for both big and small gourmets. Each illustrated workmen is busy doing a different job, all related to filling work and bricklaying. In addition, a spatula is included in the lid, which can be used to give the chocolate spread a decoratively grooved pattern on the bread.

client
T.D.G. Vertriebs GmbH & Co. KG, Hamburg

design
Kolle Rebbe / KOREFE, Hamburg

creative direction
Katrin Oeding,
Antje Hedde

art direction
Reginald Wagner

text
Gereon Klug,
Moritz Heitmüller

project management
Felix Negwer

photography
Ulrike Kirmse

illustration
Reginald Wagner

ICA Selection
[Packaging Redesign]

In the new packaging design of ICA Selection, each product features a unique design, but all of the designs are based on the same idea: an authentic design style. To achieve this, the design team put themselves in the position of a small local producer, who designs all his labels himself. Thus, standard fonts of an office computer were chosen to lend the simple packaging an authentic signature. Complemented by rustic materials, a consistent packaging design concept was developed that communicates the origin of the product.

client
ICA AB, Solna, Stockholm

design
Designkontoret Silver,
Stockholm

art direction
Steven Webb,
Niclas Öster

graphic design
Ricky Tillblad (Logotype),
Sara Modigh,
Malin Mortensen,
Pär Bauer,
Jonas Ahlgren,
Elvira Claesson
(Assistant Designer)

text
Sebastian Backström,
Johannes Rosenberg,
Eva Jönsson

strategic planning
Helena Brodbeck,
Malin Edvardsen

project management
Ulf Berlin

production designer
Monica Holm

production management
Ida Stagles

NAVARINO ICONS

[Packaging]

NAVARINO ICONS is a series of high-quality Greek food products and art objects, inspired by the history and culture of the Messenian region. The design concept of the brand packaging focuses on the narration of stories from antiquity to the present. Logo, typography and graphic elements are inspired by ideograms, the horizontal lines of clay tablets in Linear B as well as by artefacts dating back to the Mycenaean period. A contemporary interpretation created an appealing, minimalist graphic idiom.

client
NAVARINO ICONS,
P. Faliro,
Athens

managing director
Marina Papatsoni

design
LESSRAIN, London
Vassilios Alexiou,
Daniel Beattie

creative direction/concept
Helene Prablanc

graphic design
Nikos Vassilakis,
Andreas Koutouvalas,
Fox Design

project management
Ismini Bogdanou

photography
Chris Kakogiannis,
xkstudio

61

Hatziyiannakis
Dragées & "Pebbles"

[Packaging]

The packaging design of these Greek sweets (drops) puts the exceptional characteristics of the candies centre stage: the lower part of the bag is transparent, so that the different forms and colours of the drops are visible. They are produced to be reminiscent of pebbles. An illustration on the upper part of the package shows a cross section and, thus, also the fruit or nut filling of each type of candy. The product line comprises of five different flavours, which are differentiated by the names of Greek islands, such as "ios pebble".

client
Hatziyiannakis,
Athens

design
mousegraphics,
Athens

creative direction
Gregory Tsaknakis

art direction
Kostas Vlachakis

illustration
Ioanna Papaioannou

Provenance

[Packaging]

Provenance produces high-quality homeware products from recycled and renewable materials. The flexible slogan "this is now…" introduces each item's story of recycling and provenance. Consistent with the products, the newly developed packaging meets the high demands of the "cradle to cradle" ideology and has low environmental impact. It is made exclusively from recyclable corrugated cardboard and recycled paper. The branding is restricted to the paper sleeves, while the bright orange boxes achieve a high level of attention at the point of sale.

client
Provenance Homewares

design
Jog Ltd,
London

63

Liebensmittelei –
Food for Soul

[Food Packaging, Gift Box]

client
MPREIS Warenvertriebs GmbH,
Völs

design
MPREIS Warenvertriebs GmbH,
Völs

creative direction
Julia Therese Mölk

concept
Simone Höllbacher,
Johanna Mölk,
Stephanie Schumacher

graphic design/illustration
Simone Höllbacher,
Johanna Mölk

text
Stefan Österreicher

project management
Stephanie Schumacher

→ designer portrait: p. 425

The idea behind this product is that a careful selection of groceries and delicacies packed into an appealing theme box with an unusual graphic design turns food into food for the soul and, thus, makes a perfect gift for loved ones. With an extravagant design and unusual messages, the gift boxes, which are produced for various occasions and in limited editions, create a strong contrast to conventional products of this kind. The regionally produced boxes are made of environmentally friendly cardboard to fulfil the underlying principles of sustainability. The first series features three different themes: Deluxe, Tyrolean and organic products.

Dragon Tangram

[Gift Box]

client
Xue Xue Institute,
Taipei

design
Xue Xue Institute,
Taipei

creative direction
H-Yun Kuo,
Tsan-Yu Yin

art direction
Tsan-Yu Yin

strategic planning
Rebecca Hwang

photography
Po-Chao Hwang

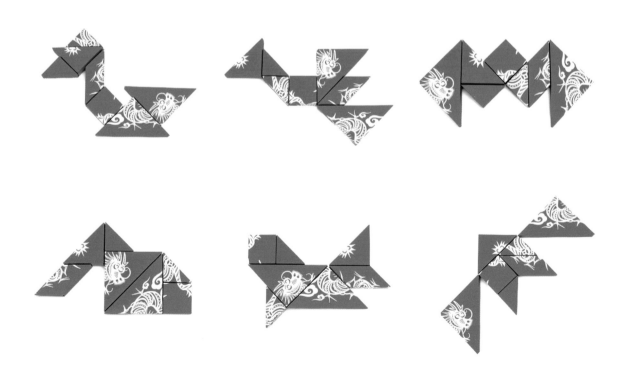

The Dragon Tangram is a gift box for the Chinese New Year 2012, the beginning of the Year of the Dragon. The structure and graphic design of the package are inspired by the classic Chinese puzzle game tangram and by the art of paper-cutting. The packaging in Chinese vermilion is structured into seven separate boxes. After consuming the delicious contents, the boxes can be used as tangram tiles and, with the included instructions, combined into various auspicious animals. The instruction card features characteristic die-cut symbols on the front. On the back are hints and assembling solutions for beginners. The objective is to encourage customers to use their imagination and create new figures and designs.

The Deli Garage
Kühlwasser
The Deli Garage
Coolant
[Packaging]

This mineral water does not enter
the market in glass or PET bottles
but according to the design
principle of workshop and garage
products. It thus seamlessly fits
into the unique and witty packaging used by the Deli Garage food
label for its product range. The
mineral water is available in
two kinds and comes filled as
"coolant" into canisters reminiscent of those used for cars.
Humorous pictograms on the
silver or gold sleeve explain the
correct use in case of overheat-
ing. The strap that connects the
lid with the canister allows fas-
tening to a backpack or bicycle.

client
T.D.G. Vertriebs UG
(haftungsbeschränkt) & Co. KG,
Hamburg

design
Kolle Rebbe / KOREFE,
Hamburg

creative direction
Rocket & Wink

text
Lorenz Ritter

project management
Kristina Wulf,
Corinna Hübl

typography
Reginald Wagner,
Alexander Rötterink

photography
Ulrike Kirmse

Baristaz Coffee Heroes To Go Cup

Baristaz combines traditional coffee with an urban lifestyle. A passion for delicious coffee, selected ingredients, the close cooperation with an aspiring young roast house and a creative approach to all the enjoyments coffee has to offer is what characterises the brand and their "Coffee Heroes". The classic takeaway cup serves as distinctive brand symbol for frequent customers: the typical black eye-mask of classic super heroes together with the cap, which is stylised into a hat, draw the attention and are true eye-catchers for style-oriented coffee lovers.

client
Jost System GmbH,
Koblenz

head of marketing
Stephan Karl

design
Flaechenbrand,
Wiesbaden

creative direction
Kai Geweniger

art direction
Marie Dowling

concept
Peter Kohl

project management
Friedrich Detering

FIVE Olive Oil

[Packaging]

This packaging concept for extra virgin olive oil from Greece was developed without a specific brief from the newly founded company World Excellent Products. The product line targets the international market and stands out through the colour of the bottle. The selected design is elegant and contemporary yet at the same time also reminiscent of potion bottles from old times. The figure "5" was chosen as a fitting brand name, with "five" standing for the quintessence of olive oil.

client
World Excellent Products,
Thessaloniki

design
Designers United,
Thessaloniki
Dimitris Koliadimas,
Dimitris Papazoglou

Etesian Gold Olive Oil
[Packaging]

This premium product is mainly marketed in the Far East, where olive oil is also considered a cosmetic item. To address the target group with specific semiotics, the design recalls symbols from the oldest civilisations. As a product from an ancient land and from a sacred plant, the "Etesian Gold" is provided in an elegant bottle. It is sealed with a symbol from an ancient Greek syllabic script that means "olive". Colour tones and hues are reduced to a discreet palette of earth colours.

client
FLB Solutions Ltd,
Athens

design
mousegraphics,
Athens

creative direction
Gregory Tsaknakis

illustration
Ioanna Papaioannou

St. Olive
Olive Oil
[Packaging]

With the aim of appealing to
a discerning target group, the
packaging design focuses on the
quality of this olive oil produced
for export. It consciously avoids
a provenance-oriented identity.
The product identity humorously
plays on the term "St. Olive" –
not in a religious context, but to
emphasise the vitalising quality
of the olive fruit. The label features a hand as spiritual symbol.
The signet was designed by an
artist specialising in Byzantine
iconography.

client
Livadaros Dascalos Gouliotis
O.E., Patras

design
mousegraphics,
Athens

creative direction
Gregory Tsaknakis

illustration
Ioanna Papaioannou,
George Kordis
(Byzantine illustration)

Razatuša Olive Oil
[Label Design]

The Croatian olive-producing region of Razatuša gave this extra virgin olive oil its name. The logo consists of the majuscule "R", composed of olives and leaves. The application of the label is kept simple, since the family business does the labelling on its own. Accordingly, the label was designed so that it can easily be slipped onto the bottle and then fixed by a wax stamp. The harvest year can be written on the label by hand, while its fabric also prevents drops of oil from dripping onto the table.

client
Ljubo Zdjelarević,
Zagreb

design
Šesnić & Turković,
Zagreb

creative direction/graphic design
Marko Šesnić,
Goran Turković

illustration
Tomislav Tomić

Fu Niang Fang
Roselle Vinegar

[Packaging]

client
Yang Da Biotec Co., Ltd.,
Pingtung County

design
Bosin Design,
Kaohsiung City

Natural brewing, without artificial additives, characterises this Taiwanese vinegar. Its high quality is based on natural ingredients, which is emphasised by the purist packaging in a limited edition. It features only one simple word, which means vinegar in Chinese. The glass bottle shows the beautiful colour of the vinegar, while a silicone material covers the bottle top, lending it a unique appeal. Paper rattans of various colours identify the different varieties of vinegar, contrasting vividly with the grey paper box.

75

Collection
Chandra Kurt

[Label Design, Packaging]

client
Provins Valais, Sion;
mediaGene, Zurich

head of marketing
David Genolet,
Provins Valais, Sion

project management
Chandra Kurt,
mediaGene, Zurich

text
Chandra Kurt

design/concept
clear of clouds,
Zurich

creative direction
Larissa Kuhl,
Stefan Huser

The "Collection Chandra Kurt" is a tribute to one of Switzerland's oldest wine regions, the Valais. Traditional Valais wine varieties are presented in a contemporary vinification for a young, international target group. The appearance reflects this idea and connects tradition and trend into a reinterpreted vintage look with original photographs from the province of Valais. Further design elements are the stories about the rare Swiss grape varieties on the label; they also explain the collaboration of the winemakers with the wine writer Chandra Kurt. The label design celebrates Swiss wine without resorting to stereotypical clichés.

Sotka

[Label Design]

With its polygraphic print, the label design of this vodka is a reinterpretation of the front side of a Soviet one-hundred-rouble note: Instead of the hammer and sickle emblem, the complex label features an illustration of the company headquarters. In addition, logo and product name are artfully integrated. Only the numerals are, apart from colour adjustments, virtually identical to the original, and allude to the particular meaning of the word "sotka" (hundred). Since in Soviet times, the average monthly salary of a skilled engineer was about a hundred roubles.

client
Russian Alcohol,
Moscow

design
UNIQA Creative Engineering,
Moscow

creative direction
Alexey Yakushik

64° Reykjavik Distillery – three Icelandic liqueurs
[Label Design]

The purist appearance of the 3x3 letter combination reflects the simplicity of the indigenous Icelandic blueberry, crowberry and rhubarb. The number "3" also reflects the number of ingredients used in each liqueur: wild-grown fruits, sugar and pure alcohol. The colouring of the labels is inspired by the nature of the fruits, and underlines the origin of the ingredients. The logo tells of the liqueur's provenance in both words and graphic symbols; the Reykjavik distillery is located on the 64th parallel north.

client
Reykjavik Distillery ehf,
Reykjavik

design
Reykjavik Distillery ehf,
Reykjavik

creative direction
Snorri Jonsson,
Judith Orlishausen

Rice Magic
Sake Japan

[Sparkling Sake Packaging]

client
Ninki Inc.,
Fukushima-ken

head of marketing
Yujin Yusa

design
GTDI Co. Ltd.,
Tokyo

creative direction
Henry Ho

graphic design
Atsuhito Enoki

illustration
Ulrica Hydman Vallien

→ designer portrait: p. 416

After the 2011 Tohoku earthquake and the devastating tsunami, many people in Japan have been working to reconstruct their home towns. Six sake producers from Tohoku are marketing a new series of sparkling sake under the name Rice Magic, hoping to stimulate the economy of their region. Emotionally appealing artworks by the Swedish glass artist Ulrica Hydman Vallien were used for the eye-catching packaging design. The two main colours, red and black, stand for Japan and its undefeatable spirit. The decorative bottles can also be reused as flower vases in memory of the catastrophe.

Kratochwill Honey Beer Packaging

Honey beer is a new product of the Slovenian brewery Kratochwill. The beer has a special taste, since honey is added to the beer in the brewing process. Echoing this ingredient, the packaging is reminiscent of a bee. A yellow and black paper bag encloses the bottle and is twisted at the top end. The unique logo has a distinctive look against the high-contrast colouring. The product denomination in various languages at the top end of the label lends the beer an international appeal and is consistent with the brand emblem that also features multi-lingual elements.

client
Pivovarna in pivnica Kratochwill d.o.o., Ljubljana

design
Futura DDB d.o.o., Ljubljana

creative direction/art direction
Žare Kerin

graphic design
Marko Piškur

project management
Ana Por

photography
Janez Pukšič

Reserva and Private Selection Esporão

[Box and Bottle Design]

The wine collection Reserva and Private Selection of the Portuguese brand Esporão features a culturally appealing label design. As true eye-catchers, the illustrations of different art objects attract the attention. Each wine is related to a particular animal, which incorporates the specific character of the wine. Further design details, such as the embossing of the brand on the glass, the changing colours of the seal as well as the high-quality paper lend the bottle an elegant appeal.

client
Esporão S.A.,
Lisbon

design
White Studio,
Porto

artwork
Joana Vasconcelos

Plagios Wine

[Label Design]

The label design for Plagios
wines was inspired by the name
of the wine (plagios means
"sideways" in Greek) by recalling
the movement of the bishop in a
game of chess. The chessboard
colours of the label are achieved
by a combination of printed
white squares with the dark glass
of the bottle. The colours are
echoed in the seal of the cork to
indicate the type of wine: white
for white wine, black for red
wine. The delicate symbol of
the bishop, the winery's crest,
complements the elegant
composition of the label.

client
Biblia Chora Winery,
Kavala

design
Beetroot Design Group,
Thessaloniki

creative direction
Alexis Nikou,
Yiannis Charalambopoulos,
Vangelis Liakos

photography
Kostas Pappas

Monocastas Wine
[Box and Bottle Design]

The purist wooden box comprises a collection of exclusive
Portuguese wines from a limited
production of 6,000 bottles.
The label encloses the bottle
almost fully, featuring an elegant
typography as the main visual
element. Several short texts
provide information about the
wine production and advice for
tasting. They contain information about the harvest, producing area, grape variety and GPS
coordinates. Embossed leaves
and the first letters of each grape
variety are used to distinguish
the different wines.

client
Esporão S.A.,
Lisbon

design
White Studio,
Porto

SOL Bottle and Outer Box – Portal to the sun

client
Heineken, Amsterdam

global management Sol
Vicente Cortina

design
VBAT, Amsterdam

strategy director
Eugene Bay

creative direction
John Comitis,
Pieter Jelle Braaksma,
Gerwin Scholing,
Martijn Doolard

account management
Susanne Leydes

→ designer portrait: p. 440

The design concept of the new SOL bottle for the international premium pils market segment was inspired by the original Mexican SOL bottle, aiming to create a balance between authenticity and a premium image. As the central design element, the sun stands for independence – Espíritu Libre. The strong and harmonious circular logo is stamped onto a transparent sun graphic. In tribute to the brand's roots, the original name of the Mexican brewery is embossed on the bottle shoulder. Two bottles of the beer are stored in a handmade, anthracite wooden box with red leather straps, which unlocks by sliding open the bottom side of the box.

Sion Kölsch

[0.5-Litre Design Bottle]

client
Haus Kölscher Brautradition,
Cologne

head of marketing
Uwe Helmich

head of advertising/concept
David Meisser

creative direction
Ralf Hofmann,
Verallia

design
RHEINSTERN, Cologne

art direction
Michael Müller

customer advisory service
Norbert Stecher

The challenge in the development of this bottle for Sion Kölsch was to reinterpret the character of traditional bottle designs without creating a retro look. Accordingly, the front of the Sion design bottle resembles the classic North Rhine Westphalia bottle design, while its profile is reminiscent of modern longneck bottles. This combination results in an expressive bottleneck, that provides space for a high-quality relief lettering. The distinctive shoulder line and the subtle waist create an ergonomic form.

Dynamax

[Motor Oil Packaging]

The objective for the new
packaging by Dynamax was a
repositioning of the entire
product range of motor oils and
technical liquids. The bottle
design is primarily determined
by ergonomics and ease of use.
An organic shape with a wide
funnel neck and solid handles
allows the oil to be poured safely.
Two separate label designs
and different container colours
assist easy recognition throughout the product range. The simple,
rounded form without sharp
edges also needs less plastic
in its production.

client
EURO-VAT spol, s r.o.,
Alekšince

design
PERGAMEN Slovakia,
Trnava

art direction
Juraj Demovič,
Juraj Vontorčík

graphic design
Juraj Demovič,
Lívia Lörinzová

photography
Jakub Dvořák

product design
Dušan Kutlík

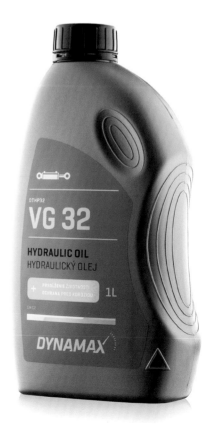

UX32 Zenbook
[Packaging]

The simplicity and elegance of the notebook packaging reflects the high artistic standard of the product design. The luxurious hardcover box is made of black cardboard, emphasising the purist design of the ZENBOOK. The illustration on the top of the box shows a slightly opened envelope, which allows a glimpse into its precious content. The packaging with separate compartments is easy to recycle and reuse, echoing the environmental protection philosophy of ASUS.

client
ASUSTeK Computer Inc.,
Taipei

design
ASUSDESIGN,
Taipei

BFF Jahrbuch 2012
BFF Yearbook 2012

With an unusual packaging design, the BFF yearbook was published as a photo box, in which paper and film used to be provided. In the style of the major manufacturers for photographic materials, KODAK, ILFORD and AGFA, it is available in three different versions, attracting an immense level of attention within the target group. On the inside, it presents a cross-section of current photo design in Germany. As a useful working manual for the industry and a unique photographic art book, it reveals new styles and documents the development of professional photography.

client
BFF Bund Freischaffender Foto-Designer e.V., Stuttgart

design
Strichpunkt Design, Stuttgart/Berlin

printing
Cantz'sche Druckerei

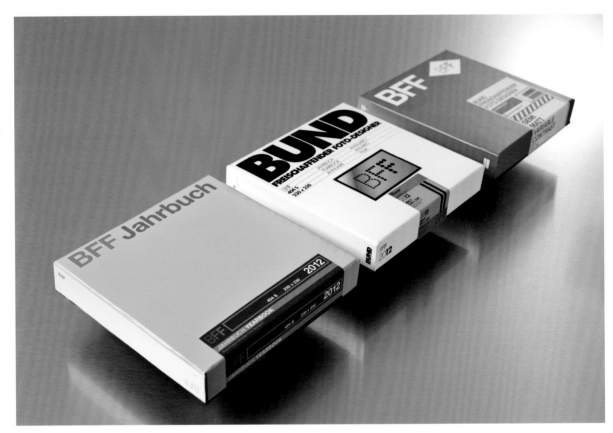

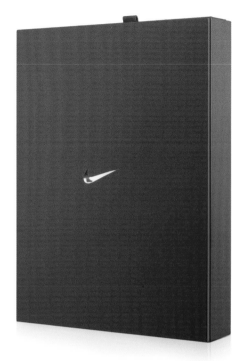

Nike 2012/2013 Korea National Football Team – Home Jersey Package

This packaging design is inspired by the product itself: the jersey of Korea's national football team. The jersey's characteristic feature are the laser-cut ventilation holes in its sides. Accordingly, the sophisticated box features a similar hole punching on its inside. The double gatefold of the box increases the excitement when opening it: at first, only the Nike logo is visible, then the claim and finally the jersey, which is framed by rays made of cords. The vermilion cardboard package can also be used as an eye-catching display case in stores.

client
Nike Sports Korea,
Seoul

design
Tae Hyun Kim,
Nike Sports Korea,
Seoul;
creative company kki,
Seoul

creative direction
Tae Ho Yoo

art direction
Seung In Baek

graphic design
Myung Woo Nam

text
Jong Dae Kim

Drift HD

[Packaging]

A reusable packaging solution
showcases the Drift HD action
camera. The design, in the shape
of the company logo, underlines
the characteristics of the camera
and serves as a transport case.
One of the main features of the
packaging is the coating, which
is the same coating that also
protects the camera and lends
it its characteristic feel. The
design also offers space to attach
anti-theft protection through
the corner of the box. The accessory case was carefully designed,
and produced from a sturdy
polymer to serve as transport
case for all necessary mounts
and accessories.

client
Drift Innovation,
London

design
Drift Innovation,
London

design director
Drew Henson

design consultant
Tom Mills

concept assistance
Milo Murphy

graphic design
Sam Chelton

Naver Photo

[Reusable Parcel Box]

As a new service provider, Naver establishes its online photo service in an already highly competitive market. The packaging design stands out from conventional photo boxes, which get damaged easily. To prevent this, the design was altered so that the box can also be used as a photo album or archive. Customers can record their memories either directly on the parcel box's label or on the enclosed photo labels, which come in ten different designs. The parcel box is assembled without adhesives or plastic tape; it is nevertheless sturdy, easy to open and eco-friendly.

client
NHN Corp.,
Seongnam-si,
Gyeonggi-do

design
NHN Corp.,
Seongnam-si,
Gyeonggi-do

head of marketing
Jo Hang Soo

creative direction
Kim Seung Eon

art direction
Jang Tae Kyung

graphic design
Kim Hyung Woo,
Ohk Hye Won

Blank

[Package Design Identity]

Blank created a strong brand identity with a uniform package design for four types of products that are vastly different in size and components. The refined design is characterised by a consistent colouring and under-lines the premium feel of the accessory brand. As an environmentally conscious packaging concept, part of the package can be reused as a tray for stationery on the desk. The simple package design with its transparent lid enables consumers to examine the respective product carefully without opening the package.

client
iriver Ltd,
Seoul

design
iriver Ltd, Seoul
Park Jisang,
Kim Juyeon

project management
Sung Baekjin

Offline Games

[Packaging]

The brand Retro Kids redesigned a number of popular classic toys: games that people loved to play with as children were given a new shape, a new name and new packaging, so that these "Offline Games" are also exciting for kids in the digital age. The illustrations of the packaging design reflect the two poles of analogue toys on the one hand and digital toys on the other. To inspire children, highly approachable instructions and tips are printed on the outer packaging as well as on the pouch, conveying also ideas about various professions.

client
T.D.G. Vertriebs GmbH & Co. KG, Hamburg

design
Kolle Rebbe / KOREFE, Hamburg

creative direction
Antje Hedde

text
Sabine Kuckuck,
Lorenz Ritter

project management
Christina Griese,
Inga Eickholt

photography
Karin Nussbaumer

illustration
Saara Järvinen,
Katja Unterkofler

97

Die 4 von der Wollga
The 4 of Woolga
[Packaging]

"The four of Woolga" is a lovingly designed wool sock packaging for the whole family. The product set contains four boxes, each with an illustration of a particular family member: father, mother, child and baby. The mother of the family, called Woolanka, was sent to customers together with a letter. If a customer replied online, he received the whole family during winter sale. The four boxes can be placed one inside the other like the Russian Matryoshka dolls and encourage buying and collecting.

client
Closed GmbH,
Hamburg

design
gürtlerbachmann GmbH,
Hamburg

text
Matthias Hardt

project management
Anna Lorenzen

illustration
Veronika Kieneke

Jazz Virus

[Packaging, CD Cover]

For the release of this Jazz album, the Moscow music label chose a cover design that by itself would be an incentive to buy the CD. The fold-away cardboard cover not only impresses with its distinctive appearance, but also has a pleasant feel that stands out from the usual plastic cases. With artful prints on the inside, the high-grade cover appears to be especially desirable compared to a download from the Internet. Illustrations full of imagination on the inside, together with the minimalist arrangement of logos and fonts on the outside, lend this edition an own and independent character.

client
Kontora Kooka,
Samara

design
General Line!,
Samara

head of advertising/art direction
Irina Karandaeva

graphic design
Inna Glazova

Placemat,
Pot Pad, Coaster

[Packaging]

New and Joy, LCC, presents a line
of decorative silicone placemats,
pot pads and coasters that are
environmentally friendly and
hygienic. The packaging design
follows the "less is more"
concept: the purist white box
features the company logo and
product name in silver print,
while on each side parts of the
logo are stamped out. By placing
several packages next to each
other, the corporate design
becomes fully visible. It also
allows customers a view of the
contents without opening the
box.

client
New and Joy, LLC,
Delaware

design
Human Paradise Studio,
Taipei

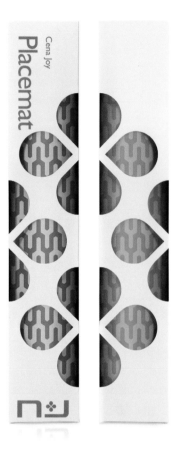

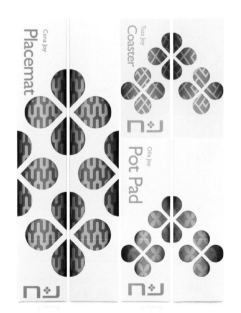
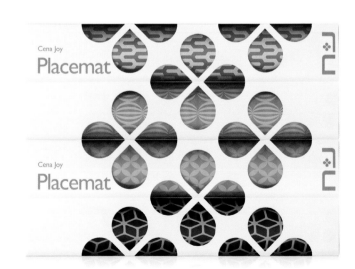

Brüken Tile Adhesives
[Packaging]

BRÜKEN is a new brand in the tile mortar market. A striking package was designed for the product launch that clearly sets the brand apart from the competition. An iconic tile design was printed on a simple white background – symbolising the adhesive base formed by the mortar. In diamond shapes and striking, bold colour combinations, the packaging design creates a distinctive vitrail or op-art effect. Eye-catching but without extravagance, the print emphasises the creative work of the tiler.

client
Petrocoll S.A.,
Athens

design
mousegraphics,
Athens

creative direction
Gregory Tsaknakis

art direction
Aris Pasouris

illustration
Ioanna Papaioannou

FOGAL
[Packaging]

client
FOGAL AG Switzerland,
Zurich

head of marketing
Marcela Palek

design
BEL EPOK GmbH,
Cologne

creative direction
Sebastian Fischenich

art direction
Judith Riemenschneider

project management
Stephanie Herse

printing
Michael Matschuck,
druckpartner

production
Patrick Rissmann,
Rissmann Packaging

From the uniquely designed paper to the special folding technique, every detail of this packaging range reflects the brand identity of Fogal. In line with the retail package, an autonomous product packaging concept for a high-quality folding box was developed, which allows flat storage and reflects the high demands of the premium product line. The packaging concept highlights the long-standing Fogal tradition in the brand's core product group, hosiery, with a new design. The main features of this relaunch are the development of a colour code and a special folding technique.

my.pen style
[Packaging, Display Units]

client
Herlitz PBS AG Papier-,
Büro- und Schreibwaren,
Berlin

design
Herlitz PBS AG Papier-,
Büro- und Schreibwaren,
Berlin

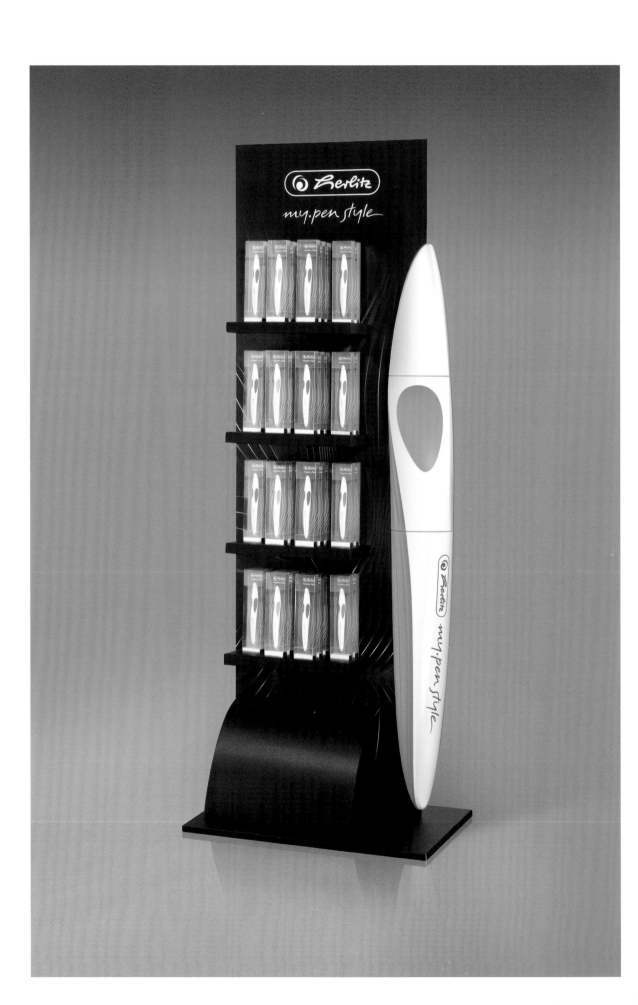

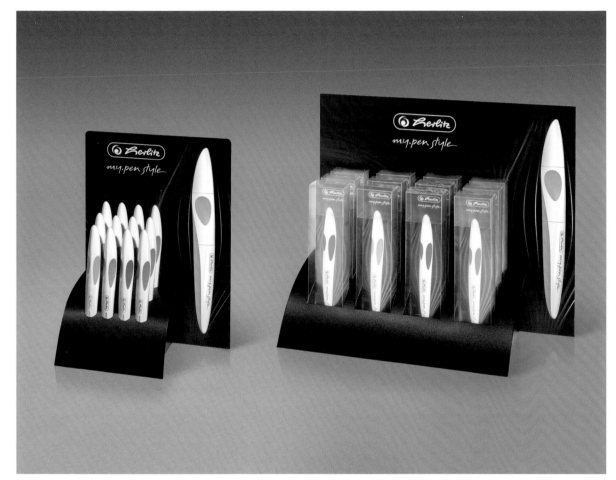

The my.pen style is a stylish new addition to the product range of Herlitz AG. The ballpoint pen was conceived as an accessory for students, apprentices and young professionals. The sales packaging and display units echo the strong colour contrasts of the product. This creates a clear order in the presentation that places the product centre stage. The organic design and the ridges and grooves that are typical for my.pen are picked up in the graphics of the background and are developed in a dynamic manner. The coloured back cards of the case packaging are reduced showing the logo and the product name, constituting a vivid background for the pen. The dark display units form a strong contrast that makes the packaging stand out and shine brilliantly.

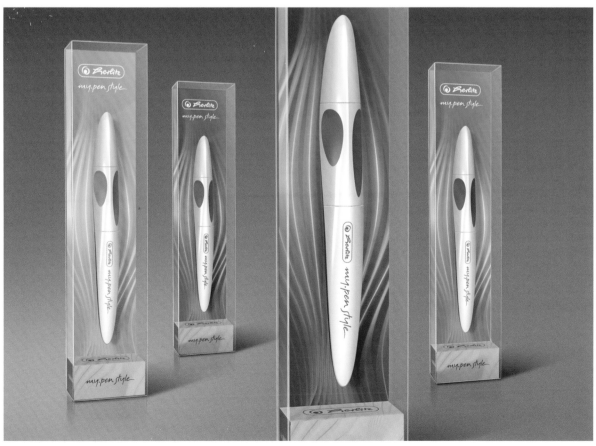

Alles ... kommt auf die Beleuchtung an
All... a matter of lighting
[Product Catalogue, Presentation Case]

client
Mawa Design,
Licht- und Wohnideen GmbH,
Michendorf

design
Mawa Design,
Licht- und Wohnideen GmbH,
Michendorf

head of marketing
Martin Wallroth

art direction
Judith Dobler,
Basel/Berlin

A quotation by Brandenburg's poet Theodor Fontane lends the product catalogue of this hi-tech manufacturer from Brandenburg its title. The company's entire range of lighting is for the first time listed in one compendium. The remarkable reading direction from both sides of the book, divided by the special colours yellow and silver, turns this catalogue into a unique reading experience. Four ribbon markers allow for easy orientation. In the middle, both parts of the catalogue meet and are complemented with photographic insights into the factory and further quotations about light by Fontane. High-quality architectural photographs illustrate the diversity of the products and enhance the catalogue visually as well as with information. The book is safely enclosed in a presentation case.

LCD/LED NB Panel Shipping Box

[Shipping Package]

This design of the LCD/LED NB panel shipping package meets the logistic requirements for safe marine transport. The box is designed with a complex structure to ensure perfect fit and protection of the product. To conserve resources, it is made of 90 per cent recycled paper and can be completely recycled after use. The symmetrical construction allows for easy adjustments and reduces tooling costs and manufacturing time by 50 per cent. The box's low weight is another convincing feature.

client
AU Optronics Corporation, Hsinchu

design
AU Optronics Corporation, Hsinchu

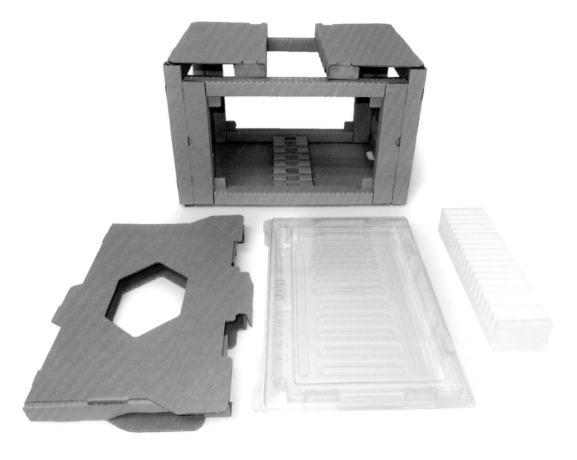

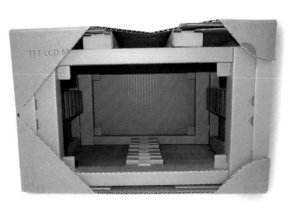

Assembly Slot
Shipping Box

The Assembly Slot Shipping Box
is specifically designed for large-
size semi-finished panel glass.
Thanks to a flexible design, all
assembly parts can be adjusted
to various panel sizes, which
significantly reduces packing
time and tooling costs. In case of
damage to the box, the damaged
components are easily replace-
able, so that it is not necessary
to buy a complete new box. The
shipping box is made of recycled
and recyclable materials in order
to ensure minimal environmental
impact.

client
AU Optronics Corporation,
Hsinchu

design
AU Optronics Corporation,
Hsinchu

Event Design

The Audi Ring –
Brand Pavilion IAA 2011

With the Audi Ring, the carmaker Audi presented itself at the Frankfurt Motor Show
(IAA) in a separate, free-standing facility. At the heart of this 100 metres long, 70 metres
wide, and 12 metres high trade show pavilion was an integrated driving track on two
levels, where visitors were given the opportunity to experience selected vehicles in a
live ride on a 400 metres long test track. Since the entire concept was geared towards
involving visitors, they were allowed to drive the cars themselves. From the Grand Hall
with the latest Audi vehicles and the Technology Park with interactive holographic
exhibits to the final highlight, the presentation of the show cars and the multimedia
brand show, the exhibition design conveyed dynamics, innovation and quality; characteristics that were also represented by the architecture of the entire facility with
its flowing forms, curved lines and surprising transitions. The core brand message
"Vorsprung durch Technik" was rendered into a fascinating and lasting sensual
experience.

Statement by the jury

»The Audi brand pavilion convinced the jury, because it was more than just a spectacular showcase. It is a combination of an exclusive design course and an authentic
experience that involves the audience. Visitors have true experiences and get in touch
with the brand. The overall concept of letting visitors experience the brand was thus
successfully achieved.«

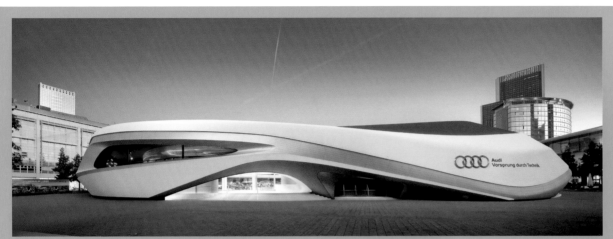

client
AUDI AG,
Ingolstadt

design
SCHMIDHUBER,
Munich
KMS BLACKSPACE,
Munich

→ designer portrait: p. 430

red dot: best of the best

Nord Stream – The Arrival

[Corporate Event]

In November 2011, the completion of the longest European offshore gas pipeline through the Baltic Sea was celebrated with an opening event. In order to turn the invisible product natural gas into a visible and tangible experience, the structure of the CH_4 molecule was chosen as the key visual throughout the entire presentation of the event. Much larger and translated into three-dimensional space, the architecture reflected this communicative core idea with five connected geodetic dome tents, a landmark that catched the eye even from far away. The biggest of these tents, a 500-square-metre dome tent, contained an elaborately produced 360-degree projection which guided the high-ranking audience from politics and economics through the engineering and logistical achievements of this European project, turning the creation of the pipeline into a spectacular and emotional three-dimensional experience.

Statement by the jury

»The idea, to not only visualise the topic of natural gas on the basis of its molecular structure, but also to let the audience experience it in film and architecture, is excellent and was applied just so. The staging impresses with a consistent concept and communication strategy that allows visitors an immediate and lasting experience of the topic.«

client
Nord Stream AG,
Zug

design
Triad Berlin
Projektgesellschaft mbH, Berlin

creative direction
Harald Lipken

head of finance
Dr. Stefan Kleßmann

head of strategic communication
Prof. Lutz Engelke

project management
Nora Penadés, Stef Detering

film production
Alexander Bartneck

media/technical engineering
Sebastian Regenauer

→ designer portrait: p. 439

The Social Kitchen

[Event Design]

The project "The Social Kitchen" presents itself as a "pop-up installation" that
combines food and design. In order to showcase outstanding achievements in
New Zealand design and appliance engineering, in combination with the changing
role of the kitchen as a social hub, visitors were received at an elegant kitchen
inside a modified shipping container and at a table for 50 persons in a temporary
blow-up cube. Here, they were treated to a range of classic New Zealand and
newly invented dishes, which were arranged like bite-sized works of art; starting
with dunking an Earl Grey biscuit into ginger nut tea. The individual steps of the
preparation were shown using large-scale photographs. The event design
furthermore included pole-based platters, uniforms with menus on the T-shirts
and a newspaper, all with a consistent appearance, and a video documenting
the design process.

Statement by the jury

»This event design combines the art of cooking with innovations in engineering
and design in a highly memorable manner. The message that, today, the
kitchen has become a versatile room where families and friends get together
is communicated with various sensual impressions in an atmosphere in which
everything is perfectly balanced and tailored, from the high-quality furniture
to the service and the food presentation.«

client
Fisher & Paykel,
Auckland

design
Alt Group,
Auckland

creative direction
Dean Poole

graphic design
Shabnam Shiwan,
 Aaron Edwards,
Dean Poole,
Janson Chau

text
Pradeep Sharma,
Dean Poole,
Shabnam Shiwan,
Ben Corban

photography
Toaki Okano,
David St George

→ designer portrait: p. 403

red dot: best of the best

smart EBALL

[Game Event]

One special feature of the smart fortwo electric drive is its surprisingly powerful acceleration, especially on the first metres. In order to demonstrate that the car is not only environmentally friendly, but also fun to drive, it was showcased with a unique test drive event at the Frankfurt Motor Show (IAA): with the game "smart EBALL", which turned the electric cars into game controllers. It is played like the classic video game Pong, with the only difference that the game is controlled by driving real cars quickly back and forth. Visitors were invited to play against each other and drive the electric cars quickly back and forth on a straight piece of road to hit the ball as shown on the projection wall. Thus, visitors had a first-hand experience of the exceptional acceleration – and a lot of fun.

Statement by the jury

»The game event impresses with the unique idea of connecting the outstanding feature of the smart fortwo electric drive, its rapid acceleration, with an interactive game. For the visitors of the trade show, this game not only offered a lot of fun, it also realised the objective of the event in a highly convincing manner.«

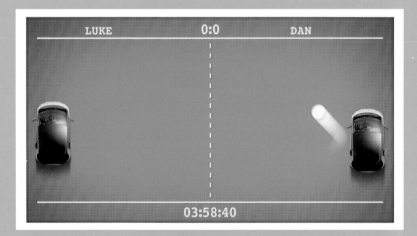

client
Daimler AG,
Sindelfingen

design
BBDO Proximity Berlin GmbH
Daniel Schweinzer,
Lukas Liske
ANR BBDO Stockholm
Fredric Antonsson,
Sebastian Forsman,
Maria Sandberg

head of marketing
Dirk Spakowski

creative direction
David Mously,
Jan Harbeck,
Ton Hollander,
Jens Ringena

project management
Jan Hendrik Oelckers,
Sebastian Schlosser,
Sandra Gesell (BBDO Live),
Frank Hägele (BBDO Live),
Fredrik Pantzerhielm
(ANR BBDO Stockholm)

→ designer portrait: p. 406

red dot: best of the best

Donation Army

[Promotion]

OroVerde Germany is a small organisation with a great goal: With only ten employees, they develop and raise funds for projects to stop the destruction of the tropical forests. In order to improve their impact they wanted to recruit new activists, mainly as donation collectors. The idea of this campaign was not to recruit expensive human donation collectors, but an entirely new breed of "activist", who would happily work the streets around the clock for free and who was a very natural and convincing advocate for OroVerde's message: trees. A whole army of 600 trees in pedestrian areas, shopping streets and parks throughout Germany were equipped with cardboard signs, calling upon the passers-by to donate: "Need money for my family in the rainforest." In doing so, the trees were turned into tireless donation collectors arousing a lot of curiosity and interest.

Statement by the jury

»The Donation Army campaign shows an extremely inventive, likeable and most of all successful realisation. By letting trees in German cities speak for themselves and their "family" overseas, the campaign draws attention to the organisation in a highly consistent and distinctive manner.«

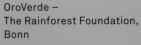

THE DONATION ARMY

client
OroVerde –
The Rainforest Foundation,
Bonn

design
Ogilvy Deutschland

creative direction
Dr. Stephan Vogel,
Peter Strauss

art direction
Sergej Chursyn,
Christian Leithner

text
Sergej Chursyn,
Dr. Stephan Vogel

project management
Michael Fucks

Naver App-Square
[Exhibition]

With this offline campaign, the Korean search portal Naver presented information in a street exhibition booth called "Naver app-square". Since many Koreans purchase their smartphones online, the aim was to promote the Naver app in public space. As an analogy of the parcel boxes in which the smartphones are delivered, the booth was conceived as a huge parcel box. The walls, props and furniture of the booth were all made from eco-friendly cardboard. Inside, professional promoters helped visitors with the installation of the app and explained its various features.

client
NHN Corp.,
Seongnam-si,
Gyeonggi-do

design
NHN Corp.,
Seongnam-si,
Gyeonggi-do

head of marketing
Jo Hang Soo

head of advertising
Yoon Yun Jae

creative direction
Kim Seung Eon

art direction
Shin Hyun Kyung

graphic design
Park Yun Hee,
Park Eun Kyung

motion design
Hwangbo Sang Woo,
Lee Seon Jae

strategic planning
Cha Ha Na,
Kim Pil Jun,
Jung Yun Young

Design Your Green Thinking

[Exhibition]

The exhibition titled "Design your green thinking" featured creative and multi-faceted artwork from 20 artists. All materials used in the exhibition space were carefully planned to be easy to disassemble and were fully recyclable. In lieu of wood walls, the standard production material, this booth was constructed with a minimised framework and felt, among other non-chemically treated materials. After the exhibition was over, the torn-down felt was used to make recycled SDF eco-bags. All proceeds of the exhibition were donated to an environmental organisation.

client
NHN Corp.,
Seongnam-si,
Gyeonggi-do

design
NHN Corp.,
Seongnam-si,
Gyeonggi-do

head of marketing
Jo Hang Soo

creative direction
Kim Seung Eon

art direction
Jang Tae Kyung,
Jung Bin Young,
Son Hye Eun

graphic/space design
Ohk Hye Won,
Park Yun Hee

motion design
Park Hyeon

mobile site design
Park Jeong Ho

Mercedes Next!
The Pulse of
a New Generation

[Trade Fair Exhibition]

The trade fair presentation "Mercedes Next!" at the International Motor Show (IAA) in 2011 followed an unusual concept. The exhibition route and the length of the average visit were seamlessly interlinked by a dramaturgical production that created a highly exciting choreography staging the automobiles, media panels and people as if in a theatre. At regular intervals, the live show drew their attention to the stage, where exhibition themes were presented in a series of different scenes. Layered, mobile media panels created a stage area for vehicles and people in ever-changing new scenes.

client
Daimler AG,
Stuttgart

design
Atelier Markgraph,
Frankfurt/Main
(Show, Communication,
Exhibition Design, Media Design)
Kauffmann Theilig & Partner,
Ostfildern (Architecture)

lighting design
TLD Planungsgruppe

→ digital presentation: DVD

Mercedes Next! A Kinetic Media Production

The presentation of Mercedes-Benz at the International Motor Show (IAA) in 2011 was defined by a 40-metre-long, media-driven strip integrated to impressive effect in the silver metal facade. The strip accompanied visitors from the foyer into the exhibition space, forming a spacious stage of ever-changing 3D impressions. Media panels arranged one behind the other on the theatre stage moved kinetically, while an LED curtain showed a panorama with a high sense of depth. Images on the LED panels behind it were visible through the curtain, creating the impression that the vehicles were moving between the different image levels.

client
Daimler AG,
Stuttgart

design
Atelier Markgraph,
Frankfurt/Main
(Show, Communication,
Exhibition Design, Media Design)
Kauffmann Theilig & Partner,
Ostfildern (Architecture)

lighting design
TLD Planungsgruppe

media feeds/integration
Atelier Markgraph, Barbecue
Mediendesign (sub company),
Group.iE (sub company)

Press Launch
Porsche 911 USA

[Interactive Presentation]

The key design characteristic
of Porsche car interiors, the
upright centre console, inspired
the stage idea of this interactive
presentation. In order to keep
the eyes of visitors on the main
attraction, the new Porsche 911
served as both input device and
projection surface at the same
time. While turned to its optimum
angle, every relevant piece of information was directly projected
onto the car, while a high-power,
tandem, HD back projection
reliably illuminated the trapezoid
main screen. Three different
projectors covered almost the
entire car with highly complex
real-time mapping.

client
Dr. Ing. h.c. F. Porsche AG,
Stuttgart

design
stereolize. GmbH,
Munich

creative direction
Reiner Knollmüller

art direction
David Sczyrba,
Patrick Wagner

project management
Isabelle Kraus

head of production
Maik Borchardt

programming
Sven Krippner,
Florian Müller

Black Box – Mercedes-Benz at Commercial Vehicle Fair RAI, Amsterdam

[Installation]

At the Commercial Vehicle Fair RAI in Amsterdam, Mercedes-Benz launched its pre-release communication for the new Mercedes-Benz city van "Citan". The challenge was to communicate all the benefits of the new city van without having the Citan on site. Inside the "Black Box" a full-size model of the Citan was impressively staged via 3D projection mapping. A comprehensive staging of the vehicle focused the dramatic and exciting four-minute-long show by using five projectors and LED technology on three surfaces.

client
Daimler AG,
Stuttgart

design
PHOCUS BRAND CONTACT
GmbH & Co. KG, Nuremberg

→ designer portrait: p. 428

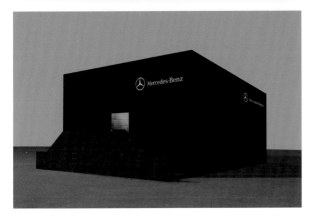

Audi connect Trade Fair Stand CES 2012

client
AUDI AG,
Ingolstadt

head of marketing
Bernhard Neumann

design
tisch13 GmbH,
Munich

creative direction/concept
Carsten Röhr

project management
Martin Mack,
AUDI AG;
Marjut Keituri,
tisch13 GmbH

photography
Gabor Ekecs

architecture
Lutz Geisel,
Bathke Geisel Architekten

Presented at the world's largest electronics trade fair, the 2012 International CES, this stand in Las Vegas was designed to convey to visitors the basic principles behind the guiding concept of "Audi connect" in an appealing, vivid form: networking, interfaces, data streams. To symbolise this, the image of a tight grid was selected and manifested in all construction elements related to both design and layout of the trade fair stand. Suspended PCBs surrounded a box that appeared to float over the visitors' heads, with the glittering light of 2,824 fluorescent lamps shining through its gaps. The reflections of the light grid on the highly polished surfaces of the architecture and the vehicles on display effectively transported the "grid" onto the visitors' level.

KUKA Systems
Energy Cinema
[Trade Fair Installation]

The trade fair installation from KUKA Systems GmbH was focused on a KUKA robot placed in an all-round translucent protection cube. The robot's monumental appearance and ease of movement were used to create a mysterious choreography of captivating, dynamic appeal. Three large monitors were mounted onto the free-moving robot arm which, programmed to move to the rhythm of music, would make the monitors start to dance. Visitors were thus offered insight into a virtual space containing several themed units that were navigated and targeted by the robot one after another.

client
KUKA Systems GmbH,
Augsburg

head of marketing
Markus Meier

design
LIQUID | Agentur für Gestaltung,
Augsburg

creative direction
Ilja Sallacz

art direction
Sönke Uden,
Claudius Gagalka

project management
Sönke Uden,
LIQUID | Agentur für Gestaltung
Sabine Neubauer,
KUKA Systems GmbH

film production
Claudius Gagalka,
Leo Bergmann

music/sound design
Marc Frank

programming
Jürgen Liepert,
KUKA Systems GmbH,
Augsburg

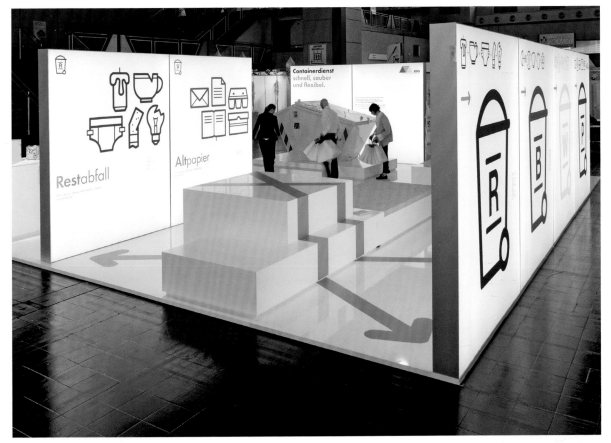

Was kommt in welche Tonne?
What goes in which bin?
[Exhibition Stand]

Developed for the waste disposal company EDG, this trade fair stand served to launch a campaign promoting waste separation. The aim was to communicate the rules and possibilities of a meaningful waste-separation system to people from all countries of origin. With this in mind, a clear and sophisticated pictographic system was developed that visualises distinctive waste types from various waste-separation categories.

client
EDG Entsorgung Dortmund GmbH

design
Paarpiloten,
Düsseldorf

creative direction
Nanni Goebel,
Christopher Wiehl

graphic design
Anna Gemmeke

trade fair construction
Projektpilot, Neuss

131

Lufthansa Trade Fair Stand ITB 2012

[Digital Event Communication]

At the Lufthansa exhibition stand at the ITB trade fair, digital attractions exuded pure holiday fun while simultaneously providing information about the services of the new brand Lufthansa Holidays. The focus was on audience-grabbing digital entertainment applications that drew upon augmented reality effects, where portrait photos of the stand visitors were "decorated" with amusing accessories or epigrams in thought bubbles. The interactive applications were presented in high-quality 3D models, such as a model of a giant camera.

client
Deutsche Lufthansa AG,
Frankfurt/Main

design
people interactive GmbH,
Cologne

creative direction
Dr. Tillman Bardt

concept
Thomas Hornstein

graphic design
Mathias Fritzen

strategic planning
Elke Mallmann

project management
Sarah Heintzmann

programming
Sven Bröker

Heidelberger Druckmaschinen Trade Show Exhibition drupa 2012

Designed in line with the motto "Discover HEI" for the drupa 2012 print media trade fair, this booth showcased a brand wall as the thematic and visual basis for the various themed zones. Real printing plates were combined to display various keywords from the latest "HEI" campaign of this Heidelberg-based company. Serving as a medium for product communication, LED screens integrated into the wall provided information about the company's products. The terrace-like platform in the middle of the booth featured a service centre that was further highlighted by a typographical sculpture.

client
Heidelberger Druckmaschinen AG, Heidelberg

design
KMS BLACKSPACE, Munich
SCHMIDHUBER, Munich

Kreon Trade Fair Stand Light + Building 2012

At the trade fair Light & Building 2012, this booth presented Kreon lighting solutions as elements that integrate naturally into architecture and interior design. Surfaces and spaces served as the main design elements which merged light and applications. A homogeneous appearance was produced by combining steel substrates with walls in black and white, whereby wall and ceiling panels were used to generate open and overlapping spaces. Lights by the manufacturer were placed in niches, wall sections and distinctive areas to illuminate and thus stage the architecture.

client
Kreon,
Opglabbeek

design
Kreon, Opglabbeek
Ueberholz GmbH,
Büro für temporäre Architektur,
Wuppertal

Alape Trade Fair Stand SHK 2012

With its reduced language of form and unusual animations, this trade fair stand fascinated visitors of the SHK 2012. The entrance led past two large portraits of a man and a woman, yet upon closer inspection it was evident that the faces had been animated on large-scale screens, with diagonals measuring over 2.6 metres in brilliant full HD quality. Inside the booth, the company Alape presented its modular system of furniture and washbasins. Combined with the sensory moments of the display, this turned the brand positioning and the claim of "Emotional Purism" into an experience.

client
Alape GmbH,
Goslar

design
Martin et Karczinski,
Munich

creative direction
Peter Martin

art direction
Birte Helms

graphic design
Johannes Kemnitzer

film production
Tina Maria Werner,
lucie_p

strategic consulting
Daniel Karczinski,
Philipp-Alexander Dietrich

architecture
Andrea Jürgens,
JI Jürgens Innenarchitektur

Audi Governance, Risk & Compliance

[Event Module]

Designed for a kick-off event, this stand introduced a newly developed and implemented in-house communication strategy for the Governance, Risk & Compliance division of the Audi company. Its asymmetrically contorted architecture of futurist appearance consists of two open modules facing each other. Distinctive slants and folds serve to symbolise the motifs "line" and "direction". Constructed on massive steel girders, the stand is self-supporting. The lighting design is highly effective, featuring white light strips and animated light control.

client
AUDI AG,
Ingolstadt

project management
Stefan Hengelmann

design
Martin et Karczinski,
Munich

creative direction
Peter Martin

art direction
Birte Helms

graphic design
Johannes Kemnitzer

text
Stephanie Schlageter

strategic consulting
Daniel Karczinski,
Philipp-Alexander Dietrich

photography
Sjoerd Ten Kate,
SCHIERKE COM/

event design
Jürgen Drändle,
Drändle 70|30

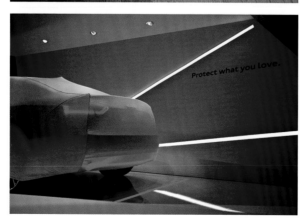

Sphinx Hall, Jungfraujoch, Switzerland

[Audio-visual Panorama]

The 360-degree audio-visual show was created in the middle of Europe's highest cave, at nearly 3,500 metres above sea level. Taking an emotional approach, it dramatises the overwhelming majesty and fragile beauty of glaciers. This film offers viewers, protected from weather conditions, an amazing panorama of the Alps projected on crystalline walls. Backed up by an orchestral soundtrack, it sensitises viewers to the human achievement of conquering the Alps. Using a 360-degree camera technique developed for this project, the dark cave is visually converted into a breath-taking panorama of Alpine poetry.

client
Jungfraubahn AG

design
TAMSCHICK MEDIA+SPACE
GmbH, Berlin

lead agency/scenography
Steiner Sarnen AG
für Kommunikation

overall concept
Steiner Sarnen AG
für Kommunikation,
TAMSCHICK MEDIA+SPACE GmbH

creative direction
Charlotte Tamschick

film direction
Marc Tamschick

concept
Franziska Fuchs

project management
Steffen Armbruster

animation/editing
Marc Osswald, Sascha Eckardt,
Matthias Wolf

music/sound design
Florian Käppler,
KLANGERFINDER GmbH

Swiss Pavilion –
Expo 2012 Yeosu Korea

[Media Scenography]

The walking tour through the
Swiss Pavilion at the Expo 2012
in Korea has been conceived to
combine a sensual experience
with insight into the importance
of the glacial landscape as a
water reservoir. Under the title
"Birth of an Ocean – it's in your
hands", the pavilion focused
on glaciers as drinking-water
reserves, staging them in immersive and emotional spaces.
Individual experiences, such
as projections on the palms of
the visitors' hands, aim to raise
awareness of water as a precious natural resource, while the
beauty and fragility of the ancient
glaciers are revealed in a three-
dimensional panoramic film.

client
Präsenz Schweiz, Bern

design
TAMSCHICK MEDIA+SPACE
GmbH, Berlin

lead agency/scenography
Steiner Sarnen AG
für Kommunikation

overall concept
Steiner Sarnen AG
für Kommunikation,
TAMSCHICK MEDIA+SPACE GmbH,
NÜSSLI (Schweiz) AG

creative direction
Charlotte Tamschick

film direction
Marc Tamschick

concept
Franziska Fuchs

project management
Steffen Armbruster, Anne Sebald

animation/editing
Akitoshi Mizutani, Marc Osswald,
Michael Trende, Fabian Tschöpl,
Sascha Eckardt, Matthias Wolf

music/sound design
Stefan Will, BLUWI

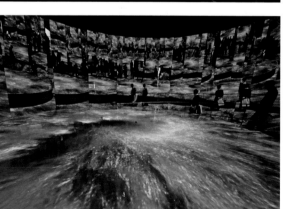

Pergamon – Panorama der antiken Metropole
Pergamon – Panorama of the Ancient City
[Temporary Exhibition]

The temporary exhibition in the Pergamonmuseum in Berlin is dedicated to the city of Pergamon and its pivotal role in antiquity. Archaeological finds have been set in their original contexts in order to offer visitors a vivid impression of the ancient metropolis. An imposing 25-metre-high, 360-degree city panorama serves to visualise a picture of the city's spatial associations; it illustrates the interaction between individual buildings and their specific components. In cooperation with the Collection of Classical Antiquities in Berlin, the panorama imparts a breathtaking impression of the overall urban space of the city of Pergamon.

client
Antikensammlung der Staatlichen Museen zu Berlin / Collection of Classical Antiquities of the National Museums in Berlin

design
asisi,
Berlin

creative direction/concept
Yadegar Asisi

art direction
Mathias Thiel

graphic design
Polyform,
Berlin

music/sound design
Eric Babak,
London

printing
Marx & Moschner,
Lennestadt

→ designer portrait: p. 405

Brunner Trade Fair Stand Salone Internazionale del Mobile 2012

This exhibition stand creates an intense spatial experience in which the innovative seating elements "plot" and "hoc" are staged. The strictly black-and-white setting takes a back seat to the colourful seating objects, which invite passers-by to pause, test them and linger. The walls reflect thoughts and inspirational ideas that arise during the contemplative act of sitting. They are completely covered in an installation of letters, forming associative figures and scenarios. Upon closer examination, poetic phrases, dialogic sequences and questioning thoughts emerge – reminiscent of Concrete Poetry.

client
Brunner GmbH, Rheinau

design
Ippolito Fleitz Group – Identity Architects, Stuttgart
Peter Ippolito, Gunter Fleitz

art direction
Axel Knapp, Martin Berkemeier

interior design
Tilla Goldberg, Jörg Schmitt, Daniela Schröder

exhibition stand construction
Hospes Team

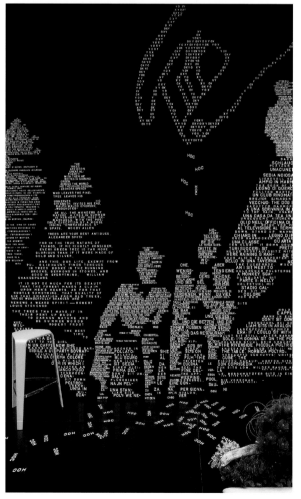

Good ideas glow in the dark
[Pavilion]

Aiming to communicate a successful business year despite the ongoing crisis, the Adris Group presented itself in a pavilion at the Weekend Media Festival, the largest media industry event in Southeast Europe. The pavilion was made to present the annual report of the Adris Group, a brochure that literally glows in the dark, illustrating how only good ideas can light up the path out of the crisis. The concept consisted of a room in which, upon entering, the lights faded out and the only things that could be seen were the annual reports glowing on the shelves and tables.

client
Adris Group,
Rovinj

design
Bruketa&Zinic OM, Zagreb
Brigada, Zagreb

creative direction
Damjan Geber,
Davor Bruketa,
Nikola Zinic

text
Ivan Cadez
(Senior Copywriter)

project management
Ivana Drvar
(Senior Account Executive)

production management
Vesna Durasin

adidas Virtual Footwear Wall – F50 Launch

[Interactive Environmental Design, Launch Campaign]

The adidas Virtual Footwear Wall (VFW) is an innovative, interactive "in-store" concept. It was utilised for this launch campaign so that customers could reserve the F50 miCoach football boot during a pre-release period. Complemented by immersive sound, the wall enabled the customer to explore high-definition, 3D models rendered in real-time, allowing them to rotate and zoom in to capture every detail of the boot. A mini, 3D-printed "BrainBoot" connected the 250 new owners to a members only online hub, while simultaneously serving as an invite to an exclusive in-store, collection event.

client
adidas AG,
Herzogenaurach

design
Start JudgeGill,
London

creative direction
Liz Sivell

project management
Nissanka Fernando

programming
Graham Pett

Henkel Forscherwelt
Henkel Explorer World
[Learning Environment]

At the heart of the 2011 "Forscherwelt" (Explorer World) learning initiative for children aged six to ten is a special educational environment. The extraordinary spatial concept interprets learning environments through a highly individual approach. Under the motto "Learning is a personal journey", up to 25 children at a time are introduced to a diverse, sensorimotor landscape featuring clear, geometric shapes, harmonious colours and appealing materials. The space thus promotes a broad field for exploration, but also experiences specifically geared towards children's perception and understanding.

client
Henkel AG & Co. KGaA,
Düsseldorf

design
wonderlabz,
Solingen

concept
Thomas Laqua,
wonderlabz

illustration
Rilla Alexander,
Rinzen

interior design
Michael Weinholzner,
visomat inc.

project management
Dr. Ute Krupp, Henkel;
Thomas Laqua,
Michael Weinholzner

MINI Pop-Up Store
London Westfield

[Temporary Store]

client
BMW AG,
Munich

design
studio 38 pure communication
GmbH, Berlin

creative direction
Kathrin Janke-Bendow,
Reinhard Knobelspies,
Mark Bendow

art direction
Yannah Bandilla

graphic design
Benjamin Fuchs,
Cathrin Roher

photography
diephotodesigner.de

programming
non-grid.jp

→ designer portrait: p. 435

Here the design task involved realising a temporary MINI brand store located in Europe's largest shopping mall in London, Westfield Stratford City, to be open for one year only. The store aims to give visitors the opportunity to browse the latest MINI models in a premium retail setting. It clearly differentiates the presentation from conventional car showroom environments and thus addresses a new target group. Realised within a period of only three months, the store showcases contemporary retail technology, including a touch-based interactive mirror that allows customers to virtually try on the outfits on sale. In addition, using a 3D car configurator, they can create their own MINI in 3D and request a test drive.

ARKHE Beauty Salon

[Interior Design]

client
Beauty Studio Therapy,
Chiba

design
Moriyuki Ochiai Architects /
Twoplus-A, Tokyo

→ designer portrait: p. 427

The concept and realisation of this beauty salon centred on the theme of water to lend it a futurist appearance. Water is interpreted as the source of all creation and a medium that connotes clarity – as an analogy of a salon that also represents a search for the source of beauty. A recyclable aluminium sheet was used to symbolise the flow of both water and hair. This sheet reflects the interior's soft light, as might emanate from the surface of water, and fills the space with elegant curves. A further effect is that the aluminium's flow changes according to the illumination, thus always providing an atmosphere suited to the surrounding area. This provides visitors with the experience of manifold atmospheres thanks to shifts in light throughout the day.

Heineken Open
Design Explorations
[Concept Nightclub]

client
Heineken,
Amsterdam

design
Heineken Design Department,
Amsterdam

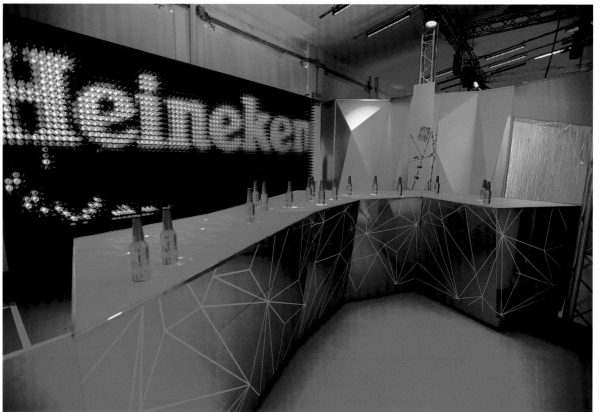

Heineken Open Design Explorations is a progressive, crowd-sourced concept in nightclub design, presented at the Milan design week. Co-created by emerging designers from New York, Sao Paolo, Tokyo and Milano, ideas were brought together in one origami themed, progressive club space that enhanced the club-goers experiences – with surprising different moods in the green refreshment, red heated dance and blue chill out areas. The interactive bar offered an inventive way to order a Heineken, and invited customers to interact with total strangers by drawing and moving light shapes across the bar's surface. A television wall made of over 2,500 Heineken bottles displayed funky images of the club-goers, while a UV-chalkboard invited guests to express their thoughts.

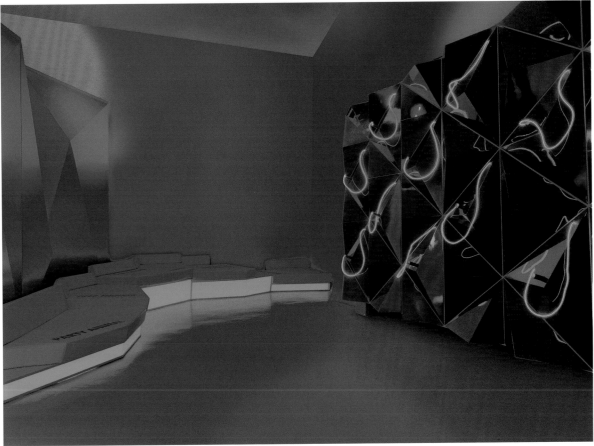

Swarovski_Xmas
[Visual Communication Concept]

client
Daniel Swarovski Corporation AG,
Männedorf

**head of retail marketing
creative concepts**
Boris A. Bihl

design
dfrost GmbH & Co. KG,
Stuttgart

creative direction
Nadine Frommer

art direction
Silke Scheytt

project management
Fabian Stelzer

Inspired by the shape of crystals, the design of an iconic pattern was at the heart of a globally uniform point-of-sale campaign launched by the company Swarovski in positioning itself for "the most beautiful crystalline time of the year". A crystal in its smallest unit which is a hexagon that stands for symmetry and future orientation was interpreted as the basic element of a visual signature, combining traditional workmanship with innovative lifestyle products. The resulting snow-flower-like icon set out to lend Swarovski a more emotional appeal during the Christmas season while symbolising symmetry and future orientation. In extensive patterns, the snow flower characterised the points of sale in an elegant and graceful way and was used for window campaigns, storefront illumination and in-store communication with on-counter displays and presenters specifically designed for Christmas.

My Green World – Dutch Pavilion Floriade 2012

My Green World, the Dutch Pavilion at the Floriade 2012 – World Horticultural Expo, takes visitors on an inspiring journey of discovery through new developments and innovations. The exhibits My Green Life, My Green Lab and My Green City are partially supported by games and animations to lend them a futuristic and sometimes experimental appeal. The sustainable building is designed as a self-carrying shield made of wood with a form inspired by an opening seed. My Green World aims to demonstrate how advanced agricultural technology changes the word.

client
Ministry of Economic Affairs, Agriculture and Innovation

design
2D3D, The Hague

creative direction/concept
René van Raalte,
Matt van Santvoord

graphics/exhibits
Jaap Bardet,
Ilona Hoogeveen,
Anke Sentker-Verhagen,
Laurens van Schijndel

audiovisual presentations
Gerben Starink

GS Caltex Pavilion – Expo 2012 Yeosu Korea

At the Expo Korea, the GS Caltex Pavilion illustrates the company mission and the future visions of this Korean oil corporation. It took the form of a dynamic ensemble that, at first glance, was reminiscent of an oversized rice paddy: 18-metre-high blades swayed like grass in the wind and became illuminated when touched. In the middle of this energy field was a mirrored pavilion building with a similarly mirrored entrance hall aimed at evoking a sense of social interconnectedness and collective networking. A 360-degree film metaphorically drew the visitors into the world of energy.

client
Peopleworks Promotion Co. Ltd. (PW), Seoul

design
ATELIER BRÜCKNER GmbH, Stuttgart

creative direction
Prof. Uwe R. Brückner

art direction
Michel Casertano

film production
TAMSCHICK MEDIA+SPACE GmbH

music/sound design
BLUWI

photography
Nils Clauss

100 beste Plakate '10
100 best posters '10
[Modular Exhibition System]

The design of this exhibition system for the presentation of the "100 best posters '10" corresponds to the corporate design of the award competition. It follows the idea of transforming the competition logo, consisting of 100 concentric circles, into a three-dimensional object. The planar circles are converted into upright rings that chain together like molecules and thus develop into ever-new, complex spatial structures. Since the system is designed on the basis of identical modules, it can be modified into variable configurations at each exhibition venue.

client
100 Beste Plakate e. V.,
Radebeul

design
büro münzing,
3d kommunikation,
Stuttgart
Prof. Uwe Münzing,
Fabian Friedhoff

corporate design
L2M3 Kommunikationsdesign

photography
Fabian Friedhoff,
büro münzing

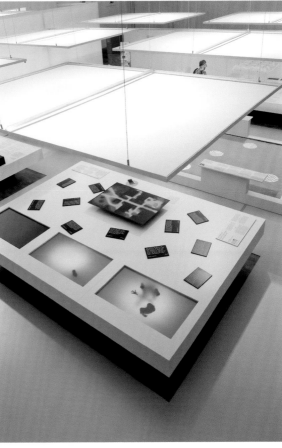

Die Zukunft unter uns
The future at your feet
[Exhibition]

The exhibition "The future at your feet" is based on an innovative research undertaking focused on soil solutions of the future. The involved projects by six creative teams of designers, artists, architects and film-makers are visualised and presented three-dimensionally as walk-in installations, film animation, or in the form of models. Six identical presentation surfaces are individually designed to suit the particular concepts. Together with the exhibits, the integrated media, and the panels of light suspended above, they form a stand-alone presentation module reminiscent of a laboratory.

client
Uzin Utz AG,
Ulm

head of marketing
Katja Kretzschmar

design
büro münzing,
3d kommunikation,
Stuttgart
Prof. Uwe Münzing,
Fabian Friedhoff

creative direction
büro münzing;
Alexander Trage,
dorten gmbh

graphic design
Daniel Fischer,
dorten gmbh

project management
Ulrike Zöllkau,
dorten gmbh

photography
Fabian Friedhoff,
büro münzing

Zeitlos – 60 Jahre Mercedes-Benz SL
Timeless – 60 years of the Mercedes-Benz SL
[Special Exhibition]

Under the theme "Timeless – 60 years of the Mercedes-Benz SL", the Mercedes-Benz Museum has dedicated a special exhibition to the legendary sports car range. The title "Timeless" serves as a hallmark and documents the aspiration of the SL series while embodying the guiding principle of the spatial concept. With floor graphics that represent a stylised clock face, ten vehicles were positioned chronologically to form a radial timeline. In the centre stands a circular showcase with selected real and media exhibits, creating thematic links to individual racing cars.

client
Mercedes-Benz Museum, Stuttgart

design
jangled nerves, Stuttgart

creative direction
Prof. Thomas Hundt, Ingo Zirngibl

art direction
Jörg Stierle

graphic design
Heiko Geiger, Stefka Simeonova

project management
Jakob Eckert

animation
Martin Maurer

interior design
Verena Pfeffer

Märchenwelten
Fairy Tale Worlds
[Travelling Exhibition]

Celebrating the 200-year anniversary of the Brothers Grimm
collection of fairy tales, the
Goethe-Institut sent fairy tales
around the world in a travelling
exhibition. The tales about magic,
heroes and villains are told at
seven groves with seven treasure
chests, while interactive sections
introduce the German language
in a playful way. Visitors have to
take tests only heroes can pass,
they are led into a world of evil
by means of a voice distorter, and
can further develop the "never-
ending story" while sitting at
escritoires. The modules may be
placed flexibly in very different
types of locations.

client
Goethe-Institut,
Munich

design
krafthaus –
Das Atelier von facts and fiction,
Cologne

concept
Robert Müller,
Patrizia Widritzki,
Kristine Fester

text
Hendrik Pletz

customer advisory service
Jörg Krauthäuser

project management
Kristine Fester

printing
Picos Grafik GmbH;
Stefan Christ, Streng & Christ
Kommunikationsdesign GbR

exhibition stand construction
Jan Mahlstedt,
Moser Design

Deutsches Filmmuseum
German Film Museum
[Permanent Exhibition]

The German Film Museum in Frankfurt am Main presents a content-generated permanent exhibition spread out across 800 square metres on two floors. The exhibition units "Filmic Vision" and "Filmic Narrative" explain the history of moving images and show the possibilities of present-day technology in an easy-to-grasp manner. Central elements are darkened spaces with spot-lit objects, analogous to a film being projected in a cinema. The design idiom on the first floor is reminiscent of film drums and tape, while the setting on the second floor is reminiscent of a film-maker's studio.

client
DIF Deutsches Filminstitut, Frankfurt/Main

design
ATELIER BRÜCKNER GmbH, Stuttgart

creative direction
Prof. Uwe R. Brückner

concept
Birgit Kadatz,
Dirk Schubert,
Tobias Geisler

project management
Frank Forell

graphic design
Jana Fröhlich,
Jutta Stüber

media production
jangled nerves

light planning
Bartenbach LichtLabor

photography
Uwe Dettmar

Kunstschätze des Mittelalters
Mediaeval Art Treasures
[Exhibition]

In the special exhibition "Mediaeval Art Treasures", the Tyrolean State Museums featured outstanding exhibits from the collection to draw attention to the significance of Tyrolean art in the early and late Gothic periods. In order to set the mode of presentation apart from the museum's permanent exhibition, the artefacts were positioned on structural elements. Reduced in terms of form and colour, these elements gave rise to new perspectives and spatial correspondences in each situation. The exhibition architecture was designed to enhance the exhibits and their auratic presence.

client
Tiroler Landesmuseum, Innsbruck

curatorial direction
Dr. Eleonore Gürtler

design
büro münzing,
3d kommunikation,
Stuttgart
Prof. Uwe Münzing,
Fabian Friedhoff

graphic design
L2M3 Kommunikationsdesign,
daz design

photography
Brigida González

PARLAMENTARIUM – The European Parliament's Visitors' Centre

The Parlamentarium in Brussels provides information on the history of the EU in an informative and experience-orientated way, while also exploring the function of the European Parliament and how it works in practice. Visitors journey through carefully harmonised, content-rich narrative spaces that offer information in all 23 official EU languages. Personal Media Guides were developed to make all of the stored multimedia data accessible to the respective target groups. This includes systems for the visual and hearing impaired visitors and a special option for children.

client
European Parliament, Brussels

design
ATELIER BRÜCKNER GmbH, Stuttgart

creative direction
Prof. Uwe R. Brückner

art direction
Britta Nagel

project management
Michelle Bühler,
René Walkenhorst

graphic design
intégral ruedi baur

media design/concept
jangled nerves

media design/production
Markenfilm Crossing

lighting design
LDE Belzner Holmes

photography
Rainer Rehfeld

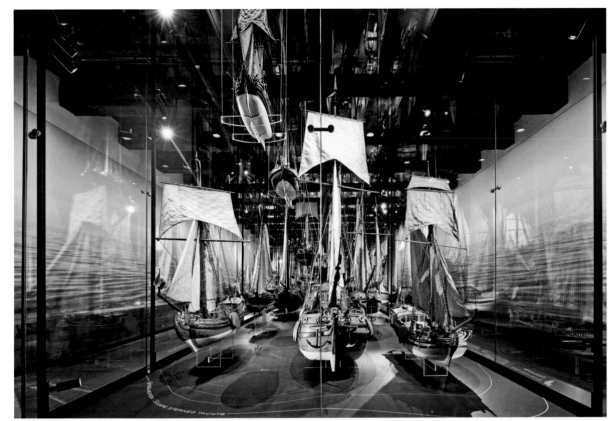

Het Scheepvaartmuseum
National Maritime Museum
[Themed Galleries]

The National Maritime Museum in Amsterdam (Het Scheepvaart-museum), which looks back on a rich history, has reinvented itself with an innovative exhibition concept. Located in a former arsenal, built in 1656, the east wing of the museum is dedicated to the most valuable exhibits in the collection, presenting them in seven themed galleries. A unique spatial arrangement with a distinctive atmosphere was developed for each gallery, using the exhibits as a starting point as they are integral to the respective settings. Digital media are integrated seamlessly into the exhibition presentation.

client
Het Scheepvaartmuseum,
Amsterdam

design
ATELIER BRÜCKNER GmbH,
Stuttgart

creative direction
Prof. Uwe R. Brückner

concept
Birgit Kadatz,
Britta Nagel,
Eva Schrade

project management
Frank Forell

graphic design
attraktive grautöne

media design
jangled nerves

media production
Kiss the Frog

lighting design
Lichtontwerpers

photography
Michael Jungblut

Moving Types – Letters in Motion

[Exhibition]

client
z zg Zentrum Zeitbasierte Gestaltung, FH Mainz/ HfG Schwäbisch Gmünd in cooperation with the Gutenberg-Museum Mainz

curators
Prof. Ralf Dringenberg, z zg
Prof. Anja Stöffler, z zg
Prof. Harald Pulch, FH Mainz

concept/ design/ creative direction
Prof. Ralf Dringenberg, z zg
Prof. Anja Stöffler, z zg

graphic design/motion design
Beppo Albrecht, Miriam Bröckel, Nicole Höfle, Julian Hölzer, Adrian Jehle, Dominic Specht, HfG Schwäbisch Gmünd
Simon Mayer, Acht Frankfurt .
Visual Catering

interface design
Adrian Abele, Onofrio Di Franco, Antonio Krämer-Fernandez, Martha Miosga, Marcel Müller, David Nickel, Luise Pescheck, Julian Schwarz, Patric Sterrantino, Dominik Witzke, HfG Schwäbisch Gmünd

programming
metaminded UG, Aalen/Kassel
Erik Freydank, Kevin Röhl, FH Mainz
Nikolaus Völzow, Karlsruhe

communication planning
Sebastian Bauer, Pia Hofmann, Till Köhler, Sandra Kühefuß, Kerstin Röcker, Philipp Schadt, Nadine Zschäk, HfG Schwäbisch Gmünd
Leonore Kleinkauf, Manfred Liedtke, Birgitta Loehr, Kristofer Oedekoven, Uwe Zentgraf, FH Mainz/img

exhibition design/interior design
Prof. Ralf Dringenberg, z zg
Prof. Anja Stöffler, z zg

architecture showroom
Bartek Wieczorek, unique assemblage, Frankfurt/Main

→ digital presentation: DVD

"Moving Types – Letters in Motion" is an interactive exhibition that documents the history of animated letters from the beginnings of film through modern times. More than 200 internationally outstanding examples of animated letters, both historical and current, are presented in this exhibition. Arranged chronologically and according to subject, the examples range from early avant-garde films to modern music videos and art films. The exhibits are presented by means of illuminated cubes with QR codes that link to the individual film sequences. These clips are accessible via iPads that the visitors can borrow. Visually, the exhibition is determined by these self-illuminating QR codes, with the cubes displaying the codes arranged chronologically. To facilitate easy orientation, each cube bears the name and date of each respective exhibit.

200 Jahre Krupp –
Ein Mythos wird
besichtigt
200 Years of Krupp –
A Survey of the Myth

[Exhibition]

client
Stiftung Ruhr Museum,
Essen

design
südstudio,
Stuttgart

creative direction
Hannes Bierkämper,
südstudio;
hg merz architekten
und museumsgestalter

art direction
Hannes Bierkämper,
südstudio

concept
Ruhr Museum,
südstudio

graphic design
Clemens Hartmann,
CLMNZ (Concept);
Karsten Moll,
Kommunikationskontor
(Realisation)

photography
Brigida González

lighting design
Jens Maier,
Maierlighting;
Ruhr Museum

Deciphering the "Krupp myth" picture puzzle was the key design idea for this exhibition, with blurred "superimpositions" serving as a design metaphor. The exhibition was staged on the 12-meter level of a former coal-washing plant, which today has been re-designated as a Ruhr area commemorative site. The space is structured by a central installation of rectangular solid elements, forming a "field of force", while different-sized cuboids follow a free play of horizontal and vertical arrangements. In terms of material and appearance, the rather dark ambience of the space is contrasted by white components creating an "enlightening" brightness. As an allegory of the mechanisation of writing, the monospaced typeface Generika, with its technical appearance, was the font selected for use in the exhibition.

Dansaekhwa – Korean Monochrome Painting

[Exhibition]

client
National Museum
of Contemporary Art,
Korea

design
National Museum
of Contemporary Art,
Korea – Design Team

design director
Yong-Ju Kim

graphic design
Hye-Min Song,
Sae-Mi Kim

space design
Hyun-Sook Kim,
Min-Hee Lee

photography
Jun-Ho Jang

→ designer portrait: p. 426

The exhibition space is designed to create an ambience of appreciating two-dimensional artworks in a three-dimensional sense of spatial experience. The works are re-created and replenished through the beauty of Korean traditional architecture, "emptying and filling": white void, space layer and windows, which are rectangular spaces cut out from the walls. The viewers are able to find out by themselves the main idea of works with an unbound gaze that penetrates the space. In the archive space, six-metre vertical wooden structures are set up, where the texture of the wood evokes a great sense of nature. The structure is composed of 360 compartments, in which all the materials documenting the artists' achievements are inhabited either through books or videos; the space forms a forest, bringing together and uniting the various and complex ideas into one.

mt ex Hiroshima

[Promotion Design]

In promoting the "mt" masking
tapes – a product originally
used as curing tape in industrial
applications, but which customers
in Japan also enjoy in interior
decoration thanks to its range
of colours and patterns – this
travelling exhibition broke new
ground. Spaces and locations
were decorated with variations
on the masking tape to raise
public attention. The exhibition
venue in Hiroshima, for instance,
was located on the seafront.
To welcome visitors, the deck
in front and the shop itself were
covered with different "mt" tapes.
Customers were thus able to
easily browse the enormous
variety of the tape collection.

client
Kamoi Kakoshi Co., Ltd.,
Kurashiki City,
Okayama Prefecture

design
iyamadesign inc.,
Tokyo

creative direction/art direction
Koji Iyama

concept
Koji Iyama

graphic design
Mayuko Watanabe,
Takenori Sugimura,
Saori Shibata

mt train
[Promotion Design]

Travelling through the whole of Japan, this promotional exhibition staged the variety of the "mt" masking tapes through presentations at unusual locations and in public space to raise attention. The promotional concept of the exhibition held in Hiroshima thus also included the tram that runs between Hiroshima's main station and the actual exhibition space at the city's harbour. The tram was decorated both on the outside and inside, with tape rolls for instance hanging down from the compartment ceilings. Thus passengers who were not yet aware of the product were also led to the exhibition.

client
Kamoi Kakoshi Co., Ltd.,
Kurashiki City,
Okayama Prefecture

design
iyamadesign inc.,
Tokyo

creative direction/art direction
Koji Iyama

concept
Koji Iyama

graphic design
Mayuko Watanabe,
Takenori Sugimura,
Saori Shibata

Edible Masterpieces Exhibition

[PR Event]

This PR event staged the launch of the brand Primor, a successful Portuguese fine charcuterie company, by visualising the brand concept of "tradition, art and masterpieces". Forming an edible exhibition, the charcuterie products were framed like well-known paintings to offer event visitors a sensual experience that merged the gustatory with the visual. Surrounded by a designer-created pig collection, visitors could delight their eyes and mouths with works such as "Pork sausage, cooked chicken breast, thin smoked sausage" (Lichtenstein), "Ham and Bacon thin strips" (van Gogh) and "Cooked ham and bacon" (Mondrian pizza).

client
PRIMOR,
Vila Nova de Famalicão

design
Ivity Brand Corp,
Lisbon

creative direction
Paulo Rocha,
Mara de Jesus

graphic design
Andre Hilario,
Catia Oliveira,
Marcos Cruz

strategic planning
Mara de Jesus

project management
Andreia Ferreira

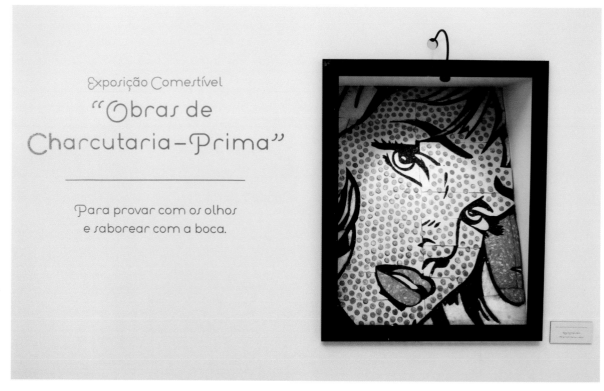

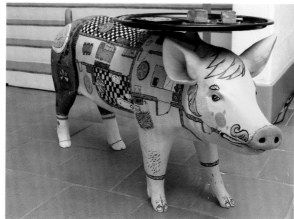

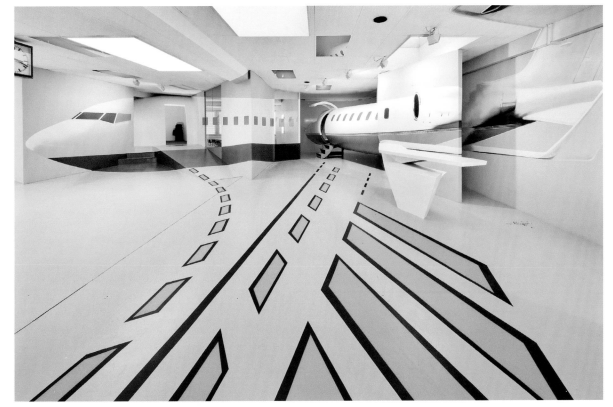

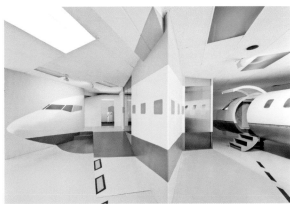

simINN
[Flight Simulation Centre]

The simINN Flight Simulation Centre presents its visitors with two fully functional flight simulators featuring the visual representation of a Boeing 737 and a Learjet X45 as full-size renditions. The built airplane elements have been complemented by graphics dispersed onto the walls, floor and ceiling. When viewed from most angles, the graphics produce the illusion of the plane in its intact form. From other perspectives, the overlapping of the built elements and the partly skewed graphics create varying compositions and distortions of both the architecture and the shapes of the airplanes.

client
simINN GmbH,
Filderstadt-Bernhausen

head of marketing
Andreas Wolf

design
banozic
architecture|scenography,
Frankfurt/Main

creative direction/concept
Boris Banozic

graphic design
Boris Banozic

photography
Kristof Lemp

construction/graphic production
Bernd Weinmann,
Christoph Meyer,
Jan Haas

Lebendige Erinnerung
Vivid Memories
[Exhibition]

Raum-D is a therapeutic studio for people with dementia. Following a creative working approach, the studio offers patients new ways of dealing with their memories. Aiming to raise awareness for the Raum-D therapy programme in the region and in the local media, and also to sensitise the public to this complex topic, this exhibition traces the life story of a theoretical Alzheimer's patient. A three-dimensional model of a brain invites visitors to learn about this person's life story, memory by memory. The personal and historical milestones in the person's life thus become accessible once more.

client
Raum-D, Atelier für Menschen mit Demenz, Düsseldorf

design
Ogilvy Germany, Düsseldorf

head of advertising
Thomas Schwarz

creative direction
Andreas Steinkemper

art direction
Paul Kuna

text
Kajo Strauch

project management
Anke Breuer

illustration
Casper Franken, Shotopop Ltd, London

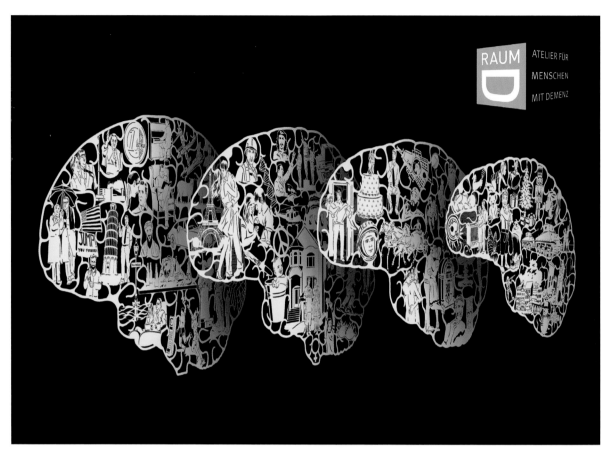

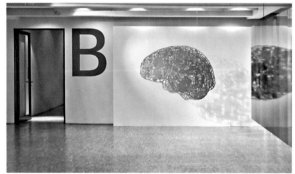

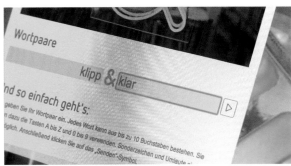

This is the AND
[Installation and Online Event]

With an aim to connect "people with people, brands and themes", this installation visualises the core competency of the agency Milla & Partner. The pivotal symbol of the new corporate design translates this core competency into a universal sign: the ampersand. The iconographic element of the installation, consisting of the ampersand sign and vintage Telefunken displays, was developed to launch the new corporate design: the installation "This is the AND", which was combined with a communication chain encompassing diverse media channels as well as a live link to the analogue installation at the heart of the agency.

client
Milla & Partner,
Stuttgart

design
Milla & Partner,
Stuttgart

creative direction
Johannes Milla

art direction
Claudius Brodmann,
Simon Pertschy

concept
Ingo Wörner,
Claudius Brodmann

project management
Patrick Pickert

programming
Ingo Wörner

screen design
Thomas Frenzel

→ digital presentation: DVD

Radler raus!
Bikes get out!
[Promotion]

client
Europcar Autovermietung GmbH,
Hamburg

design
Ogilvy Deutschland

creative direction
Dr. Stephan Vogel,
Peter Strauss

art direction
Ute Sonntag

graphic design
Nadine Reich

text
Peter Strauss

project management
Stefan Molter,
Julia Adrian

In order to promote a reasonable rental offer by Europcar among city-bound bike enthusiasts, with the offer involving a rental car plus bike carrier, this campaign needed to address the target group despite its small budget. The solution was to present the offer at a perfect touch point which had never been used before: at the bike lanes in German cities that were marked with an iconic bike symbol. That very symbol became part of the advertising – which was sprayed directly below, so that the bike looked as if it were mounted on a car. Bikers literally came across this "enhanced" bike lane sign all around the participating Europcar stations, causing demand for the rental package to soar. And when the season was over, the offer just vanished from Germany's streets, because the environment-friendly chalk spray was washed away by the first autumn rain.

Driller Killer

[Promotion]

client
nie wieder bohren AG,
Hanau

design
Ogilvy Deutschland

creative direction
Michael Kutschinski,
Jens Steffen,
Uwe Jakob

art direction/text
Christian Urbanski

project management
Larissa Pohl

art buying
Martina Diederichs

production
Bernhard Schmidt,
Red Works

Driller Killer was a promotion campaign for the product "nie wieder bohren" (no more drilling), which makes drilling holes unnecessary. Without a media budget, the challenge was to find a simple idea to promote the product features in a tangible way, to enhance website traffic and to increase sales. Based on a bold and purposefully shocking concept, the campaign illustrated how drilling holes is annoying and how life is easier without it. The approach involved affixing product samples with screws to the doors of parked cars in the parking lots of hardware stores in Stuttgart, Dortmund, Munich and Frankfurt. Shocked at first, car owners soon relaxed again: the screws were magnetic and could easily be removed without leaving residue, just like the promoted product itself.

Information Design/
Public Space

red dot: grand prix

Dauro Oliveira Orthodontics Clinic
[Signage System]

The concept of the signage system for the Dauro Oliveira Orthodontics Clinic is inspired by multi-bracket appliances, more specifically the wires that keep them together and fix them on the teeth. In the implementation of the system, these brackets are represented by small silver-coloured squares and the wires by rubber band that can easily be tied around the squares. Based on this design idea and on the materials which are used in these elements, a family of pictograms was created along with numbers which, placed on glass surfaces and doors, serve to identify the different clinic areas and immediately convey an association with the profession of the client. In combination with a distinctive typography, which reflects the strength of the rubber band, this resulted in a system that is easy to install and has a very simple yet clear and friendly appearance that helps create a positive environment. The aim of placing the aesthetic perception centre stage and thus minimise patients' inhibition and fear of pain, has been implemented optimally.

Statement by the jury

»The idea for this signage system is fantastic and works perfectly well – especially against the backdrop of the client. Inspired by the genuine daily work of orthodontists, it reflects their identity in a manner that is just as authentic as it is original and appealing.«

client
Dauro Oliveira
Orthodontics Clinic,
Belo Horizonte

design
Greco Design,
Belo Horizonte

creative direction
Gustavo Greco

graphic design
Tidé

graphic design assistance
Fred Fita

illustration
Bruno Nunes

motion design
Ricardo Donato,
Victor Magalhães

account management
Victor Fernandes

printing
Dani Pires,
Alexandre Fonseca

→ designer portrait: p. 415

Amnesty International Light Sculpture

[Installation]

As part of the Ai Weiwei exhibition in the Martin-Gropius-Bau in Berlin, the Amnesty International mission statement "Amnesty shines a light into the darkness" was turned into a light sculpture. Beholders see this statement projected onto the middle of a white wall, complemented by a figurative mark of a candle. This candle, which is both the international symbol for hope and the logo of the human rights organisation, has an LED at its base so that it illuminates a template, which is attached to the wall, from below. As soon as the LED is activated by a visitor stepping up to the installation, an apparently realistic shadow of a scene in which human rights are violated is projected onto the wall – the change of the ambient light turns the previously neutral viewer instantly into a shocked eyewitness. The installation conveys the message that human rights are violated unnoticed and in secrecy until Amnesty International makes such incidents visible and brings them to the world's attention, in a highly effective manner.

Statement by the jury

»The outstanding achievement of this installation is that it makes its mission statement unmistakably clear. In addition, it integrates viewers into the presentation by having them activate it unknowingly, turning them into both actors and witnesses. The light sculpture thus embodies a convincing and well-staged implementation of the message.«

client
Amnesty International,
Sektion der Bundesrepublik
Deutschland e.V., Berlin

design
Scholz & Friends

head of advertising
Martin Pross,
Matthias Spaetgens,
Wolf Schneider

creative direction
Wolf Schneider

art direction
Olivier Nowak,
Jürgen Krugsperger

customer advisory service
Anna Kubitza,
Nicole Krumrei

photography
Jürgen Krugsperger

illustration
Olivier Nowak

→ designer portrait: p. 431

red dot: best of the best

A50 Motorway Information Graphic

This regional tourist information graphic was part of an art project in the service area of Sonse Heide on the Dutch A50 motorway and aims to bring attention to regional tourist sites. Instead of presenting the information on familiar-looking boards and signs, as is usual, it was engraved in the form of line charts on the hardwood planks of picnic benches and tables. Showing the tourist sites and places of interest located along the route as pictograms emerging from a single line, the benches and tables serve as banners advertising the region. The pictograms feature smooth, simple contours and are set around six touristic themes, grouped by individual colours such as green for nature, dark blue for art and pink for religious sites. They refer to specific places in the region, while a geographical wall-map, which also shows motorway information, serves as a legend to the icons. Both the icons and the accompanying low-contour typography were designed particularly with regard to machinability.

Statement by the jury

»This information design impresses with its highly original implementation. The idea to advertise tourist sites on objects typical of motorway service areas, such as benches and tables, is smart and makes perfect sense. The graphically minimalist yet highly distinctive design in particular turns the work into an outstanding eye-catcher.«

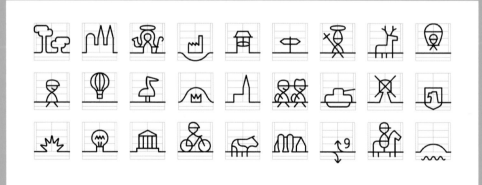

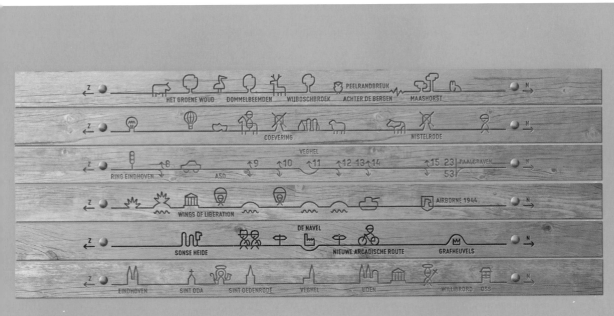

client
Stichting Kunst langs de A50
Dutch Province of Noord-Brabant
Dutch Ministry of Infrastructure
and the Environment
(Rijkswaterstaat)
BKKC, Brabants Kenniscentrum
voor Kunst en Cultuur

design
Pier Taylor,
Amsterdam

project management
Marcel Smink

strategic planning
Bas Veldhuizen, BKKC,
Tilburg

programming
Paul Roncken,
Wageningen University

engraving
Jeroen Brouwer, ID Lite BV,
Westzaan

→ designer portrait: p. 437

Architectural
Particles

[Information System,
Exhibition Design]

The theme of the exhibition
"Architectural Particles" is
consistently implemented
through a three-dimensional
information system: modular
octahedrons and tetrahedrons
serve as the basic shapes and
grids of all information displays,
which seem to flow and evolve
across the room. Texts, drawings,
photographs and films are rigor-
ously but playfully placed in an
unusual baseline grid. With their
unconventional character, they
encourage visitors to take in the
information while remaining easy
to read and comprehensible.

client
Museum für Angewandte Kunst
Köln / Museum of Applied Arts
Cologne

**head of communication/
education**
Dr. Romana Breuer

design
großgestalten
kommunikationsdesign,
Cologne
Tobias Groß,
Jazek Poralla

exhibition concept
STUDYO ARCHITECTs*
Olivia Ferguson-Losier,
Ayşin Ipekçi

exhibition design
STUDYO ARCHITECTs*
Olivia Ferguson-Losier,
Ayşin Ipekçi
responsive design studio
Hans Sachs,
Johann Eckartz

text
Ayşin Ipekçi

printing
Werbetechnik Kleiner

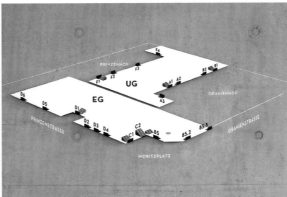

Aufbau Haus

[Signage System,
Orientation System]

This individual signage and orientation system was developed for the Aufbau Haus at Moritzplatz in Berlin, which houses an exciting mix of tenants, such as the publisher's group Aufbau Verlag, the Planet Modulor with its adjacent "planets", as well as galleries, designers and photographers. The design concept combines typography and material in the second and third dimensions. Excerpted bylines – flexibly arrayed and complemented by seemingly three-dimensional symbols – lend the Aufbau Haus its unique identity. The black-and-white colour scheme emphasises its rough concrete architecture.

client
Moritzplatz 1
Entwicklungsgesellschaft mbH,
Berlin

design
Moniteurs GmbH,
Berlin

art direction
Heike Nehl

concept
Heike Nehl,
Anne von Borries

graphic design
Christian Witt

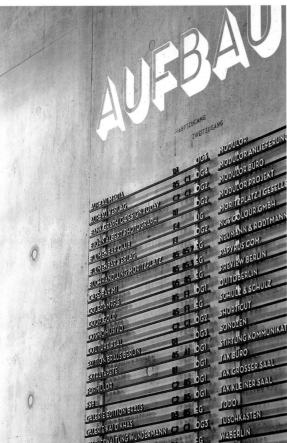

adidas laces

[Signage System, Interior Design]

client
adidas AG,
Herzogenaurach

design
büro uebele
visuelle kommunikation,
Stuttgart

graphic design
Carolin Himmel,
Prof. Andreas Uebele

project management
Carolin Himmel

photography
Werner Huthmacher,
Christian Richters

interior design
ZieglerBürg
Büro für Gestaltung

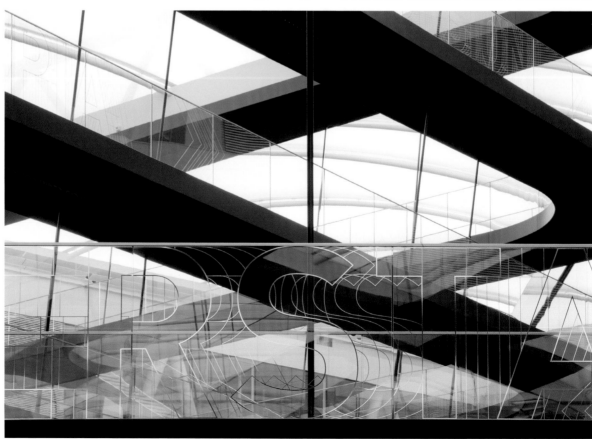

A metaphor of laces is the key element throughout the entire architecture of the adidas building, capturing the essence of sport: constant movement. A "moving" typography runs through the new adidas centre and is also reflected in the typeface of the signage system. Swift and light, the font leaps and bounds across walls and balustrades, its form vibrating and altering in the process. Words identify places, translating into coloured surfaces, reliefs and sculptures. In the meeting areas on the upper floors, the white lettering appears to have been frozen mid-movement, forming a mural relief. On the glass balustrades of the high walkways that criss-cross the interior of the building, the letters look as if they had been stamped from super-fine, transparent gauze.

Space Dot One

[Information Design]

client
Daum Communications,
Jeju/Seoul

design
Daum Communications,
Jeju/Seoul

creative direction
Lee June Hyeong

lead design
Baek Seung Wan

graphic design/illustration
Bae Soo Hyun

head of design
Kim Mi Yeon

photography
Kim Young Soo

project management
Park Dae Young

→ designer portrait: p. 409

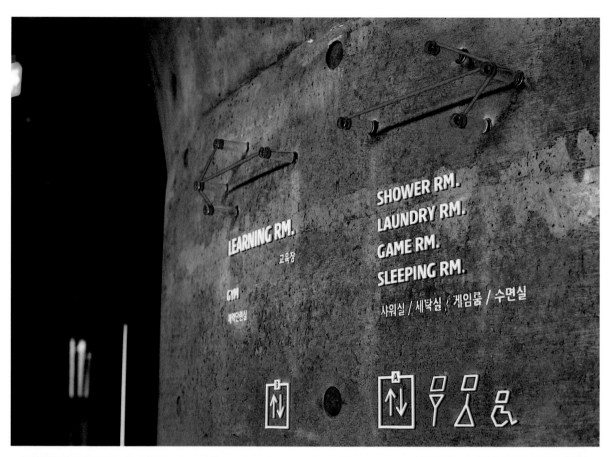

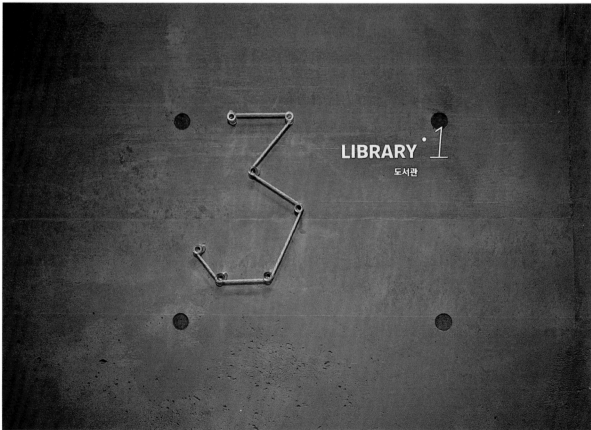

The signage system for the headquarters of Daum Communications, a building called Space Dot One in Jeju, Korea, illustrates the corporate philosophy of sustainability while simultaneously underlining the architectural individuality of the building. Another objective of this signage approach was to facilitate efficient communication between the binary workplaces and to gain the trust of the public. The concept focuses on a story that is based on the metaphorical motif of a thread, which also reflects the aspect of sustainability. The complex relationship between human, company and public is represented by an association of canvas and dot, with the thread as the central connecting medium.

Memory Loops

[Website]

Memory Loops is a virtual
memorial for the victims of
National Socialism created by
the city of Munich. Collages of
voices and music were developed
from the transcriptions of historical and recent audio material
from victims and surviving witnesses. The collages are thematically linked to the topography
of National Socialism in Munich.
This audio artwork was realised
in collaboration with the Bavarian
Broadcasting Corporation.
It consists of 300 German and 175
English audio tracks, which are
made available on www.memory-
loops.net for listening and free
download.

client
Landeshauptstadt München /
City of Munich

concept/illustration
Michaela Melián,
Munich

graphic design
Markus Weisbeck,
Surface,
Frankfurt/Main

music/sound design
Michaela Melián,
Munich

programming
MESO Web Scapes,
Frankfurt/Main

user interface design
Stefan Ammon,
MESO Web Scapes

Städel Museum

[Multitouch Installation]

With the reopening of the new Städel Museum in Frankfurt, a multi-touch table was introduced that fosters unprecedented value in the experience of art. Intentionally located among the Old Masters, the table invites visitors to change their thinking process while consuming art. It intentionally provokes an emotional and personal dialogue with the works of art – an interactive application based on an associative and didactic approach to art education. The visitor intuitively selects a topic and is presented with five out of 2,200 questions.

client
Städel Museum,
Frankfurt/Main

design
Cosalux GmbH,
Offenbach/Main

Packaging Design

Event Design

Information Design /
Public Space

Corporate Films

TV, Film & Cinema

Corporate Films

red dot: grand prix

The first mark

[Recruitment Film]

It is said in the arts that the first brush stroke defines the work. What happens after that has its own momentum. This recruitment film also centres on the idea of the first brush stroke as the first stroke of a signature and the starting point of a professional career. It thus emphasises the career entry as an important mark that sets the course of personal future development. The film draws a parallel to the art world by showing an artist drawing the first stroke on a canvas and elaborating it into a beautiful, richly detailed landscape. Meanwhile, a voice-over is talking about the life of a passionate artist, actively creating an environment that allows him to tap into his skills and unleash the courage to think out of the box. The idea of the artist that people may view the world with slightly different eyes owing to their work and unmistakable signature is equally important for a work of art as it is for somebody's lifework. The film thus elegantly and entertainingly closes the circle from the arts to the inspiring and satisfying work of a consultant.

Statement by the jury

»The outstanding achievement of this film is that it conveys its content through a metaphor and communicates the challenge and high demands of a company by analogy to the art of painting. The skilfully realised film promotes thinking outside the box – as a requirement to its future employees.«

client
McKinsey & Company, Inc.,
Munich

head of marketing
Dr. Fabian Hieronimus

design
Heimat Werbeagentur GmbH,
Berlin

creative direction
Ole Vinck, Ove Gley

film production
Pixelbutik by Deli Pictures

film direction
Michael Reissinger,
Pixelbutik by Deli Pictures

music/sound design
Deli Sounds

motion design
Rafael Ahamad,
Robert Rhee,
Axel Schmidt,
Michael Matthias,
Nico Feindt,
Gunnar Wittig

→ designer portrait: p. 429
→ digital presentation: DVD

Followfish. Good Catch.

[Film]

The image film of the company Followfish is about tuna. Tuna is highly overfished and industrial tuna fishing leads to 100,000 tons of marine species wasted as unused by-catch every year. In a highly engaging and attention-grabbing approach, the animation film aims to show that it does not have to be this way and that there is a sustainable alternative to industrial tuna fishing: the Followfish tuna is caught by hand with a fishing rod and processed and canned directly on site. The film animation is based on simple illustrations that look like paper cutouts made from packing paper. They feature a reduced colour scheme that consistently reflects the subdued colours of the brand's visual identity. The message that tuna is particularly delicious when caught in a sustainable way, and that it contributes to the protection of both its stocks and the local economy, as for example on the Maldive Islands, is conveyed by "Good Catch" in a fresh and convincing approach that visualises the philosophy of the company.

Statement by the jury

»The image film "Good Catch" succeeds in two ways: on the one hand, it conveys its message to the consumer in a highly positive and concise manner; on the other hand, it communicates the philosophy of the company, which is active in the fight against the overfishing of the oceans. Moreover, the film is technically well made and impresses with a consistent narration.«

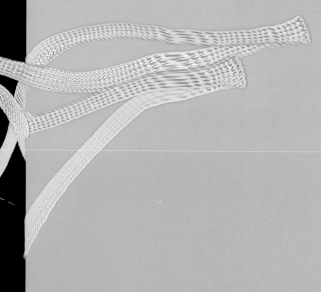

client
Fish & More GmbH,
Friedrichshafen

head of marketing
Jürg Knoll

design
Leagas Delaney Hamburg GmbH,
Hamburg

creative direction
Stefan Zschaler,
Michael Götz,
Florian Schimmer

art direction
Jan Berg

text
Oliver Kohtz

illustration
Veronika Kieneke

motion design
Nico Uthe

music/sound design
Supreme Music

→ designer portrait: p. 422
→ digital presentation: DVD

MEWA
[Image Film]

Developed for Internet users who
are researching information on
the MEWA company, this image
clip creatively gives an overview
of the company's spectrum of
products and services while also
presenting MEWA's long tradition.
Instead of boring viewers with
annual figures and shots of working halls or auto washes, the clip
aims to turn figures and facts into
thrilling pictures. To achieve that,
a metaphorical narrative level
has been realised in an animation
style reminiscent of watercolours.
A second, complementary level
features "real" pictures to present the company's products.

client
G2 Germany GmbH,
Frankfurt/Main

design
dyrdee Media GmbH & Co. KG,
Berlin

creative direction
Ole Keune, Ljubisa Djukic,
dyrdee Media;
Carsten Lukas, Anita Stoll, G2

project management
Sven Henrichs, dyrdee Media

technical director
Mesut Can, dyrdee Media

film production
Björn Knechtel,
Oliver Köppel

compositing
Ian Hutchinson,
Jochen Weidner,
Konrad Müller,
Marcel Krumbiegel,
Raffael Calleja,
Christian Schwarz

3D design
Radoslaw Jamrog,
Stephan Sacher,
Lars Krüger,
Alexander Pohl,
Nico Kahmann

→ digital presentation: DVD

DART
[Image Film]

For the repositioning of owner-managed advertising agency d'art Visuelle Kommunikation as a strategic communications consultancy with creative competencies, this image film features a piece of paper that exceeds itself. This simple piece of paper – a classic medium and carrier of thoughts and ideas – symbolically links the print media roots of the agency with its future and comes alive on screen, growing into a three-dimensional object. With a sense of lightness and sovereignty, it conveys the strategic qualities of the creative agency playfully.

client
DART Beratende Designer GmbH, Stuttgart

design
DART Beratende Designer GmbH, Stuttgart

→ digital presentation: DVD

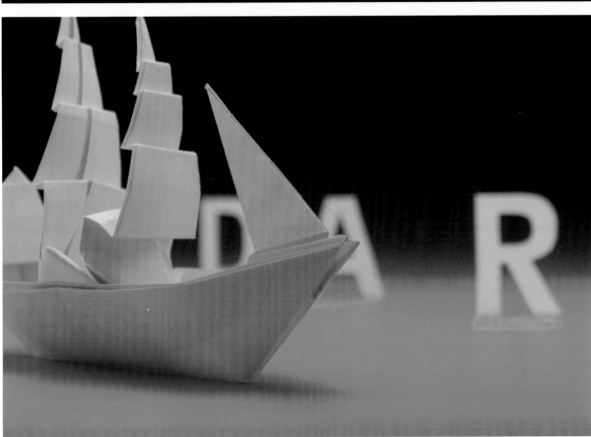

The Speaking House – seven films on saving energy

[Animated Film Series]

Presented by this animation film series is a new and overall charming approach to addressing customers of energy providers and public services in reminding them of the rather unpopular topic of energy conservation. Seven short animation clips were created in which a house, from its own perspective, tells viewers how its inhabitants have learned to save energy. A new topic is the subject of each clip: lighting, insulation, household, heating, home office, kitchen and garden. The films offer a reasonable (licensing) model for using the medium of film in or for different businesses.

client
Trurnit & Partner Verlag, Munich

design
Ina Findeisen, Dresden

creative direction
Florian Cossen, Munich

concept
Claudia Görgen, Trurnit Filmmedien

text
Elena von Saucken, Munich

illustration
Ina Findeisen

film production
Martin Burkert, Trurnit Filmmedien

music/sound design
Knut Jensen, Basel

→ digital presentation: DVD

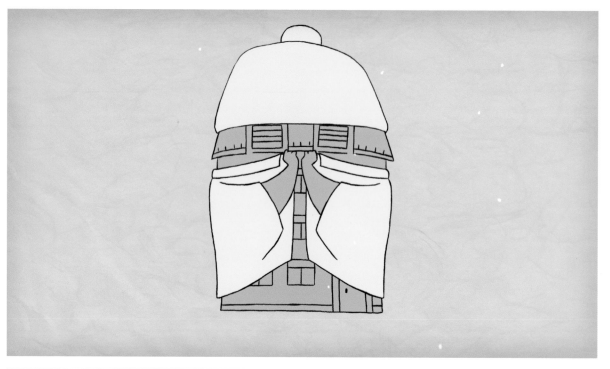

The story of the fisherman
[Computer-Animated Spot]

The Fisherman Story is a successful analogy which vividly demonstrates the benefits of the InfoZoom software, an invention by the Fraunhofer Institute. The computer-animated film demonstrates how this software offers companies a solution to "fishing in the dark" when it comes to the sheer amount of data they have to manage. The story of the fisherman, with characters fashioned from data textures, gets right to the heart of the core benefit and reveals the uniqueness of the InfoZoom software in a way that any viewer can grasp.

client
humanIT Software GmbH, Bonn

design
spot°entwicklung, Tübingen

creative direction/motion design
Marc Böttler

concept/text
Theo Eißler

project management
Ulrike Schaal

music/sound design
Thomas Eifert

→ designer portrait: p. 433
→ digital presentation: DVD

I'm Somewhere

[Motion Graphic Video]

client
Organic Motion Graphic Ltd.,
New Taipei City

design
Organic Motion Graphic Ltd.,
New Taipei City

graphic design
An-Ru Liu

motion design
Po-Wei Su

→ digital presentation: DVD

Starting from the abstract assertion "I'm somewhere", this motion graphic video addresses the complex relation between a location, individual perception, and creativity. It visualises the peculiar images that emerge in the mind of a person who simply exists at any given place. This film sets out to show that it is the artist within each of us who defines the distinctiveness of a place. The source of artistic creativity is everyday life, with art being based on personal experience and preferences. Transferred to the agency Organic Motion, this implies that artistic minds have created an "Organic We" and postulated that "our creations exist in our hearts".

Pause Fest –
Organic

[Motion Graphic Video]

client
Organic Motion Graphic Ltd.,
New Taipei City

design
Organic Motion Graphic Ltd.,
New Taipei City

illustration
Wen-Chang Peng

animation/motion design
Po-Wei Su

music/sound design
Radium Audio Studio

→ digital presentation: DVD

This expressive motion graphic video is based on the conviction that human feelings can be translated into visual form, just as in painting or any other art form. "Organic" represents various emotional states, such as the feeling of nearly crashing down. The emotions visualised in this video tell of having overcome the initial pain caused by these emotional states after the first wave of perceptual "black and white" has passed. The film uses a paper-like texture to represent the skin of the human body, while any hair shown is perceived by viewers as hand-drawn lines – thus creating a natural semblance of the human world of emotions.

On your marks

[Image Film]

"On your marks" is an image film that stages the core of the Porsche brand in an emotionally engaging manner, building a bridge between tradition and future. Conceptualised to convey brand identity, the film also explores current and future Porsche models and drive systems, but also the allure of sports cars, "intelligent performance" and the fascination this holds for both young and old. The preparation of the race track for a prototype test serves as a background story used to communicate the message that the future of the Porsche brand is raring to go.

client
Dr. Ing. h.c. F. Porsche AG,
Ludwigsburg

design
Kemper Kommunikation GmbH,
Frankfurt/Main

creative direction
Lars Vollert

film direction
Bernd Seiboldt,
bee Film

→ digital presentation: DVD

A sharper drive

[Showroom Film, Internet Film]

To impress existing and potential customers at Audi dealerships with the new, more precise design of the Audi A5 Coupé, Audi A5 Sportback and Audi A5 Cabriolet, this showroom film builds on the classic campaign titled "A sharper drive". The slogan was taken literally, as an A5 model "cuts" through the paper on which it stands, thus visualising the sharper look and new features of the new A5 model. This image was also translated into the showroom film, where the A5 vehicles "cut up" an entire desert landscape – carving out new streets, bridges and underpasses with sovereignty.

client
AUDI AG,
Ingolstadt

design
Philipp und Keuntje GmbH,
Hamburg

creative direction
Diether Kerner,
Jan Krause

art direction
Jan Gericke

text
Sandra Eichner

project management
Andreas Bilgeri,
Kristian Siewert

film production
Parasol Island GmbH

film direction
Philip Hansen

→ digital presentation: DVD

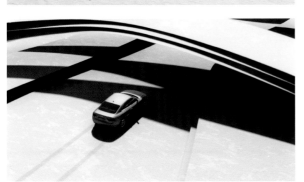

Asus Zenbook

[Screensaver Video]

Inspired by "the beauty of timepiece design", this laptop computer screensaver was conceptualised with an aim to underscore the original Asus Zenbook design concept. The objective is to show that embracing the embedded "precision craftsmanship" concept from the wristwatch-making industry involves, in terms of design, applying numerous unique production processes in order to create such a high-quality notebook. The screensaver video serves as a visual tool to communicate with end users. It possesses high aesthetic value and offers a visually compelling experience.

client
ASUSTeK Computer Inc., Taipei

design
ASUSDESIGN, Taipei

→ digital presentation: DVD

Movement is Everything – The Experiment

[Image Film]

The image clip developed for Böhm Stirling-Technik, a manufacturer of refined Stirling model engines, employs highly detailed imagery. It stages the claim "Movement is Everything" by oscillating between the paradigms of reduced pictorial language and aesthetic dynamism. Showroom aesthetics, with an elegant yet improvised appearance, is interspersed with humorous design elements to foster a dazzling visual effect. The clip conjures up the charm of pre-industrial hot air engines that, basically, are toys for grown-ups.

client
Böhm Stirling-Technik e. K., Neustadt an der Aisch

design
Elastique. We design., Cologne

art direction
Wolfgang Schmitz

concept
Andreas Schimmelpfennig,
Wolfgang Schmitz,
Karz von Bonin

project management
Luzi Kahn

film direction
Andreas Schimmelpfennig

director of photography
Sven Lützenkirchen

music
Jonas Förster

sound design
Andreas Schimmelpfennig

→ digital presentation: DVD

211

Packaging Design

Event Design

Information Design /
Public Space

Corporate Films

TV, Film & Cinema

TV, Film & Cinema

Progress
[TV/Cinema Commercial]

"Poverty causes illness" – this fact is what the commercial "Progress" builds social awareness about, in connection with the appeal that everybody deserves health. In order to illustrate this message, the commercial plays with fascinating surreal-beauty images such as time lapse recording of sprawling excrescence, symbolising the world of viruses and bacteria. However, no matter how fascinating the beauty of the tremendousness and how encouraging the voice-over – the end is disenchanting. While medical science has eliminated killers such as small pox, typhus and plague, it is powerless against the most serious cause of disease: poverty. This is conveyed in the last shot of the film by showing an elderly man's haggard face that suddenly crystallises statically out of the visual flow of sensuously dynamic animation. Specifically cultured viruses were used for the animated sequences and elaborately shot in a special medical studio.

Statement by the jury

»The outstanding achievement of this film is that it condenses the complex topic into a highly dramatic narrative. Both sound and images are aesthetically convincing and latently disconcerting. The film refrains from forcefully imposing multi-layered meanings but instead lets them arise in the minds of the viewers.«

client
Deutscher Caritasverband e.V.,
Freiburg

design
BBDO Proximity
Düsseldorf GmbH
Anne Katrin Hüsken,
Antje Schnottale

head of marketing
Verena Schoedel

creative direction
Sebastian Hardieck

project management
Andreas Bintz

film production
Cobblestone Filmproduktion,
Hamburg

film direction
Nico Beyer

music/sound design
Christian Meyer

dop
Michael Mieke

voice over
Matthias Brandt

→ designer portrait: p. 407
→ digital presentation: DVD

reddot design award
grand prix 2012

215

red dot: best of the best

Followfish. Good Catch.

[Film]

The worldwide operating tuna fishing industry is a highly destructive business that leads to 100,000 tons of by-catch every year. Many kinds of tuna are overfished or on the brink of extinction. With the film "Good Catch", organic frozen foods brand Followfish aims to communicate that there is an alternative. The animation film is based on naively reduced, yet highly charming illustrations, which almost possess the appearance of paper-cuts. It depicts the aggressive fishing techniques used by the tuna industry and compares them to the sustainable technique used on the Maldive Islands. That is where Followfish support both the century-old, simple method of catching fish by hand and the further processing of the products on site, thus contributing to the protection of the local economy and the stocks of those fish. The message that tuna is delicious, particularly so when knowing how it was caught, is conveyed in a fresh and distinctive approach.

Statement by the jury

»The animated film "Good Catch" excels with its consistently implemented pictorial language of high recognition value, which was superbly translated not only into movements but also into sound. The idea of sustainable fishing is thus presented in an interesting and innovative manner.«

client
Fish & More GmbH,
Friedrichshafen

head of marketing
Jürg Knoll

design
Leagas Delaney Hamburg GmbH,
Hamburg

creative direction
Stefan Zschaler,
Michael Götz,
Florian Schimmer

art direction
Jan Berg

text
Oliver Kohtz

illustration
Veronika Kieneke

music/sound design
Supreme Music

→ designer portrait: p. 422
→ digital presentation: DVD

Back Seat Holiday

[TV Commercial]

Is there a nicer way to start the family holiday than an endless, exhausting drive on the motorway in a fully packed family van? The little darlings tired and whining on the back seats, and the parents sitting in the front, annoyed and staring straight ahead. The answer to this ironic question – that holiday travels can easily be comfortable and relaxing with the German Rail Family Special ticket – is communicated by this commercial in a highly original manner: a boy in the back seat of a car is drawing a picture of his family. Suddenly he looks up, turning to his sister: "Tell me, do you remember what they look like from the front?" He has forgotten, seeing them only from behind. The next shot shows the two kids again, sitting next to each other, eating ice cream and joking around – in a four-seat compartment of an ICE, sitting relaxed opposite their parents, looking at their faces. The commercial thus aims to convey that travelling by rail is not only more comfortable, it enables the family to spend the journey time together and is therefore more fun.

Statement by the jury

»The fantastic cast and staging of this TV commercial manage to tell a slightly exaggerated yet amusing story in a few scenes. The story line is dramatically condensed to culminate in an antithetical final shot, which both resolves the story and optimally conveys the advertising message.«

Urlaub im Auto ist kein Urlaub.

client
DB Mobility Logistics AG,
Berlin

design
Ogilvy Deutschland

creative direction
Dr. Stephan Vogel,
Matthias Storath

art direction
Bent Kroggel,
Catrin Farrenschon

text
Bent Kroggel

project management
Martina Huschka

film production
Michael Schmid,
JO! SCHMID

film direction
Martin Schmid,
JO! SCHMID

→ digital presentation: DVD

Media Markt Christmas Campaign
[TV Commercials]

PlayStations, iPads, flat-screen TVs, smartphones and notebook computers are among the top products on Christmas wish lists in Germany. The pure joy of receiving them is expressed in the TV commercials of Media Markt's seasonal campaign through happy faces and people bursting out shouting in joy and excitement. All commercials are set on Christmas Eve, with young and old having gathered in the festively decorated living room, opening their presents. And when unwrapping a present reveals an electronic product, there is no holding back their happiness and joy. In a charming and humorous way, the advertisements demonstrate that Christmas is a feast of joy, and that this joy is limitless when receiving the right present. Instead of professional actors, ordinary people were cast for the commercials while the camera suggests that they were shot by one of the family members. The shrill campaign with the motto "Christmas is decided under the tree" is thus conveyed in a particularly authentic manner.

Statement by the jury

»The Media Markt TV commercials impress by adapting a video aesthetic well known from a number of viral Internet films, which turns them into a successful production. Their sound-image world complements the basic idea of this campaign very well.«

client
redblue Marketing GmbH,
Munich

design
Ogilvy Deutschland

creative direction
Dr. Stephan Vogel,
Matthias Storath,
Peter Römmelt,
Simon Oppmann

art direction
Julia Schäfer,
Eva Stetefeld

text
Taner Ercan,
Holger Gaubatz

project management
Yves Rosengart,
Jonas Bailly,
Nadine Ries,
Eva Hoffmann

film production
Robert Tewes,
Markenfilm Berlin

film direction
Jan Wentz

→ digital presentation: DVD

Scratch
Decibel

[Product Spots]

Invoking minimalist images,
the Scratch Decibel product spot
strives to visualise the benefits of the Wagner QuickClick
system. Impressively staging
different forms of scratching, it
illustrates that the repainting of
a luxury sports car is only half as
expensive as the replacement of
scratched flooring. Illustrated on
a different level is how the shrill
sound generated when moving
a chair in an enclosed space can
exceed the volume of a chainsaw.
The QuickClick furniture slider
system is presented as a consistent solution that avoids both
deafening noise and damaging
scratches.

client
Wagner System GmbH,
Lahr

design
Bar Vinya Film,
Ohlsbach

film direction
Jan Reiff

→ digital presentation: DVD

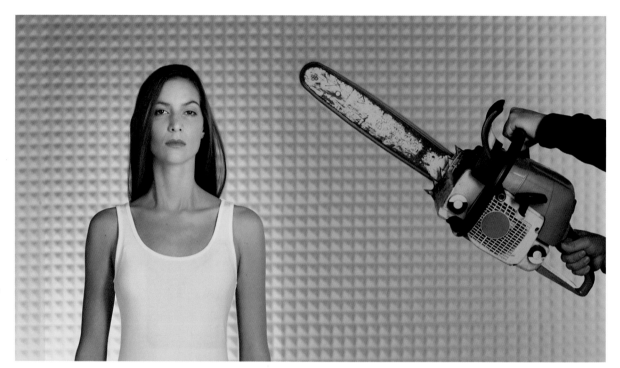

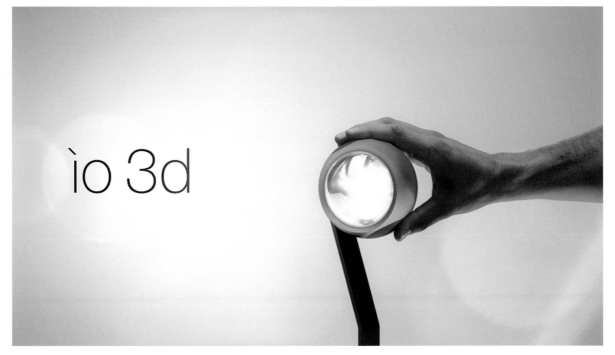

Occhio io 3d
[Image Film]

Visualising the product world of the Occhio io 3d lamp in an emotionally engaging visual language is the aim of this 3D image film. The aesthetically animated setting shows how the lamp evolves step by step from a basic sphere element, tracing the process of gradual transformation from this rather abstract form into the final product. The film thus stages the exciting three-dimensional world of the lamp in different combinations of colour and surface while explaining its features and functions in a way that is both playful and easy to follow.

client
Occhio GmbH,
Munich

design
Martin et Karczinski,
Munich

creative direction
Peter Martin

art direction
Simon Maier-Rahmer

strategic consulting
Daniel Karczinski,
Philipp-Alexander Dietrich

motion design
Nastuh Abootalebi,
Chris Faber,
Sunday Digital

music/sound design
Michael Fakesch

→ digital presentation: DVD

Discovery Science
Human Element
[Channel Ident]

client
Discovery Networks Asia-Pacific,
Singapore

design
+AKITIPE STUDIOS,
Taipei

creative direction/art direction
Sawoozer Wang

concept
Sawoozer Wang,
Chris Leow

animation
James Chen,
Juin Chang,
Lance Ni

→ designer portrait: p. 402
→ digital presentation: DVD

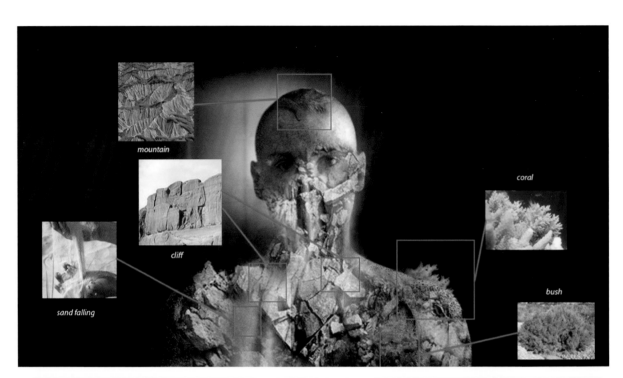

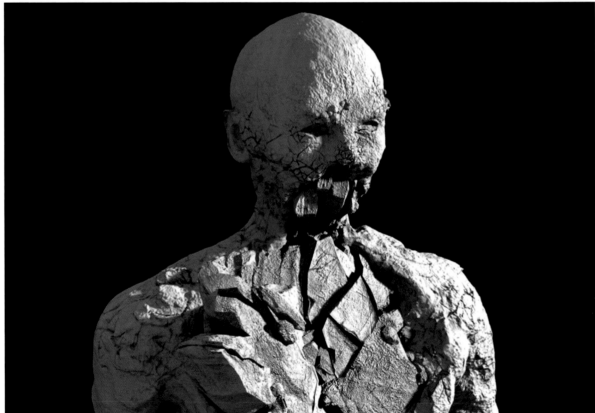

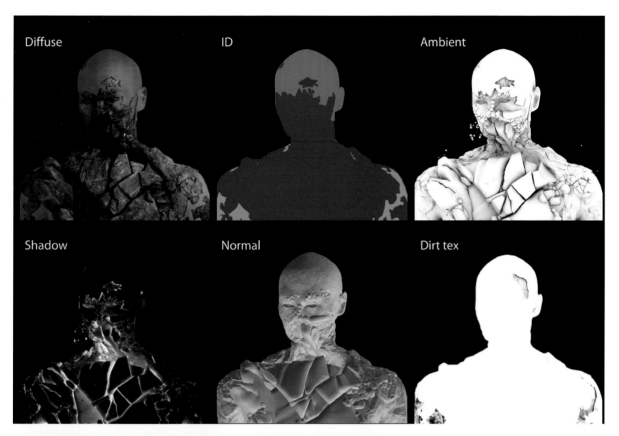

The "Human Element" communicates the brand content of Discovery Science, a television channel dedicated to making science programming relevant and entertaining. Placing the human being centre stage and inspired by Plato's four classical elements, this image spot visualises the "human" endeavour in the field of scientific discovery. With a treatment that visually merges mythology, philosophy and technology, a human figure is shown in the midst of a complex thinking/dreaming process that may arise when exploring the mental world of science. Stylised scientific elements literally burst forth from the protagonist in a seamless series of surreal epiphanies.

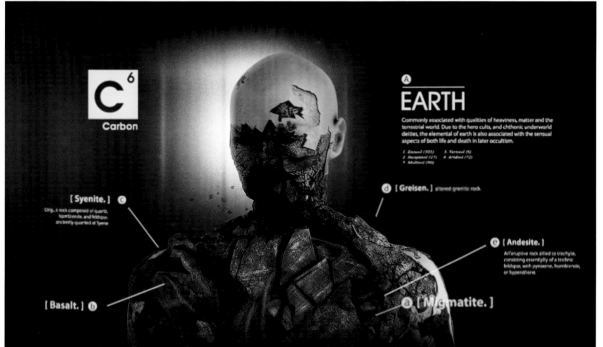

n-tv app campaign (Merkel, Memorial and Hillary)
[TV Commercial]

In the TV commercial that references an app campaign communicating how the n-tv news channel
delivers first-hand news, an invisible god-like finger intervenes
in the course of global events.
We see German chancellor Angela
Merkel sleeping at an official
meeting, when the finger enters
frame to wake her up. A different
scene shows some politicians lost
in thought at a memorial, when
the god-like finger flips a floral
bouquet at one of them. In the
third app, we see Hillary Clinton
ready to board Air Force One,
when suddenly the finger pushes
her inside.

client
n-tv
Nachrichtenfernsehen GmbH,
Cologne

design
Havas Worldwide Düsseldorf
(Euro RSCG Düsseldorf)

creative direction
Felix Glauner,
Martin Breuer,
Martin Venn

art direction
Ingmar Krannich

text
Christian Kroll

project management
Harald Jaeger,
Simone Klinke

film production
JOTZ! Filmproduktion GmbH
Jan Behrens

post-production
PIRATES 'N PARADISE Film &
Video Postproduction GmbH
Martin Basan, Jochen Becker

music/sound design
Studio Funk GmbH & Co. KG

→ digital presentation: DVD

Leica "Go play!"

[Product Film]

The lightness of taking photographs with the Leica V-Lux 30 camera is visualised in film by accompanying "Go Play" Danny MacAskill, one of the best street-trial bikers, through Cape Town. Just like young photographers discovering a city through pictures, MacAskill can easily turn a city into a playground for his enormous skill and artistry. In this case, Internet users could interactively choose between three teaser videos and thus decide which thrilling stunts they wanted Danny MacAskill to dare. The resulting "users' cut" achieved more than 520,000 views on YouTube and 2,900 "likes" within six months.

client
Leica Camera AG,
Solms

design
G2 Germany GmbH,
Frankfurt/Main

creative direction
Felix Dürichen,
Anita Stoll

art direction
Sabine Brinkmann

text
Sabine Weber,
Christin Leonhardt

project management
Maik Hofmann,
Silvana Meyer

photography
Maik Scharfscheer

film direction
Thomas Stoll

→ digital presentation: DVD

Wanna ride?

[TV Commercial]

client
DB Mobility Logistics AG,
Berlin

design
Ogilvy Deutschland

creative direction/art direction
Dr. Stephan Vogel

text
Dr. Stephan Vogel

project management
Martina Huschka,
Roland Stauber

film production
Michael Schmid,
JO! SCHMID

film direction
Martin Schmid,
JO! SCHMID

→ digital presentation: DVD

"Wanna ride?" With this question, an overly self-confident man featured in this TV commercial tries to chat up a woman in a bar by boasting about his sports car parked out front. The response to this question epitomises the central claim expressed in the commercial about the advantages and attractiveness associated with travelling on Inter City Express trains in Germany. Here, the woman reveals to the man that she drives a much faster and more powerful machine: the lady is a train driver with Germany's main rail-services provider, Deutsche Bahn. The authenticity conveyed in this commercial is enhanced by the fact that the woman is not played by a trained actress but is actually a "real-life" train driver.

Online World

Save as WWF, Save a Tree

[Online Advertising]

Each year, millions of square metres of rain forest are cut down to make paper –
paper that is used all over the world to often senselessly print out documents. In
order to stop unnecessary printing and encourage a new awareness about the use of
paper, a new green file format was developed that cannot be printed: WWF. Available
for download and installation from the WWF website, the free software converts many
common file formats into the new format with a single click. The recipient of this
green format is informed automatically, since the last page of each WWF document
functions as a response element with instructions and a link to the website. This
online advertising thus does not turn smart communication into a product but instead
an intelligent product into communication, with the message "Save as WWF, Save a
Tree". In addition to the idea of saving trees, both companies and individuals are able
to make their contribution by using and spreading the WWF format. Today there are
already more than 53,000 users all over the world.

Statement by the jury

»This online advertising impresses with a fantastic concept that not only works
seamlessly, it is also useful, meaningful and beneficial for us all. The message of
this sustainable project to save the rain forests creates a direct added value that
leads to immediate and concrete action.«

Online World
Online Advertising

Interfaces & Apps

Games & Electronic Art

Sound Design

Junior Award

Designer Portraits

Das erste grüne Dateiformat der Welt: das WWF.

Millionen von Quadratmetern Regenwald werden jedes Jahr abgeholzt. Nur für Papier. Papier, mit dem überall auf der Welt sinnlos Dokumente ausgedruckt werden. Wir wollten das unnötige Ausdrucken stoppen und den bewussten Umgang mit Papier starten.

Deshalb haben wir ein neues, grünes Dateiformat erfunden: Das WWF.
Ein Dateiformat, das man definitiv nicht ausdrucken kann. Eine simple Idee, die Bäume rettet. Jeder Einzelne und jedes Unternehmen konnte durch Nutzen und Verbreiten des WWF Formats einen aktiven Beitrag zum Umweltschutz leisten.
Hier ist nicht schlaue Kommunikation das Produkt, sondern ein schlaues Produkt macht die Kommunikation. **Unsere große Botschaft:**

SAVE AS WWF, SAVE A TREE

client
WWF Germany,
Berlin
Dr. Dirk Reinsberg

design
Jung von Matt,
Hamburg

executive creative direction
Jan Rexhausen,
Dörte Spengler-Ahrens

art direction
Michael Kittel,
Alexander Norvilas

text
Henning Müller-Dannhausen

account management
Florian Paul

film productiona
Florian Panier

programming
Michael Behrens

→ designer portrait: p. 421

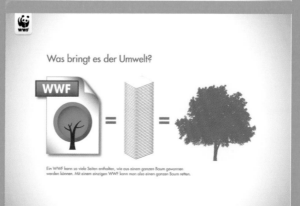

China Tours

[Travel Configurator]

With the novel presentation of
an itinerary in timeline form,
users of this travel configurator
are given a straightforward tool
to simplify the complex process
of planning a trip. A drag-and-
drop function allows travellers
to take an exploratory approach
to organising an individual trip,
supported by filter options and
a clear informational structure.
Timeline, slideshow and map
displays all make it possible to
experience the intended trip
in advance in an exciting way.
The mode of transport between
the individual stop-off points
can be configured directly on
the timeline.

client
China Tours Hamburg CTH GmbH,
Hamburg

design
Büro Persch,
Hamburg

creative direction
Matthias Persch

art direction
Christian Schäfer

concept
Matthias Persch,
Christian Schäfer

programming
Philipp Kruse

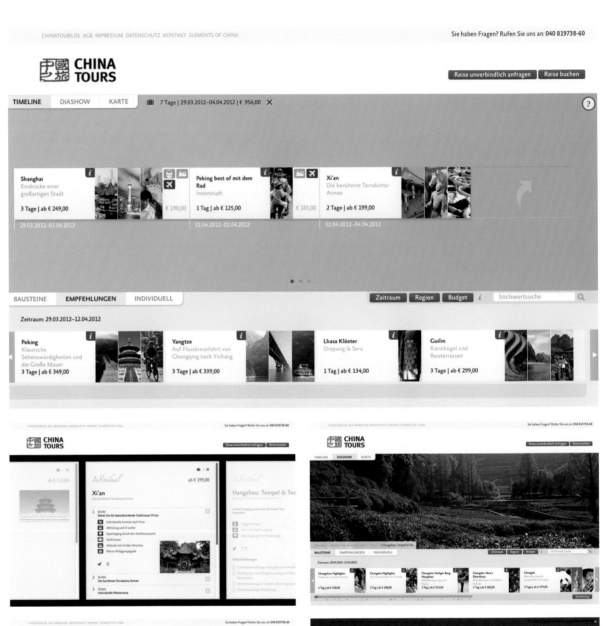

Online World
Online Communication

Interfaces & Apps

Games & Electronic Art

Sound Design

Junior Award

Designer Portraits

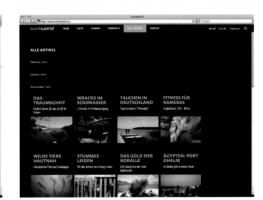

silentworld.eu

[Web Magazine]

The relaunch of the web magazine "Silentworld" strives to make the beauty of the underwater world and the experience of diving come alive online. Expressive images by well-known photographers are combined with reports from the worlds above and below sea level: they tell of oceanic creatures, their visitors and their protectors. A map shows exciting diving sites and bases that divers may visit. Users are able to find and filter articles on this microsite using the menu categories "Leute" (People), "Themen" (Topics) or "Produkte" (Products).

client
PROJEKTBUERO .HENKELHIEDL, Berlin

design
PROJEKTBUERO .HENKELHIEDL, Berlin

creative direction
Andreas Henkel

art direction/graphic design
Anne Wittorf Kojima

concept
Sigrid Jositz,
Daniela Künne

project management
Christiane Altmann

editorial work
Manuela Kirschner,
Matthias Bergbauer

programming
Christian H. Riss,
Kathrin Furtlehner,
Inostudio, Berlin

Böhm
Stirling-Technik

[Corporate Website]

The clear design of this website, based on magazine-style aesthetics, communicates the company's core offering as well as the claim "Movement is Everything". Extremely high-definition photos and slow-moving image films impressively demonstrate the precision of the products and manufacturing techniques. Humorous design elements entertainingly interrupt the otherwise elegant website and illustrate the charm of the models of pre-industrial, hot-air-powered engines that are, in fact, toys for adults.

client
Böhm Stirling-Technik e. K., Neustadt an der Aisch

design
Elastique. We design., Cologne

creative direction
Andreas Schimmelpfennig

art direction
Wolfgang Schmitz

project management
Luzi Kahn

sound design
Andreas Schimmelpfennig

programming
Stefan Klug,
Karz von Bonin

director of photography
Sven Lützenkirchen

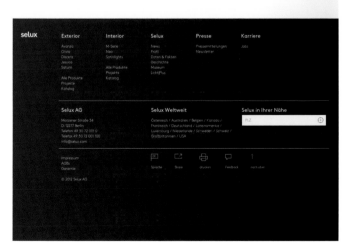

selux.com

[Website]

As part of the repositioning of the brand, the selux.com website has been redesigned. Since it is essentially aimed at architects and light planners, the focus of the site is to provide tools that give rapid access to specific data on over 2,000 products. An intelligent search engine, which can be combined with a filter and a dynamic product selector, allows the user easy access to all planning tools for lighting solutions in just a few steps. The information may be subsequently stored in a personalised area for further processing.

client
Selux AG,
Berlin

design
CDLX/Codeluxe,
Berlin
Martin Christel,
Hugo Göldner

Centraal Museum Utrecht

[Website]

"Discovery" is the central theme of this website for the Centraal Museum in Utrecht. The site encourages users to create their "own" Centraal Museum by storing individual objects from the collection, combining sets and adding the corresponding description. In a tagging game, everyone is challenged to name as many keywords for each exhibit as possible. The information on the website is justified to the right, thereby positioning the logo at the centre of the page and displaying the collection on the left-hand side at all times.

client
Centraal Museum Utrecht

design
Fabrique
[brands, design & interaction],
Delft

concept
Paul Stork,
Sjoerd van der Kooij

interaction design
Bette Burger,
Jeroen van Geel

production
Goeie Jongens

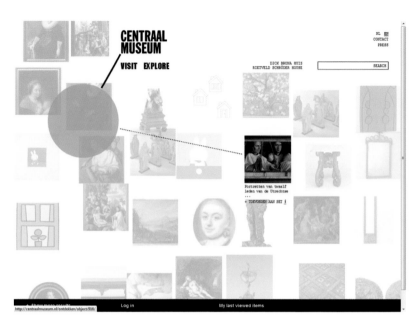

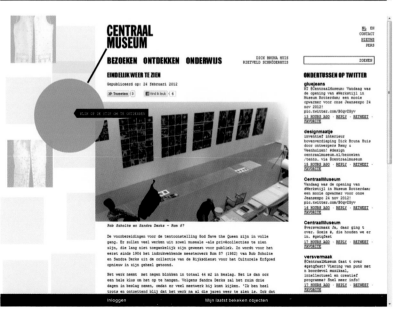

OVERVIEW / EVENT / BLOG

OVERVIEW / EVENT / BLOG

TRANSMISSION LA:
AV CLUB

EVENT | CURATOR | EXHIBITION | MUSIC | LOCATION

WE WOULD LIKE TO SAY THANK YOU?
Thank you for 17 incredible days of TRANSMISSION LA: AV Club. Over 30,000 guests attended! We thank all the artists, all the great performers, all the guests, workers, organizers, all the staff, - simply everyone who has been part of this great project. And, last but not least, we would like to thank our curator Mike D for making it happen.

THE SECOND ISSUE OF THE AVANT/GARDE DIARIES
TRANSMISSION SERIES TOOK PLACE IN LOS ANGELES!
None less than Mike D from the legendary Beastie Boys was the patron and creative head of the festival. The music and entertainment icon invited 17 outstanding artists from multiple disciplines to create an exceptional 17 days event consisting of concerts, DJ

OVERVIEW / EVENT / BLOG

Honor to Whom Honor

Busy days for Mike "Mike D" Diamond! While the building of "Transmission LA: AV Club" went on in Los Angeles the curator visited Cleveland to take part at the induction ceremony of his band The Beastie Boys into the Rock n Roll Hall of Fame last Saturday. Amongst the inductees were Guns'n'Roses, Red Hot Chili Peppers and The Faces, presenters included Bette Midler, Chris Rock, LL Cool J and ZZ Top.

The Beastie Boys became just the third hip-hop act to be immortalized in the museum, joining Run-DMC and Grandmaster Flash and the Furious Five. The trios planned performance had to be canceled as Adam "MCA" Yauch was unable to join his group mates Mike D and Adam "Adrock" Horovitz. The band did share the honor with fans, saying it is as much theirs as the band's.

SHARE

AVANT/GARDE DIARIES
[Microsite]

"AVANT/GARDE DIARIES" is a digital, web-based interview magazine for young, individualist representatives of the post-modern market segment who are not per se keen on Mercedes-Benz. It is devoid of branding and eschews the standard staging of vehicles, preferring instead to focus on renowned artists, cura-tors and events of strictly limited attendance. By communicating this content, the site aims to establish an emotional connection with the target audience and to underline similar aesthetic values and intellectual attitudes.

client
Daimler AG,
Stuttgart

design
Scholz & Volkmer GmbH,
Wiesbaden

creative direction concept
Christoph Tratberger

creative direction design
Mario Jilka,
Jörg Waldschütz

art direction
Anastasia Lyutikova

content/concept
K-MB,
Berlin

account management
Nina Grams

technical direction
Daniel Haller

unit direction
Thomas Nolle

Dutch National Ballet

[Website]

The Dutch National Ballet website allows visitors to look behind the scenes of the ballet like never before. The Netherlands' largest dance ensemble boasts over 80 dancers, who enjoy pop-star fame. To match this popularity, the website brings enthusiasts right up close to the dancers and choreographers. Massive background photos create a visual and emotional proximity to the viewers, while well-prepared stories reveal what inspires the dancers and their choreographers.

client
Dutch National Ballet,
Amsterdam

design
Fabrique
[brands, design & interaction],
Delft

creative direction
Jeroen van Erp

art direction
Matthe Stet

project management
Tine Leeuwerink

programming
Dodi Raditya

photography
Erwin Olaf,
Angela Sterling

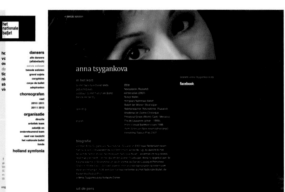

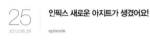

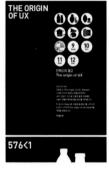

A plain convergence with INPIX

[Online Communication]

Giving the brand identity of the Korean company Inpix – as expressed by the slogan "a plain convergence" – an honest and authentic appearance was at the forefront of the development of the company's online communications. A clear, emotionally appealing and simultaneously functionally reduced design conveys the message of "convergence" and thus alludes to the company's values and visions. The intention was to create an authentic and easily understandable world online, one that also communicates a new user experience of the company's technical equipment.

client
INPIX,
Seoul

design
INPIX,
Seoul

creative direction
Hyun Woo Lee

→ designer portrait: p. 419

Tribute to the Mont Blanc

[Microsite]

To mark the launch of the new Montblanc collection "Tribute to the Mont Blanc", the user of this microsite becomes a passenger on a sightseeing flight around Europe's highest mountain. In creating this microsite, Mont Blanc was filmed for the first time from the air with a special 360-degree camera. This unique video footage enables the user to experience a scenic flight at an altitude of 4,810 metres while also offering exciting interactive access to the history of the mountain. The microsite can be viewed without additional plug-ins or other programs.

client
Montblanc International GmbH, Hamburg

design
Scholz & Volkmer GmbH, Wiesbaden

creative direction
Katja Rickert,
Judith Schütz

art direction
Nicole Derscheid,
Tai Lückerath

concept/text
Stefan Ulfert

text
Lutz Brocker

technical direction
Philippe Just

flash programming
Matthias Volland

Online World
Online Communication

Interfaces & Apps

Games & Electronic Art

Sound Design

Junior Award

Designer Portraits

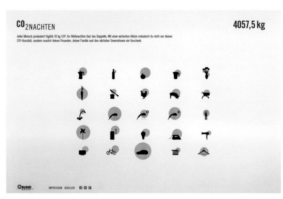

CO₂nachten:
Kleine Geschenke
erhalten das Klima
CO₂nachten:
Small gifts protect
the environment

[Microsite]

A highly motivated Christmas
campaign by Scholz & Volkmer
highlighted the problems caused
by excessive CO_2 emissions.
Using clearly structured information, the microsite conveyed
the fact that the Western world
produces tons of CO_2 gas every
year. Since emissions almost
double at Christmastime because
of increased consumption, this
campaign sets in at exactly this
time of year. Twenty-five sustainable ideas to reduce CO_2 emissions
were compiled in conjunction
with Friends of the Earth Germany
(BUND), Germany's largest
environmental organisation.

client
Scholz & Volkmer GmbH,
Wiesbaden

design
Scholz & Volkmer GmbH,
Wiesbaden

creative direction concept
Michael Volkmer

creative direction design
Katja Rickert

text/concept
Lutz Brocker,
Kerstin Bones

art direction
Katharina Köhler,
Tai Lückerath

technical direction
Peter Reichard,
Philippe Just

flash development
Matthias Benfer

Nike –
Catch the Flash

[Microsite]

Catch the Flash is a game based on the idea of "making the invisible visible". Fifty runners raced through the night-time streets of Vienna as "Flashrunners", thereby communicating the qualities of the new Nike Vapor Flash Jackets they were wearing. Chased through the streets, in real life, by inhabitants whose aim was to photograph them, the flashing of the cameras made the number on the runners' backs visible. At the same time, the event details could be followed virtually on a microsite, because the 50 runners transmitted their GPS data with an app in real time to the Catch the Flash online game.

client
Nike Gesellschaft m.b.H.,
Vienna

head of marketing
Edgar Jorissen,
Sebastian Bayer

head of advertising
Oliver Eckart, Andreas Roitner

design
Jung von Matt/Neckar GmbH,
Stuttgart

creative direction
Kai Heuser, Joerg Jahn,
Jacques Pense

art direction
Matías Müller

graphic design
Christoph Kock, Alexa Petruch

text
Gün Aydemir, Matthias Hess

project management
Manuel Colloseus, Björn Hansen,
Denise Winter

photography
Mat Neidhardt

programming
Nils Doehring

post-production
Recom

Samsung NX System

[Microsite]

On this microsite, high-quality images and Flash-based motion graphics provide an impressive platform for Samsung NX System products, including the corresponding lenses. In order to graphically convey the high-end quality and performance of these products for the website visitor, all of the features on the microsite are interactive. Images of the various different available cameras can be viewed via a menu gallery. Since the models shown here and their corresponding lenses are matched together, users obtain a favourable overview of all possible configurations.

client
Samsung Electronics Co., Ltd., Suwon

design
Cheil Worldwide, Seoul
designfever, Seoul

head of advertising
Seokjoon Hong

creative direction
Johannes Faeth,
Cheil Worldwide;
Donghyun Choi,
designfever

art direction
Joohee Lee,
Cheil Worldwide;
Juhwan Lee,
designfever

graphic design
Kwangsun Ryu,
Seungtae Kim,
Yumi Jeong,
Dongmin Choi

project management
Meehyun Song,
Cheil Worldwide;
Seungae Jang,
designfever

programming
Youngsu Han,
Hyunil Park,
Kwanyoung Choi

www.faz.net

[News Portal]

The news portal of the Frankfurter Allgemeine Zeitung embodies the broadsheet's view of itself as the premium brand among German newspapers. The multi-column layout of both home and subject pages allows editors to evade Internet dictates for speed and topicality by teasing longer, analytical pieces prominently positioned at the top of the screen. Journalists can easily provide additional background material on pieces originally written for the printed page with the help of several buttons on the article pages that trigger links to image galleries, videos, maps and social media.

client
Frankfurter Allgemeine Zeitung GmbH, Frankfurt/Main

design
KircherBurkhardt GmbH, Berlin

creative direction
Paul Wagner

art direction
Andrea Rohner

concept
Reinhard Dassel

customer advisory service
Diana Schniedermeier

Online World
Online Communication

Interfaces & Apps

Games & Electronic Art

Sound Design

Junior Award

Designer Portraits

Bewegen /
What Drives Us
BMW Online Annual
Report 2011

This iPad-enabled online version of the 2011 BMW Annual Report enhances the already available yearbook in the form of an interactive rich-media version. Communicating the annual report in HTML format and as a PDF download, the report is reduced to its functional aspects in the process. The layout, the various navigation mechanisms of PC and iPad, and the technical features have been specifically reconceptualised. In addition, interviews and film sequences, for example with chief designer Adrian van Hooydonk or with customers picking up their vehicles from BMW Welt, have been integrated online.

client
BMW AG,
Munich

design
häfelinger + wagner design,
Munich

creative direction
Frank Wagner

art direction
Stefan Kaderka

concept/graphic design
Dirk Habenschaden

programming
Equity Story

Lightweight.info

[Corporate Website]

The minimalist product philosophy of a German manufacturer by the name of Lightweight is reflected by the company website. Visualised through the creative concept and presented via expressive black-and-white photography is the perfect nature of the products. Emotive videos are juxtaposed with real racing shots, which are interwoven with technical details and surprising animations, just like the carbon fibres of every wheel. The website offers its target audience a wealth of information, ranging from sponsoring right through to the pick-up service and the company's history.

client
CarbonSports GmbH,
Friedrichshafen

design
Stockhausen Group GmbH

creative direction
Mario Stockhausen

text
Dirk Fliesgen,
Tim Winkelmann

strategic planning
Benjamin Baumann

photography
Peter Muntanion,
Mathias Baumann

film production
Moritz Ripprich,
Philipp Grolle

programming
Markus Vetten

→ designer portrait: p. 434

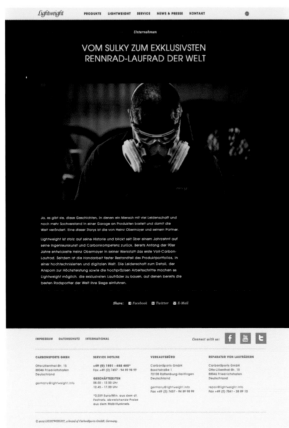

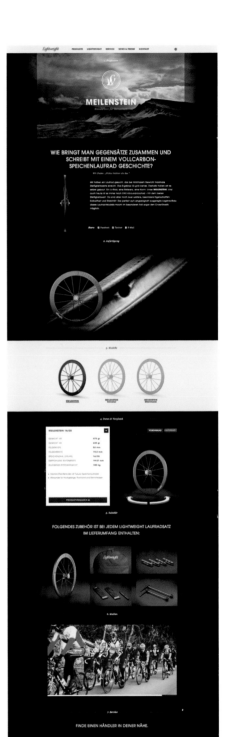

Mercedes-Benz.com

[Website]

The re-launch of the Mercedes-Benz.com website was implemented in the style of an innovative premium-brand magazine. Content, visual appearance and methods underline the transformation from a classic website to an e-zine. All content, subject matter and messages are edited and sorted by relevance and topicality. Strategically, the re-launch coincides with the consolidation of the digital Mercedes-Benz world, which is why platforms such as "Mercedes-Benz.tv", "Mercedes-Benz Reporter" and "Mercedes-Benz Magazine online" have been integrated into the website.

client
Daimler AG,
Stuttgart

design
Scholz & Volkmer GmbH,
Wiesbaden

creative direction concept
Christian Daul,
Christoph Tratberger

creative direction design
Mario Jilka,
Jörg Waldschütz

art direction
Mohshiour Hossain

text/concept
Jin Jeon

technical direction
Andreas Klinger

unit direction
Thomas Nolle

Egon Eiermann
Collection by VS

[Microsite]

client
VS Vereinigte
Spezialmöbelfabriken
GmbH & Co. KG,
Tauberbischofsheim

project management
Dietmar Speuser

design/concept/programming
Zum Kuckuck /
Büro für digitale Medien,
Würzburg

text
Josef Mang

design history consulting
Dr. René Spitz

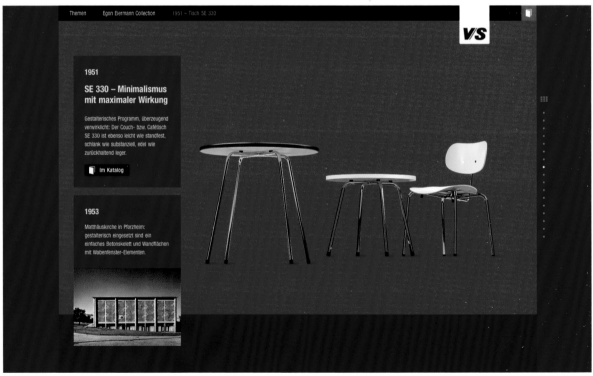

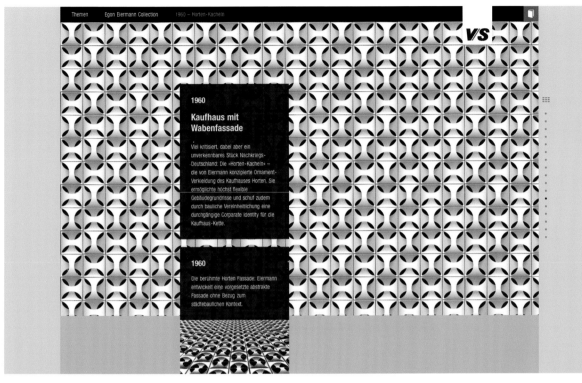

The Egon Eiermann Collection microsite consciously follows the designer's principles of functional aesthetics and constructive clarity. It pays tribute to the style-defining creative powers of Egon Eiermann by linking his minimalist furniture design with impressive, historic photos from his professional biography. Site users can navigate their way through 15 of the virtual show's exhibits via an interactive timeline. The colour scheme and positioning of the graphic details are well coordinated with the object on view. With access as easy as child's play, users are invited to interactively experiment with the functionality of the furniture and to obtain information about each object in the company catalogue.

"pass on your passion" initiative

[Microsite]

client
Deutsche Bank AG,
Frankfurt/Main

project management
Heike Merkle,
Jens Tangemann

design
zeros+ones GmbH,
Munich

art direction
Luca Capelletti

programming
Daniel Sucké

motion design
Kristof Dreier

→ designer portrait: p. 443

Online World
Online Communication

Interfaces & Apps

Games & Electronic Art

Sound Design

Junior Award

Designer Portraits

12 Monate, 12 Projekte – und 100 % Begeisterung

In der Region, für die Region und für 'ihre' Stadt: Ein ganzes Jahr lang haben Heike Erhardt, Ingo Ottmann und 120 andere Deutschbanker die Ärmel hochgekrempelt – um 12 Projekte zu ermöglichen, die Kunden und Essener Bürger vorgeschlagen hatten. Dazu gehörte zum Beispiel, eine Grundschule zu verschönern und einen Hühnerstall zu bauen.

⊙ mehr zu Mitarbeiter-Engagement

„Be! Fund" hilft jungen Sozialunternehmern – Joris Hensen trägt zum Erfolg mit bei

Plastikmüll von der Straße räumen und damit Arbeitsplätze schaffen: Das ist eine der Geschäftsideen, die ohne „Be! Fund" kaum verwirklicht werden könnten. Denn die Gründer solcher Start-ups sind arm, Gründungskapital ist knapp. Der Deutschbanker Joris Hensen hilft der gemeinnützigen Organisation bei ihrem Aufbau – und überzeugt Sponsoren vom Erfolg der Projekte.

⊙ zum Blog von Joris Hensen

For over 20 years, Deutsche Bank has encouraged its employees to undertake social-responsibility projects. The "pass on your passion" initiative is dedicated to the people behind these activities, to their passions and goals, and is now supported by this microsite. In order to allow enough space for each project, a dynamic parallax effect is employed. By scrolling down, the visitor of the site can "open" each project and access a variety of multimedia-based information. This effect, along with the movement of the people shown at a horizontal level, makes the site very dynamic. Both the appearance and the responsive nature of the microsite reflect the energy that drives Deutsche Bank employees.

Urban Mood

[Microsite]

client
Telefónica Germany
GmbH & Co. OHG,
Munich

design
Ogilvy Deutschland

creative direction
Uwe Jakob,
Michael Kutschinski,
Petra Berghäuser

art direction
Uwe Jakob,
B-Reel

graphic design
Cerstin Scheuten,
Klaus-Martin Michaelis,
Michael Longerich

text
Hans-Peter Junius,
Achim Bokeler,
Sebastian Kraus

project management
Oliver Rosenthal,
Chaichana Sinthuaree,
Frank Dittrich

development
Jens Steffen,
Jens Lauer

programming
B-Reel

O₂ Stimmungsbild
Wie zufrieden ist Deutschland

o2 denkt immer daran seine Kunden glücklicher zu machen. Um zu sehen wie glücklich sie wirklich sind, haben wir Deutschlands erstes Gefühlsbarometer entwickelt: Das **o2 Stimmungsbild**.

Es misst und visualisiert die Stimmung von 10 deutschen Städten anhand von Social Media Posts und lokalen Meldungen, wie Tweets, Flickr Fotos, Fussballergebnisse oder Wettermeldungen. Aber nicht faktisch und nüchtern, wie es Datenvisualisierung normalerweise macht, sondern emotional und spielerisch.

Aufwendig animierte Origami Icons verwandeln die Daten in ein lebendiges Erlebnis. Interaktiv, in Echtzeit und anfassbar, um schon beim Betrachten Freude zu verbreiten. Was für die Betrachter schön aussieht, hilft o2 herauszufinden wo ein wenig bessere Stimmung benötigt wird, um entsprechend darauf zu reagieren.

10 Städte mit ihrem eigenen Stimmungen, Farben und Sounds stehen zu Auswahl.   Das Archiv zeigt im Detail die Entwicklung der Stimmung in den letzten Woch

Online World
Online Communication

Interfaces & Apps

Games & Electronic Art

Sound Design

Junior Award

Designer Portraits

Origami Figuren symbolisieren die Gefühle, die täglich in Deutschland geposted werden.

Urban Mood was developed as an interactive microsite that acts as a measure of people's states of mind and creates a picture of urban mood. It records the atmosphere of ten German cities using social-media posts and local reports, such as tweets, Flickr photos, football-match results or weather forecasts. Urban Mood's aim is to establish which city is in need of a better atmosphere in order to be able to react in an appropriate way. The essence of the development of this microsite was a desire to present the data in an emotional and playful way rather than as neutral facts and figures. Complex Origami icons mutate into a lively experience, and users encounter the results authentically and in real time.

nklicken der Origami Figuren werden die Posts hinter den Gefühlen sichtbar.

Aus den Daten aller Städte errechnet sich in Echtzeit die Stimmung für Deutschland.

www.beetroot.gr

[Website]

The website design of the Greek agency called beetroot reflects the characteristics of its creative processes, development and future expectations. Conceived as a white-toned, minimalist communication platform, the site focuses on pictorial elements. Since beetroot's projects elude a uniform style, making it impossible to group them in a systematic way, they are presented together through a general overview. The mosaic resulting from this arrangement represents flowing and ever-changing creativity.

client
Beetroot Design Group,
Thessaloniki

design
Beetroot Design Group,
Thessaloniki

creative direction
Alexis Nikou,
Yiannis Charalambopoulos,
Vangelis Liakos

graphic design
Ilias Pantikakis,
Alexis Nikou

text
Paris Mexis

music/sound design
Karolos Gakidis

programming
Giorgos Lemonidis

Online World
Online Communication

Interfaces & Apps

Games & Electronic Art

Sound Design

Junior Award

Designer Portraits

Elastique.

[Corporate Website]

Elastique's Internet presence consistently puts the work of the design agency in the foreground. So as to keep the agency as such in the background, the company logo is not immediately apparent but rather virtually "hidden" in a retractable black bar. The generous typography and the complete flexibility of the image grid showing the projects make the webpages appear diversified and lively, despite the formal reduction. Technical details, as well as a project collection with a personalized PDF edition, underline its usefulness.

client
Elastique. We design.,
Cologne

design
Elastique. We design.,
Cologne

creative direction
Andreas Schimmelpfennig

art direction
Betty Schimmelpfennig

text
Wiebke Lang

project management
Luzi Kahn

programming
Karz von Bonin,
Jörg Heinzelmann

Nachhilfe
per E-Mail
Private Tuition
by E-Mail

[Mailing]

Supporting children from socially vulnerable families, the non-profit organisation Lüttenhilfe e.V. for instance offers them free private homework tutoring. This surprising e-mail has been designed to convince former supporters of the organisation to donate again for this purpose. In the e-mail, recipients see a sentence written by a child with many spelling mistakes, and how it gradually improves as the recipient reads through the handwritten text. The idea behind the e-mail is to communicate how both the orthography and the handwriting of children can improve – progress that is rendered possible thanks to donations.

client
Lüttenhilfe e.V.,
Hamburg

design
Elephant Seven Hamburg GmbH,
Hamburg

creative direction
Kai Becker

art direction
Oliver Baus

graphic design
Julia Kestner,
Katja Borsdorf

text
Nils Liedmann

programming
Hanno Rippe

Lange Fahrt
Long Drive

[Banner]

This banner utilises the natural scrolling behaviour of website visitors to visualise the advantages of Mercedes' innovative, fuel-efficient automobile technology. The trajectory covered when scrolling symbolises the distance that this new technology can take vehicle drivers without having to refuel. While users are scrolling down, the new C-Class accompanies them to the bottom of the page. Yet when the end is reached, the journey is far from over – because thanks to this novel technology, the new C-Class goes much further than expected.

client
Mercedes-Benz Vertrieb
Deutschland, Berlin

design
Elephant Seven Hamburg GmbH,
Hamburg

creative direction
Kai Becker

art direction
Oliver Baus

graphic design
Julia Kestner

text
Julia Molina,
Nils Liedmann

programming
Sebastian Moormann

Online Stolpersteine / Stones Telling Stories – Online Holocaust Memorial

The online presence of the Stones Telling Stories project visualises the magnitude of the Holocaust, in particular to young Germans who know little about it. Every brass stone stands for a person murdered during the Third Reich and is placed in front of the building from which the person was deported. While taking a virtual tour through a city, website visitors stumble upon these stones, discovering the names of the victims along with pictures and biographical data. The "stumbling stones" can also be found on Google Maps, on street posters and via an iPhone app that features additional details.

client
Gunter Demnig

design
Jung von Matt, Hamburg

executive creative direction
Jan Rexhausen,
Dörte Spengler-Ahrens

creative direction
Felix Fenz

art direction
Alexander Norvilas,
Eric van den Hoonaard

graphic design
Eric van den Hoonaard

online design
Kuborgh GmbH,
Till Kubelke

executive account direction
Raphael Brinkert

project management
Benjamin Wenke,
Sara Teckenberg

mobile application
Phi Mobile Services,
Florian Herzberg

→ designer portrait: p. 421

Online Straßenmusiker
Online Street Musicians

In order to raise awareness for street musicians in Germany – people who are finding it harder than ever before to earn money from passers-by – the Online Street Musicians campaign gave them a virtual presence on the Internet. Instead of having them play music in front of shops as they usually would, the campaign had the musicians play on inter-active banners in front of online shops. Positively surprised by this idea, website visitors could donate money to the German Red Cross with a single click. The pro-motion resulted in 3.5 million page views, many new members for the German Red Cross and more than 12,000 euros in donations.

client
Deutsches Rotes Kreuz / German Red Cross, Berlin

design
Jung von Matt, Hamburg

executive creative direction
Jan Rexhausen,
Dörte Spengler-Ahrens

creative direction
Felix Fenz

art direction
Eric van den Hoonaard,
Cathrin Hoffmann, Pedro Pahl,
Robert Menzel (RIA)

concept
Felix Fenz

text
Andreas Hilbig, Marc Freitag,
Christina Drescher

executive account direction
Raphael Brinkert

account direction
Natalie Martens

project management
Rabea Huthmann

online design
Andreas Kiesel, Frederik Mellert

web development
Georg Hemprich

261

www.droom.de

[Online Shop]

Developed with the aim of offering customers a high degree of design freedom, this online shop centres around a sophisticated configurator that allows them to create individual designs for the printable DROOM products in real time. Motifs provided by the design label or by the customers themselves can be configured freely on tables, lampshades, seat elements, partitions and wallpaper: they may be scaled, tiled, rotated, moved and changed in terms of colour. The display formats in the webshop thus offer a realistic presentation of the product portfolio.

client
DROOM / DESIGN YOUR ROOM,
DROOM GmbH & Co. KG,
Cologne

design/concept/3D configurator
Zum Kuckuck /
Büro für digitale Medien,
Würzburg

online shop programming
iWelt AG,
Würzburg

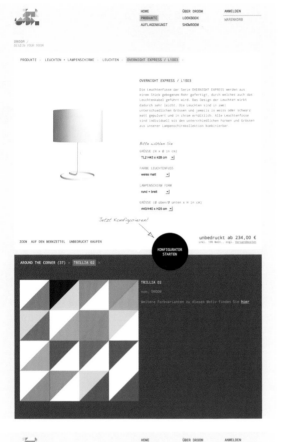

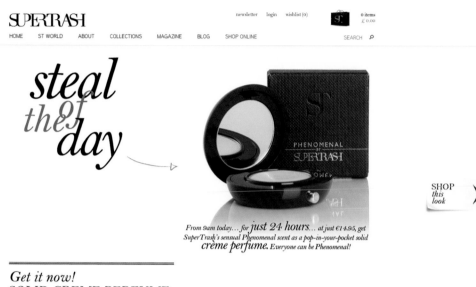

SuperTrash

[Online Shop]

The SuperTrash online shop is an extension of the brand image: international, feminine, sexy and innovative. The visual identity of the shop is defined by full-screen photographs with distinctive and refined feminine details. In order to increase the website conversion rate, the innovative tool of persuasive design has been used. The webshop gives female visitors a heightened sense of interactivity by placing the style advice of designer Olcay Gulsen directly next to selected products. The shop integrates the current collection, blog posts, fashion shows, tweets and magazine appearances.

client
SuperTrash,
Amsterdam

design
Fabrique
[brands, design & interaction],
Delft

concept
Nils Mengedoht,
Bram Stege,
Pieter Jongerius

project management
Wouter Dirks

account management
Pieter Jongerius

programming
XSarus

Shout for Red

[Social Media Marketing]

Shout for Red was a digital campaign that facilitated fan support of the Korean national football team for a qualification game in the World Cup. Via a Facebook app accessed by way of the Nike Football Korea homepage, users could change their Facebook profile to the national team colour of red and send it directly to the football team together with a supportive message. The profile pictures were then assembled to form the image of a tiger, which was exposed on banners installed inside and outside the stadium. After the game, Facebook users could tag their own face on the tiger image.

client
Nike Korea,
Seoul

design
PostVisual.com,
Seoul

head of marketing
Jung-Won Lee

concept
Tae-Hyung Lee,
Hyun-Hee Park

graphic design
Mina Seo,
Sora Lee

project management
Songeh Han,
Woo-Young Lee

programming
Seol-Baek Shon,
Won-Seok Cho,
Hyun Lee

motion design
Sung-Wook Kim,
Jiho Lee,
Sihyun Kim

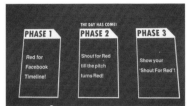

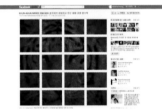

Online World
Social Media

Interfaces & Apps

Games & Electronic Art

Sound Design

Junior Award

Designer Portraits

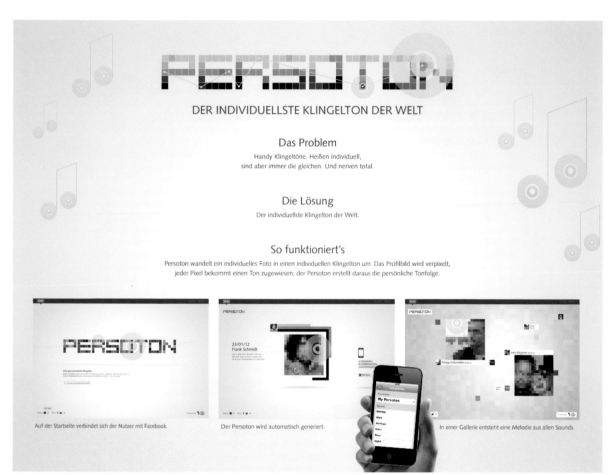

Persoton
[App, Website]

Persoton enables users to turn a personal photo into an individualised ringtone. First, users visit the persoton.de website and log in with Facebook from there. Persoton then takes the Facebook profile picture, pixelates it and allocates a sound to each pixel. These sounds are then turned into a personalised sound sequence. In an online gallery, the sound sequences of hundreds of people are interwoven to create a never-ending melody, making each a part of a huge symphony of individuality.

client
E-Plus Mobilfunk GmbH,
Düsseldorf

design
Kolle Rebbe GmbH,
Hamburg

creative direction
Jan Hellberg,
Lorenz Ritter

art direction
Robert Jähnert

text
Ales Polcar,
Lorenz Ritter

music/sound design
Robert Jähnert

programming
Interactive Pioneers GmbH

Blog Chocolate

[Crowdsourcing Campaign]

With this crowdsourcing campaign, the Ritter Sport brand aimed to redefine the interactive web for their fans. The "Blog Chocolate" concept implied a new kind of crowd sourcing event, giving the brand's fans full power over the development of a new product. Users were invited to invent a new chocolate product and submit it to a vote. The winning chocolate, Cookies & Cream, was then produced by the company. The campaign reached 30,000 Ritter Sport blog readers and achieved lively participation on all brand platforms – entirely without a media budget.

client
Alfred Ritter GmbH & Co. KG,
Waldenbuch

design
elbkind GmbH,
Hamburg

creative direction
Stefan Rymar

art direction
Lisa Bengs

strategic planning
Maik Königs

project management
Tobias Spörer

social media management
Benjamin Wittkamp

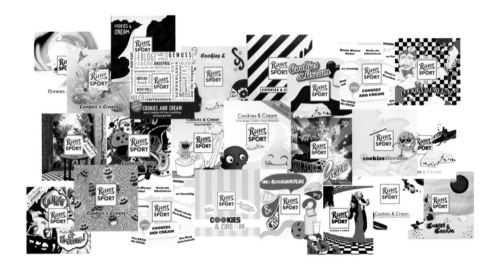

Online World
Social Media

Interfaces & Apps

Games & Electronic Art

Sound Design

Junior Award

Designer Portraits

Mercedes-Benz
A-Class
First Impression
[Web Special]

The world premiere of the new A-Class was presented via a web special live from the Geneva Motor Show. Since no company product details of the new A-Class were to be disclosed, the idea was to inform the target group via trade visitors and online users talking about their first impressions. With a mobile camera team and hosts at the booth, the online users could ask about vehicle details and the visitors at the trade fair responded by describing their live impressions. Fixed cameras, showing the A-Class from different angles, rounded off the overall impression of the vehicle.

client
Daimler AG,
Stuttgart

design
Scholz & Volkmer GmbH,
Wiesbaden

creative direction
Christian Daul,
Jörg Waldschütz

art direction
Anastasia Lyutikova

text/concept
Jin Jeon,
Christopher Schwarz

project management
Kris Rauch

technical direction
Peter Reichard,
Andreas Klinger

NX200
Feel & Share
[Facebook Campaign]

client
Samsung Electronics Co., Ltd.,
Suwon

design
Cheil Worldwide,
Seoul
designfever,
Seoul

head of advertising
Seokjoon Hong

creative direction
Johannes Faeth,
Cheil Worldwide;
Donghyun Choi,
designfever

art direction
Joohee Lee,
Heungkyo Seo,
Cheil Worldwide;
Juhwan Lee,
designfever

graphic design
Sukkyoung Choi,
Sanghyuk Park,
Kwangpyo Kim,
Changsu Kang

project management
Meehyun Song,
Cheil Worldwide;
Seungae Jang,
designfever

programming
Youngsu Han,
Hyunil Park,
Innobirds

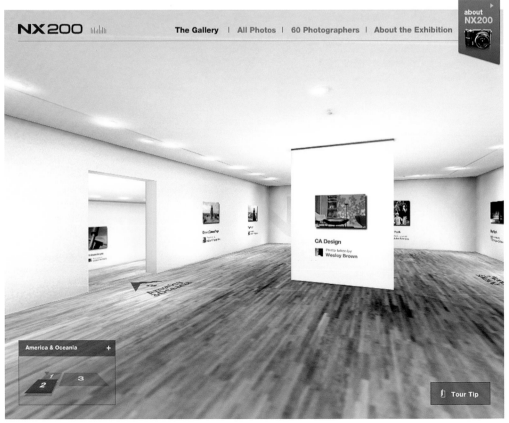

Online World
Social Media

Interfaces & Apps

Games & Electronic Art

Sound Design

Junior Award

Designer Portraits

As part of this Facebook campaign, 60 photographers worldwide were invited to take photos with the Samsung NX200 compact system camera. With these photos, they documented their skills, their personal environments as well as their individual photography styles. The photographs were then compiled into a three-dimensional NX200 photo gallery in which users, after choosing their continent, can view and move the images by clicking the mouse. The campaign also offers users the possibility of becoming jurors – voting for and commenting on their favourite shots and sharing them as postcards.

聽&說
iListen

語音溝通

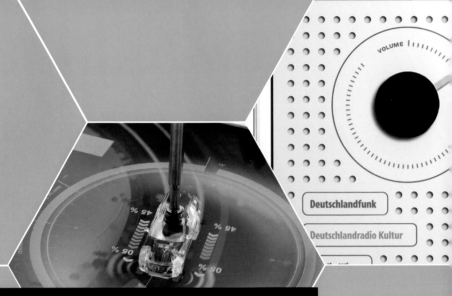

Interfaces & Apps

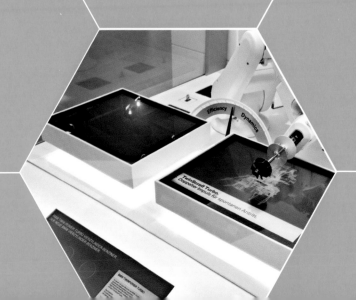

red dot: grand prix

Experience Exhibits IAA 2011

[Robotic Exhibits with User Interface]

"Enter a new era" is the title of BMW's trade show tool at the IAA 2011, which showcased robots with user interfaces to present the company's trade fair themes of BMW Individual, BMW Lines (1 Series) and BMW M as interactive experiences. Housed in glass displays, each exhibit comprises a sculpture with a dynamic robotic arm, the movements of which can be controlled via touch screens, inviting visitors to engage in dialogue. The objective of the user interfaces was to redevelop the exhibits following a comprehensive approach and create cognitive stimuli that enable visitors to experience each theme in a three-dimensional way. Based on systematic movement and behaviour patterns, the agile and harmonic movements of the jointed-arm robots take on an almost "human" appearance that intensifies the interaction between user and exhibit. The combination of digital media with real moving components thus turns into an experience that communicates the complex themes in an emotional as well as a rational manner.

Statement by the jury

»The outstanding aspect of this trade show tool is how it stages complex themes, so that visitors will long remember the content and presentation. Combining concrete exhibits with an interactive user interface, the innovative concept thus not only embodies a new experience but also offers a glance into the future.«

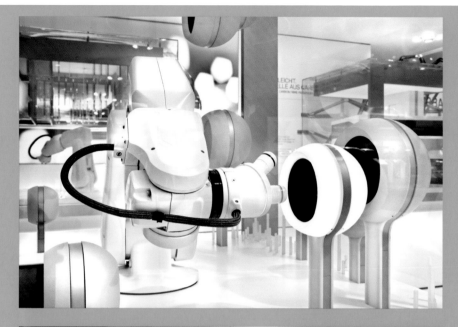

client
BMW AG,
Munich

design
Meso, Frankfurt/Main
Mutabor, Hamburg
Yellow Design, Cologne
Schusterjungen und Hurenkinder,
Munich

creative direction
Sebastian Oschatz,
Patrick Molinari,
Ulf Plihal,
Andreas Eric Meyer

strategic planning
Christian Pressler

project management
Michael Papst

→ digital presentation: DVD

red dot: grand prix

FontBook App

The FontBook app for the iPad opens up a new chapter: it turns the bulky print compendium of the FontBook into an electronic collection of maps that allows 700,000 typeface samples to be intuitively spread out, searched, layered, moved, scrolled and combined. The practical and well-designed tool for the world's most comprehensive lexicon on digitised fonts – the definitive source documenting and classifying the typefaces of past centuries until today – uses live, over-the-air updates to add new content releases on a regular basis. Direct links and five gateways invite users to browse the world of typography visually, categorised by class, foundry, designer, year or name. In addition, a quick text search takes users directly to the font families, foundries or designers. Further new features are a specially curated font lists and two types of bookmarks that serve as tools for compiling lists and comparing chosen typefaces. The easy-to-operate tool allows mailing FontBook samples directly from the app, saving them in personal photo albums or posting them to Twitter or Facebook.

Statement by the jury

»This iPad app is characterised by a very clear and simple design, as well as a user interface that is entirely self-sufficient in terms of form and function. The app is easy to navigate, distinctly structured and, as a whole, presents priceless added value for designers.«

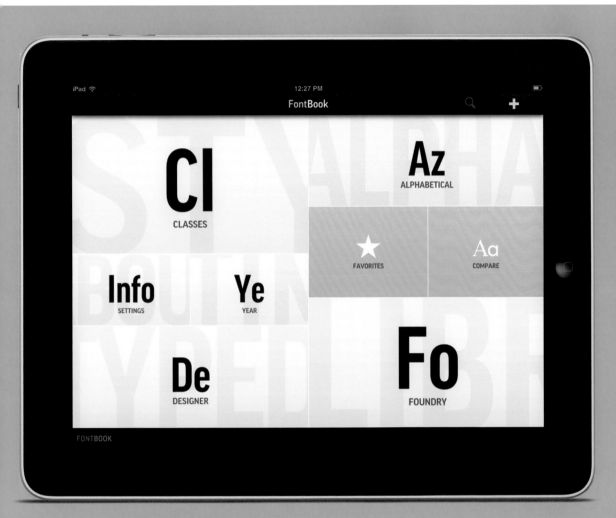

client
FontShop International GmbH,
Berlin

project management
Jürgen Siebert

design
Jan Rikus Hillmann,
burningbluesoul,
Berlin

programming
Andreas Pieper,
null2,
Berlin

database
Mai-Linh Truong

classification
Indra Kupferschmid

→ designer portrait: p. 412

red dot: best of the best

Loewe Assist Media

[iPad App]

The Loewe Assist Media app for the iPad is a one-of-a-kind TV remote control: it enables users to control and programme the Loewe TV set with a simple swipe of the finger – and this, in turn, also has a new experience in store for the successful tablet PC. The interface features a graphically clear, reduced design that offers easy and playful operation. With the light colour of the text set against a dark grey background, its high elegance and functionality tie in directly with the characteristic design of this manufacturer for home electronics. Serving as a digital remote control, the app also features a TV guide and a video library. Browsing through the iPad electronic programme guide and the cross-channel overview, users are informed at a glance about what is on air and what is coming up next – everything complemented by background information and preview images arranged for easy orientation and navigation. In addition, the app proves that creating favourites, programming and launching instant recording can be done with ease.

Statement by the jury

»The user interface of this app is outstanding because it features both technical sophistication and an excellent design, and opens up a new approach. Several media have been merged into one so that mobile devices can be used to choose a TV programme. Furthermore, the information management offers added value in that it was integrated into the Loewe product design concept.«

client
Loewe Opta GmbH,
Kronach

design
Loewe Opta GmbH,
Kronach
Marc Joschko,
Jasmin Kastner

programming
Grand Centrix

→ designer portrait: p. 423
→ digital presentation: DVD

red dot: best of the best

Kia Rio

[iPad App]

This iPad application presents the Kia Rio with its broad range of talents and abilities. It gives users the chance to get to know this compact car, which, alongside innovative convenience features and eco-friendly powertrains, also possesses a dynamic exterior as well as an elegantly designed interior, through a range of comprehensive features as well as photo and video galleries. Both the exterior and the interior of the car are presented in 360-degree panorama views that allow zooming and tilting. Furthermore, a customisation tool allows users to see the new model in all available colours and with all wheel options. Thanks to interactive virtual reality clips, a wide range of the Rio's innovative features can be previewed and experienced: thus users are shown how the air conditioner works when they set a specific temperature, while different shots of the trunk demonstrate the trunk's spaciousness. Not only all performance details, but also the sensation of driving the car, including road handling, agility and safety aspects are conveyed by this app in an entertaining and exciting manner.

Statement by the jury

»The Kia Rio iPad app piques curiosity and invites users to discover this compact car within various presentation media. The application is fun to use, easy to understand and operates and presents itself in a design that reflects the sporting dynamic characteristics of the Rio.«

client
Kia Motors Corporation,
Seoul

design
JNS Communications,
Seoul

head of marketing
Yong-Tae Shin

**creative direction/
strategic planning**
Man-Hee Jang

art direction
Sang-Moon Nam

graphic design
Hyun-Ji Kim

film direction
Do-Gyun Kim

→ designer portrait: p. 420

red dot: best of the best

Occhio App

The new io 3d app for Occhio gives a comprehensive presentation of the outstanding innovative range of lamps and lights that offer an exciting light experience owing to their three-dimensional adaptability, the latest LED technology and fascinating design solution details. As well as providing professional advice and convincing and time saving on-the-spot presentations, it also renders an aesthetic experience that inspires and entices both business partners and customers all over the world. With its highly purist and elegant appearance, the app presents the latest highlights by manufacturer Occhio and convinces with its clear design idiom, high-quality product pictures and intuitive user guidance. Vertical and horizontal navigation guides users through the entire product range, allowing them to choose playfully between an exhaustive information level and an inspiring configuration level, and thus to conceive new lighting both freely and with individually specified style options.

Statement by the jury

»The app for the io 3d range of lamps is special in that it features a clear and minimalist design elegance that highlights the product centre in all its facets and style options. It is complemented by an equally clear typography and easy-to-use, self-explanatory user guidance.«

client
Occhio GmbH,
Munich

design
Martin et Karczinski,
Munich

creative direction
Peter Martin

art direction
Simon Maier-Rahmer

concept
Christian Begusch

graphic design
Christian Begusch,
Ulrike Gottschild,
Björn Matthes

→ designer portrait: p. 424

BMW Magazin
iPad App
BMW Magazine
iPad App

Thanks to a clever navigation
system and stylistically sophisticated technology, the BMW
Magazine iPad app allows users
to easily swipe, tap, rotate and
balance their way through a
broad range of themes. Designed
to be informative and playful,
this app offers numerous photo
series, videos, sound files and
exciting games – all directly integrated into the layout. Through
a parallax effect, in which text
and image are situated in different layers, the layout is imbued
with dynamism. The iPad app is
inspired by the quality of content
and aesthetics found in the
print version of BMW Magazine.

client
BMW AG,
Munich

publisher
HOFFMANN UND CAMPE
Corporate Publishing,
Hamburg

design
ringzwei,
Hamburg
Dirk Linke

programming
cranberry production,
Hannover
Swipe Studio,
Hamburg

RWE /NEXT iPad App

As a digital supplement to a premium customer magazine, this iPad app offers not only the content of the print magazine but also additional features, such as image galleries, links to related websites, full-screen videos and animated illustrations. Intuitive navigation and clear mechanics make it easy for users to familiarise themselves with the app, motivating them to rotate, slide, swipe or tilt the content so as to discover many new functions in the process. The visually exciting and future-oriented design appeal fits in with the array of displayed topics related to energy.

client
RWE Vertrieb AG,
Dortmund

publisher
HOFFMANN UND CAMPE
Corporate Publishing,
Hamburg

project management
Jutta Groen

design
ringzwei,
Hamburg
Dirk Linke

programming
cranberry production,
Hannover
Swipe Studio,
Hamburg

→ digital presentation: DVD

PRADA 3.0 GUI

[Smartphone Graphical
User Interface]

"PRADA 3.0 GUI" was the third
collaboration between LG and
Prada. The interface is based
on the LG strategy that smartphones should have luxury
brands. The unique feature of
this product lies in that both the
appearance and user interface
were modified distinctively while
designing the product with Prada
in joint. An ultimate black GUI
concept was created, based on
the Prada's minimalism design
philosophy without any modi-
fication. Also, the design was
created for the "people who want
to distinguish themselves" by
securing the identity of "luxury
brand phone" that is differentiated from general IT devices.

client
LG Electronics Inc.,
Seoul

design
LG Electronics Inc.,
Seoul
Mee-Yeon Choi,
In-Young Hwang

→ digital presentation: DVD

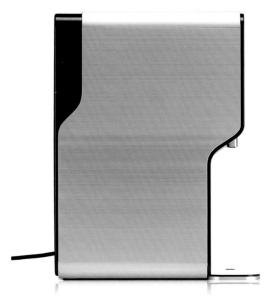

SMART Water Purifier

[User Interface]

The Smart water purifier features an innovative four-step filter system. It has been designed for installation in kitchens to purify polluted tap water and provide clean drinking water. The design of the display and interface focuses on intuitive ease of use so that users may obtain information – more easily, exactly and quickly – about the precise temperature and amount of clean water. In addition, frequently used buttons are larger, and the purifier provides other useful information in the kitchen, such as quick recipes, the time of day and the weather.

client
Woongjin Coway Co., Ltd.,
Seoul

design
Woongjin Coway Co., Ltd.,
Seoul
Hun-Jung Choi,
Seung-Woo Kim

→ digital presentation: DVD

Nautilus Hyosung ATM 8700 GUI

[Graphical User Interface]

The concept of the ATM 8700 graphical user interface realises the qualities of "transparency", "ease" and "comfort". Despite being a virtual experience, this GUI provides customers with a reliable and familiar experience by focusing on emotional communication, as if they were in a real bank. The input and transaction areas have been placed in the same location to make them easy to recognise and use. Furthermore, the complex process of self-banking has been simplified to foster an intuitive and instant reaction and to allow various functions to be accessed in a single step.

client
Nautilus Hyosung Inc.,
Seoul

head of marketing/advertising
Yoo Mee Min

design
designfever,
Seoul

creative direction/art direction
Jaehyung Park

graphic design
Kwangmin Jung,
Sanghoon Lee,
Daeill Moon

project management
Seungae Jang,
Heehyun Kim

→ digital presentation: DVD

Make Your Race

[Digital Installation]

In order to offer the 30,000 participants of the We Run Seoul 10K 2011 event a personal goal and incentive for running, the idea was to develop a digital installation utilising a transparent display. A running shirt was on view behind the screen. Runners could have race T-shirts printed with their own messages and photos using innovative technology. A transparent touchscreen simulated how the customised design would look on an actual T-shirt. Furthermore, the slogan "Race of my life" became reality with a post-race printing service which allowed runners to have their personal records printed on a race T-shirt.

client
Nike Korea,
Seoul

design
PostVisual.com,
Seoul

head of marketing
Jung-Won Lee

creative direction
Euna Seol,
Tae-Hyung Lee,
Hyun-Hee Park

graphic design
Sin-Ae Kim, Sora Lee,
Sung-Hae Choi

strategic planning
Kyung-Hee Lee, Myoung-Soo Kim,
Chang-Hyo Yoo

programming
Seol-Baek Shon, Won-Seok Cho,
Hyun Lee, Seung-Wook Chen

motion design
Sung-Wook Kim, Jiho Lee,
Bok-Ro Lee, Hanna Shin,
Ye-Nee Park

→ digital presentation: DVD

Troi 5

[Project Software]

client
Troi GmbH,
Munich

design
Martin et Karczinski,
Munich

creative direction
Peter Martin

art direction/concept
Christian Begusch,
Meike Rott

graphic design
Christian Begusch

→ digital presentation: DVD

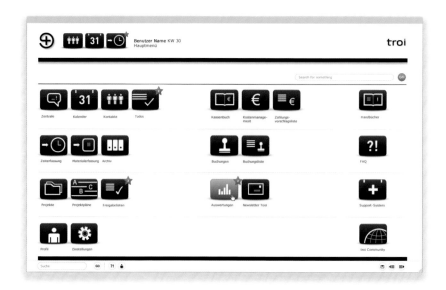

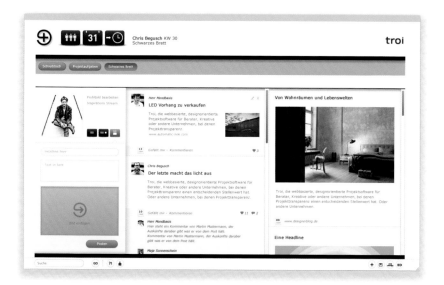

For the Troi 5 project software, an optimised graphical user interface was developed. It makes navigation easier while simultaneously illustrating the company's high standard of design. The greater use of graphic elements in the interplay of function and form facilitates direct access to the software and its functions. In addition, Troi 5 offers a large number of innovations, such as an entirely new desk design, a bulletin board with social media functionality, and a selection of widgets offering optimum assistance with everyday work processes.

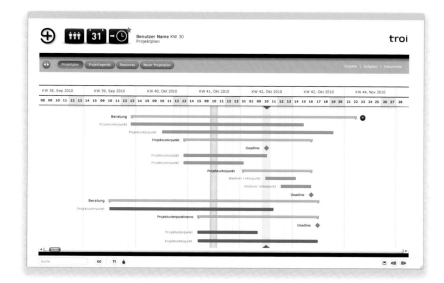

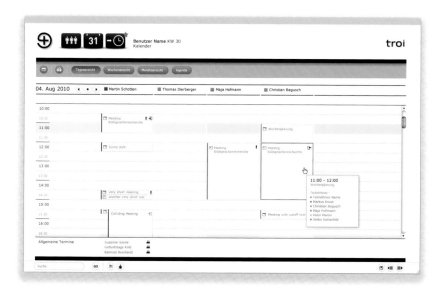

Postcard

[App]

Adopting the bright and friendly design language of Deutsche Telekom, the app Postcard enables users to send digital photos as real postcards, to edit their photos, enter text easily and select addresses directly in the app. This saves long searches for postcards and stamps while enabling users to share personal emotional moments from the digital world in an analogue way with people who do not own a smartphone. Another attractive aspect of the design is the convenient billing process, whereby the postcards are automatically billed to the user's mobile phone invoice.

client
Deutsche Telekom AG,
Bonn

design
Deutsche Telekom
Product Design,
Bonn

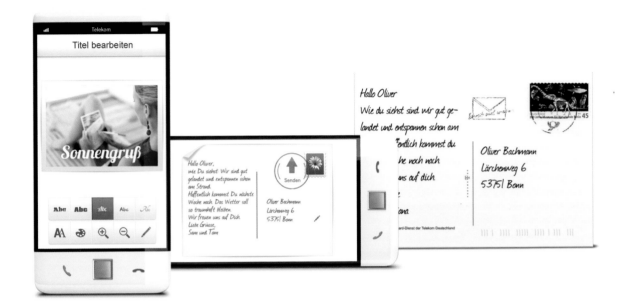

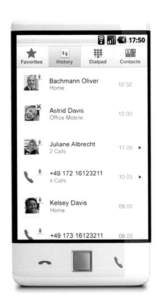

HomeTalk

[App]

HomeTalk allows a smartphone to be used as a fixed-network telephone at home. With the new IP-based Deutsche Telekom connection, users only have to enter their fixed-network number once to register via their smartphone. HomeTalk supports access to personal smartphone contacts, the compilation of a list of favourite contacts with images, toggling between two calls, and conference calling. The intuitive user interface is easy to use, and HomeTalk is equipped with HD Voice for outstanding voice quality.

client
Deutsche Telekom AG,
Bonn

design
Deutsche Telekom
Product Design,
Bonn

Das DRadio

[Mobile Radio App]

The concept of Das DRadio focuses exclusively on the purpose of listening to the three radio stations broadcast by Deutschlandradio. The interface of the app is designed to visually integrate the entire smartphone or tablet and turn it into a radio. Depending on the colour of the respective device, users can choose between a black or a white surface and thus personalise the app accordingly. For a more traditionally minded target group, there is also the option of selecting a wood-like surface.

client
Deutschlandradio, Cologne

design
nondesign, Cologne
Sebastian Kutscher

Sports Tracker

[GPS-Based Workout Tracker]

After years of internal research and prototyping, the first real incarnation of Sports Tracker was launched as a beta version by Nokia Beta Labs on Symbian devices in 2006. During the long process of its development, the visual appearance, typography and layout of this successful app were designed, tested and then meticulously modified again and again to satisfy the needs of iOS users. The result makes the current version of Sports Tracker very easy to use and conveniently controllable via the touchscreen, offering users a wide range of highly interesting features.

client
Sports Tracking Technologies, Helsinki

head of marketing/advertising
Jussi Solja

design
Great Apes Ltd, Helsinki

creative direction
Niko Sipilä, Antti Sorvari

art direction/graphic design
Niko Sipilä

project management
Antti Sorvari

→ designer portrait: p. 414

2012 Nike Women's Race: Running Styling Guide

[App]

client
Tae Hyun Kim
Nike Sports Korea,
Seoul

design
ahn graphics Ltd.,
Seoul

art direction
Young-Hoon Park

graphic design
Yu-Won Choi

strategic planning
Kyeong-Ok Kim

project management
Ji-Hyun Lee,
Tae-Sung Kang

programming
Jae-Yeon Won

A new kind of catalogue, "2012 Nike Women's Race: Running Styling Guide", showcases Nike's 2012 Spring/Summer collection, authentically situated around urban Seoul. This catalogue offers the exciting new way to find, select and match products and their colours for the individual styling. The catalogue is installed at various Nike stores throughout South Korea, helping their customers with the new shopping experience. It is also available for download from the iTunes store, allowing users to share their ideas with others at their convenience. The structure of the catalogue is kept minimal for easy navigation. Rather, the catalogue concentrates on offering attention-catching, fun-to-use navigation system with the interactive-moving types floating around the screen, reflecting the movement of the iPad.

QisBattery

[App]

The QisBattery app for smartphones and tablets communicates wirelessly with a home
battery bank and thus facilitates
individual energy management.
The application bundles all power
supply information together –
including that originating from
solar sources, power plants and
battery banks – for an easy
overview of energy supply and
reserves at home. There is a
setting for off-peak purchasing
of less expensive power, and
the electronic volume may be
adjusted based on projected
needs for emergency use during
a power outage. Moreover, Qis-
Battery's analysis of the solar
power supply can give users
a better understanding of the
benefits of green energy.

client
Qisda Corporation,
Taipei

design
Qisda Creative Design Center,
Taipei

Busch-ComfortTouch App

Offering a high degree of user comfort, this app enables an entire home's automation to be controlled via a smartphone or tablet. Designed as a remote control, the new Busch-ComfortTouch app can operate all building-related functions of the Busch-ComfortPanel from any room via iPhone, iPod touch, iPad or Android device. A matrix allows users to scroll easily through the rooms and navigate horizontally between the particular appliances in each room. In addition, the app allows the house to be monitored and operated from afar via the Internet.

client
Busch-Jaeger Elektro GmbH, Lüdenscheid

design
Human Interface Design, Hamburg
Konradin Windhorst,
Fee Fröiland

creative direction
Prof. Frank Jacob,
Claudia S. Friedrich

art direction
Andi Kern

concept
Jobst Prinzhorn

programming
Symphony Teleca

→ designer portrait: p. 418

Audi Konfigurator
Audi Configurator

[App]

For the first time ever, a car
brand has enabled customers
and fans to configure their perfect vehicle via a mobile application. Using their smartphones
(iPhone and Android), users can
virtually build and customise an
Audi from the very first bolt to
the last drop of paint. The design
challenge consisted in incorpo-
rating the huge amount of data
related to equipment and accessories, along with the potential
combinations thereof, into a
seamless user experience which
fits the Audi brand values.

client
AUDI AG,
Ingolstadt

strategic planning
Bettina Rühle,
AUDI AG

design
SapientNitro

art direction
Marc Benz

concept
Stefan Schroder

project management
Alex Scheidgen

programming
Thorsten von Vietinghoff,
Stefan Jager

back-end
Das Büro am Draht GmbH
Randolf Nawrath
(Technical Project Management),
Steffen Lehn
(Software Engineer)

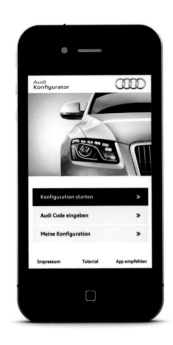

Gira
Designkonfigurator
Gira
Design Configurator

The development of this iPad app centred on creating a new form of planning aid for building contractors, architects and spatial planners. With the Gira design configurator, diverse frame variants from the Gira switch ranges can be combined with selected functions in various colours and materials according to customer wishes. The configurator is accessible online and also available as a free app for the iPhone and iPad. For smartphones and tablets with other operating systems, such as Android, an optimised web display is available.

client
Gira Giersiepen GmbH & Co. KG,
Radevormwald

design
schmitz Visuelle Kommunikation,
Wuppertal
Hans Günter Schmitz,
David Conrad

Chinese Traditional Furniture

[App]

design
Central Academy of Fine Arts,
Beijing
Prof. Feng Yan

→ designer portrait: p. 442
→ digital presentation: DVD

Chinese Traditional Furniture offers exciting insight into furniture from the Ming Dynasty period, filigree pieces of furniture that were designed without the use of nails. Thanks to a highly consistent digital media design, users are shown the diversity of traditional Chinese design patterns and forms of construction. They can learn about the steps involved in making these unique pieces of furniture, and will find answers to questions such as how Ming Dynasty artists drew and designed their furniture. Tapping on the image at the start page gives access to well-structured details on the piece's history, size and function, as well as the tools used. The four options in the navigation bar cover all relevant information for a better understanding of each piece of furniture.

F.A.Z.

[iPad App]

The claim made by the Frankfurter Allgemeine Zeitung, commonly referred to as the F.A.Z., that it is a newspaper offering high-quality journalism for decision-makers in politics and business is also reflected by this iPad app. It places the daily print edition centre stage and underscores this focus through a navigation bar situated above the respective newspaper pages. Highly functional features that enhance the reading experience include an article-reading mode, a topic monitor and a notepad. Rounded off by an archive feature for older editions, the app represents a well-thought-out symbiosis of classic newspaper experience and digital research tool.

client
Frankfurter Allgemeine Zeitung GmbH, Frankfurt/Main

design
KircherBurkhardt GmbH, Berlin

creative direction
Paul Wagner

art direction
Andrea Rohner

concept
Reinhard Dassel,
Frank Gürgens

customer advisory service
Diana Schniedermeier

project management
Sophie Lindenstruth

F.A.S.

[iPad App]

The high-quality journalism and visual design of the Frankfurter Allgemeine Sonntagszeitung, launched successfully just ten years ago, provided inspiration for the concept and design of the F.A.S. iPad app. A high demand placed on layout and design is apparent throughout the entire application, offering a user-friendly navigation experience that provides access to a broad spectrum of content. Each of the presented articles is designed with loving attention to detail. The clear focus is on the optimal reproduction of the articles, enriched with small, sophisticated animations.

client
Frankfurter Allgemeine Zeitung GmbH, Frankfurt/Main

design
KircherBurkhardt GmbH, Berlin

creative direction
Lukas Kircher

art direction
Andrea Rohner

customer advisory service
Diana Schniedermeier

project management
Stefanie Pursche

303

BMW Magazin
iPad App
BMW Magazine
iPad App

The BMW Magazine iPad app offers users a comprehensive multimedia experience of the brand. Extensive photo series, exciting videos and interesting animated clips justify BMW's claim to premium quality in a manner that is fully in line with international lifestyle publications. The app shares the quality content and aesthetics of the print version of BMW Magazine and transfers them in a creative and innovative way to this enhanced communication channel. The aim is to fascinate and thrill readers through the interactive content specially created for the iPad medium.

client
BMW AG,
Munich

publisher
HOFFMANN UND CAMPE
Corporate Publishing,
Hamburg

design
ringzwei,
Hamburg
Dirk Linke

programming
cranberry production,
Hannover
Swipe Studio,
Hamburg

Deutscher Bundestag, V. 3.0
German Bundestag, v. 3.0

[App]

Giving users quick and easy access to the latest information from the German Bundestag was the design objective of this newly developed app. It features ease of navigation in combination with a design that is both modern and reliable. Content is continuously updated on an hourly basis, which includes meeting agendas and video recordings. When developing the iPad version, particular attention was paid to ensuring a medium-appropriate realisation. Furthermore, the design was ideally adapted to the large iPad screen using a two-column display.

client
Deutscher Bundestag /
German Bundestag, Berlin

head of marketing/text
Dr. Maika Jachmann

design
Babiel GmbH,
Düsseldorf

→ digital presentation: DVD

Christophorus – The Porsche Magazine

[iPad App]

The design of the iPad app accompanying the print magazine "Christophorus – The Porsche Magazine", a sophisticated customer retention tool by Porsche, combines the reading experience of a print product with a high-value design appearance. The magazine's conceptual aim is to serve as a stage for the Porsche brand – for the cars as well as for the people who invent, produce and drive them. As an extension of this aim, the Christophorus app offers interactive storytelling, a distinctive pictorial language and innovative navigation features.

client
Dr. Ing. h.c. F. Porsche AG, Stuttgart

design
KircherBurkhardt GmbH, Berlin

head of marketing
Antje Saborowski

graphic design
Sarah Röse

text
Elmar Brümmer

project management
Özden Durmus

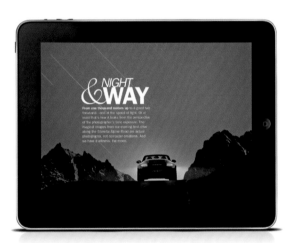
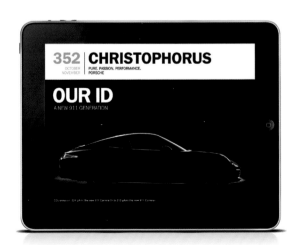

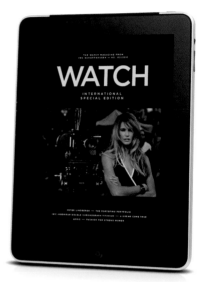

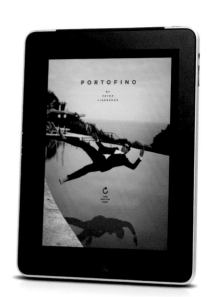

IWC WATCH
International 02/2011
[Customer Magazine, iPad App]

The concept of this iPad app was modelled on the quality of the IWC magazine Watch International, which has established the foundation for the entire communications family and is oriented towards the communication needs of the company's various target groups. It documents the brand's quality claim and offers users a variety of interactive features that simultaneously enhance the value of the actual magazine. When it comes to photography, however, the app offers a broader range of impact, with video and audio files complementing the content through a high sense of vibrancy.

client
IWC International WATCH Co. AG,
Schaffhausen

project management
Christian Gattiker,
Richemont

brand publisher
Keren Eldad,
IWC Schaffhausen

design
ringzwei,
Hamburg

creative direction
Dirk Linke,
ringzwei

art direction
Lukas Niehaus,
ringzwei

editor-in-chief
Medard Meier,
GMRZ

production
Hanspeter Eggenberger,
Duktus AG

programming
Bastian Hoyer,
Cranberry Production

NCsoft
iactionbook –
Baseball Picture
Dictionary

[App]

client
NCsoft,
Seoul

design
designfever,
Seoul

creative direction/art direction
Jaehyung Park

graphic design
Sukkyoung Choi,
Sanghyuk Park,
Kwangpyo Kim,
Giyong Rhee,
Taeyeon Kim

project management
Sunny Jung,
Heehyun Kim

The Baseball Picture Dictionary is a cleverly designed app for people who are interested in learning more about baseball. Based on appealing interactive animation and unique characters, this iactionbook makes learning practically everything about baseball fun and easy for everyone. With its consistent design approach of using a variety of actions and illustrations, the app presents the basic rules of baseball and also explains the more difficult terminology in an easy-to-understand way.

Packaging Design

Event Design

Information Design /
Public Space

Corporate Films

TV, Film & Ci

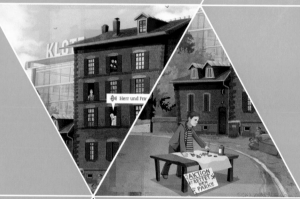

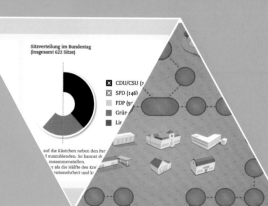

Games & Electronic Art

Nike –
Catch the Flash
[Online Game]

client
Nike Gesellschaft m.b.H.,
Vienna

head of marketing
Edgar Jorissen,
Sebastian Bayer

head of advertising
Oliver Eckart,
Andreas Roitner

design
Jung von Matt/Neckar GmbH,
Stuttgart

creative direction
Kai Heuser,
Joerg Jahn,
Jacques Pense

art direction
Matías Müller

graphic design
Christoph Kock,
Alexa Petruch

text
Gün Aydemir,
Matthias Hess

project management
Manuel Colloseus,
Björn Hansen,
Denise Winter

photography
Mat Neidhardt

programming
Nils Doehring

post-production
Recom

→ digital presentation: DVD

For the launch of Nike's Vapor Flash Jacket, a fully reflective jacket for enhanced safety, the Catch the Flash game followed the idea of "making the invisible visible". Fifty runners set out on the dark streets of Vienna as "Flashrunners" with the whole of Vienna chasing them. The chaser who flashed the most Flashrunners with his or her camera, thereby revealing their jacket numbers, won a 10,000 euro platinum bar. Simultaneously, people could take part in the chase on a microsite: using an app, all 50 Flashrunners transferred their GPS data in real time to the Catch the Flash online game.

Eugen's World

[Browser-Based Serious Game]

"Eugen's World" is a multimedia production complementing the eponymous TV series on Germany's school programme. The character illustrations and the dark setting in a run-down house prominently portray the style of the series. The plot is embedded in a clear graphic interface design. Developed as an educational game for use in classrooms from 5th to 8th grade, this "serious game" aims at active opinion formation. It seeks to encourage young people to understand and assert their rights within a democracy for the greater good of the community.

client
SWR Südwestrundfunk,
Stuttgart

design
outermedia GmbH,
Berlin

art direction
Eva Duwenkamp

concept
Kerstin Stoll,
Anne Sauer

graphic design
Mariano Procopio,
Sabine Reichel

project management
Martin Talmeier

illustration
Elke Hanisch

programming
Simon Oldeboershuis,
Mike Wendeborn,
Stephan Allner,
Gunnar Daugs

→ digital presentation: DVD

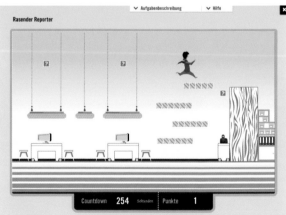

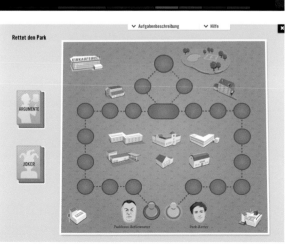

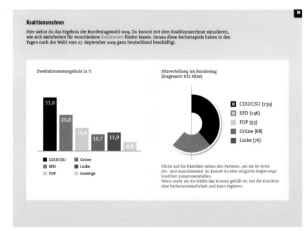

The Flower – Poetic Short Messaging System

This short message service offers an interactive and poetic approach to sending unusual text messages. After users have entered their text into the smartphone app, the single letters are transformed interactively into a beautiful flower. By touching the flower on the display, the individual letters shift back again to spell out the message. On an iPhone, the flower can be shaken, moved, touched and even blown away. The Flower knows all languages and is compatible with the iPhone keyboard. The messages may be sent by e-mail as a video attachment or an e-card, and they can also be posted on Facebook and Twitter.

client
undSchwieger,
Hamburg

head of marketing
Marc Schwieger

design
Artificialduck Studios,
Hamburg

creative direction/art direction
Dirk Hoffmann

project management/ programming
Wolfgang Müller

→ designer portrait: p. 404
→ digital presentation: DVD

Sound Design

red dot: best of the best

The Absolute Pitch

[Radio Commercial]

Young people with absolute pitch are a rather small, highly specific target group. Conceived as the "first official radio-based application procedure", this radio commercial aims at this very target group, inviting young musicians to apply for courses in classical music at the Academy of Music, Theatre and Media in Hanover. In order to make sure that applicants are talented and possess the rare gift of absolute pitch, the radio commercial features a tone sequence that needs to be identified. When decoded, the sequence of note names forms the individual letters of the e-mail address to which applicants have to send their documents. Since people with the gift of absolute pitch can identify every tone on the musical scale without any device, they can easily decode the sequence by just listening to the melody and using the German scale system (C, D, F or A). Played on a piano, the musical sequence serves as a first challenge for applicants and thus turns the radio commercial into the first round of a qualifying examination.

Statement by the jury

»The trick of this radio commercial is that it links a call for applications to study music with a qualification test. The e-mail address applications have to be sent to is exclusively encoded as a musical sequence. This ensures that applicants belong to the target group and, in itself, represents a sophisticated design solution and implementation.«

Script „The Absolute Pitch" (Translation)

(VO:)
Welcome to the first official application procedure of the University of music Hannover. We are searching for students with an absolute pitch. If you can hear that this (Piano-Sound: A) is an A, and this (Piano-Sound: C) is a C, then we are looking forward to receiving an email from you. Just send it to (Piano-Sound: C-H-E-F)@hmtm-hannover.(Piano-Sound: D-E).

Once again, so you can write it down:
(Piano-Sound: C-H-E-F)@hmtm-hannover.(Piano-Sounds: D-E).

Script „Absolutes Gehör" (Original Language)

(Off-Sprecher:)
Willkommen zum ersten offiziellen Radio-Bewerbungsverfahren der Hochschule für Musik, Theater und Medien Hannover. Wir suchen Studenten mit absolutem Gehör. Wenn Sie hören können, dass das (Klavierton: A) ein A ist und das (Klavierton: C) ein C, dann freuen wir uns auf eine Mail von Ihnen.
Einfach an (Klaviertöne: C-H-E-F)@hmtm-hannover. (Klaviertöne: D-E)

Und jetzt nochmal zum mitschreiben:
(Klaviertöne: C-H-E-F)@hmtm-hannover. (Klaviertöne: D-E) .

Additional information / regional characteristic:

Please note: The German musical scale goes C, D, E, F, G, A, H (instead of B), C. So the encoded mail address is:
CHEF@HMTM-HANNOVER.DE

The German word „Chef" means „Chief".

client
Hochschule für Musik,
Theater und Medien Hannover /
Academy of Music,
Theatre and Media Hanover

design
Ogilvy Deutschland

creative direction
Dr. Stephan Vogel,
Matthias Storath

text
Manuel Rentz

project management
Michael Fucks,
Sophie Gudat

music/sound design
Studio Funk, Berlin

→ digital presentation: DVD

FIsound

[Corporate Sound]

A triad in the key of F sharp served as the basis for the corporate sound of Finanz Informatik. The tripartite structure is also reflected in all relevant company and product names, with the individual letters in the German designation for F sharp – "fis" – interpreted as the DNA of the brand. Moreover, since the abbreviation "FI" stands for Finanz Informatik and the "S" for Sparkasse, the corporate sound was also created from various perspectives: the "brand" version is a scoring of the FI pattern and the "group" version is coupled with the jingle for Sparkasse.

client
Finanz Informatik,
Frankfurt/Main

head of marketing
Claudia Lensker

head of advertising
Christoph Rutter

strategic planning
Claudia Ellerbrake

project management
Andreas Honsel

design
beierarbeit GmbH,
Bielefeld

creative direction
Christoph Beier

music/sound design
Rainer Falkenroth

→ digital presentation: DVD

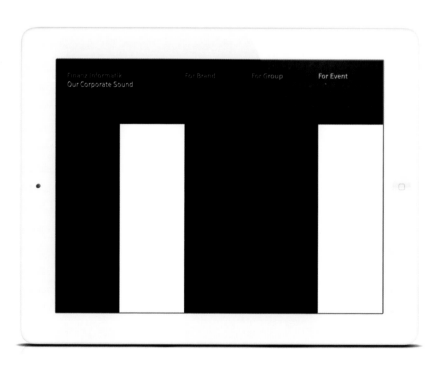

OLYMPUS
[Sound Branding,
Sound Identity Development]

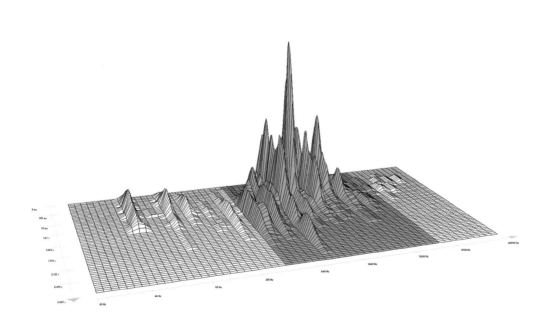

The core element of the Olympus sound identity is the sound logo, which provides a synergetic effect by creating cross-modal interaction between acoustic and visual communications. The three syllables of "O-lym-pus" are thus reflected in the rhythmic three-tone structure of the sound logo. Additional sound elements are implemented in touchpoints, such as TV spots, exhibitions, online presence, telephone and events, as well as in the products themselves. So, when switching on an Olympus product for instance, users are greeted by the sound logo to enhance instant brand recognition.

client
Olympus Europa Holding GmbH,
Hamburg

head of marketing
Heino Hilbig

creative direction
Satoru Tanio

design
GROVES Sound Branding GmbH,
Hamburg

head of sound branding
John Groves

project management
Christoph Groß-Fengels

→ digital presentation: DVD

SCA Libero
[Sound Branding]

client
SCA Libero,
Moscow
LHBS Consulting GmbH,
Vienna

music/sound design
Max Kickinger,
Max Kickinger Soundbranding,
Vienna

head of marketing
Peter Hedenberg,
SCA Libero

senior brand manager
Tatiana Novoselova,
SCA Libero

strategic planning
Joanna Bakas,
Stefan Erschwendner,
LHBS

project management
Joanna Bakas,
LHBS

→ digital presentation: DVD

The sound branding for the Russian diaper brand Libero reflects the brand essence of "Nature & Know-how" as well as the brand strategy "Seriously good nature in a playful way". The Libero sound logo consists of a three-note motif, inspired by the rhythm of the brand name. The melody line was derived from the idea of a simple lullaby and therefore uses only instruments made of natural materials, without resorting to electronic sounds of any kind. The Libero brand music is therefore based on the sound logo and is flexibly adaptable for all different customer-oriented sound applications.

Packaging Design

Event Design

Information Design /
Public Space

Corporate Films

TV, Film & Cinema

Junior Award

red dot: junior prize

Hochschule Niederrhein
University of Applied Sciences

[Image Film]

The motto of the Niederrhein University is "crossing borders". True to this philosophy, the corporate video crosses visual borders by doing without shots of real-life scenes. Instead, by an analogy to school and learning, it starts off with an animated drop of blue ink: firstly, the drop symbolises the world in which the Niederrhein University offers orientation by giving its 10,800 students the opportunity to "write their future" to suit their own individual goals. The drop then starts to move, illustrating the university's 150 years of history and tradition in facts and figures, leaving lines of blue ink on a white paper background. Retracing the development of the university into a global network and esteemed academic institution, the lines become ever more filigree and convey a firmly rooted image. With this unusual, creative approach to the topic, the film not only builds the university's profile and distinguishes it from other universities, it also implements the university's mission statement in a coherent and sophisticated manner.

university
Hochschule Niederrhein /
University of Applied Sciences

supervising professor
Prof. Thorsten Kraus

design
Damon Aval,
Stephen Erckmann

motion design
Jens Kindler

→ designer portrait: p. 449
→ digital presentation: DVD

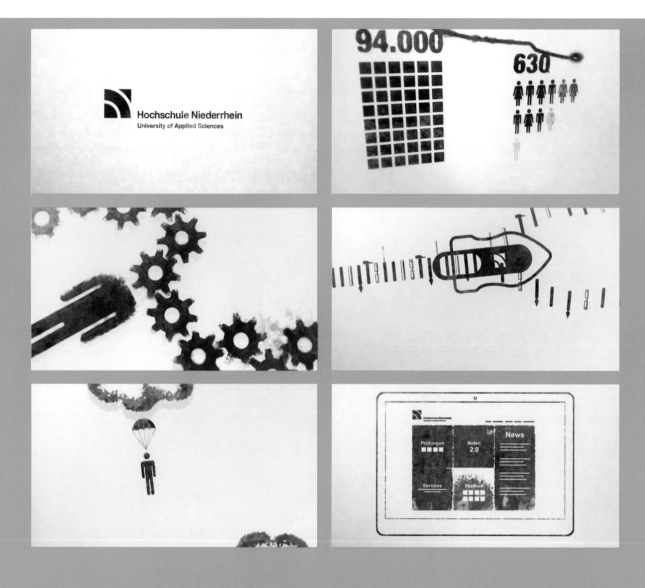

red dot: junior prize

"Transcending limitations" – an ink mark as starting point for the history and the visions of a university

[Laudation by Prof. Dr. Linda Breitlauch]

As professor for game design I am frequently asked whether it is possible to impart creativity through a degree course and if so, how this can be done. The role of universities and professors for design degree courses is to enable students to discover and channel their own talents, and thereby to allow them to unfold. Exceptional design stands out because of its novel approach to established thinking, its effective execution and the ability to convey a clear, unequivocal message and vision. A design course offers students the opportunity to experiment bravely, to depart from well-trodden paths, to take inspiration from the tasks set and to crystallise their intentions.

If a design degree course wants to present its university in an image film, it is faced with the challenge of not only portraying information effectively and entertainingly, but also of giving a comprehensible and appealing overview of the degree course. In addition, professional film design criteria demand no less than masterly handling of the audio-visual media, as well as an understanding of their effect on the target audience.

The team of students surrounding Prof. Thorsten Kraus has succeeded admirably in achieving just this with their image film of the Niederrhein University.

The vision is unequivocal. What should a university be for its students? A support and guiding light – which does not have to be followed – to help them turn their concept of life into reality. The film, which is based on the general idea of "transcending limitations", develops from an ink mark, the starting point for all conceptual work in this image film. The structure and history of the university evolve from the initially visionary concept like from a seed. As is the case with the initial concept of a design, the vision turns into the foundation that underpins the end product. Starting from an ink mark, the film develops a fascinating dynamic of images, numbers, figures and events that ultimately paint an animated picture of a highly creative and professional academic education.

A university should enable its students to shape their professional future in the best way possible. The film impressively demonstrates that teams of students are capable of managing the complex task of producing an image film, which contains much supposedly dull information, in a way that is appealing both visually and aurally. They have done so professionally and with remarkable creativity. The key idea of transcending limitations applies in particular to the talent of these students who, with this film, have mastered the move to the professional market with apparent ease. The jury honours the filmmakers with the "red dot: junior prize", knowing that the winners will continue to accomplish exceptional projects in the future and will furthermore act as an inspiration for designers and filmmakers alike.

reddot design award
junior prize 2012   329

red dot: best of the best

T

[Corporate Design]

This work is the corporate design for a tea brand that sells only tea leaves and tea beverages. In order to endorse the image of tea on all products of this brand, a logo was created modelled on the letter "T" and inspired by the typical shape and curling of tea leaves. This logo can be used independently or in conjunction with the various products of the brand. In order to complement the logo, an illustration of the "T" was created that depicts the familiar visual impression of tea leaves being infused in hot water. The letter slowly blurs and infuses just like tea leaves slowly infuse water when brewed. The illustration is employed in many ways: on print ads, on various merchandise articles as well as on the packages. In addition, visitors of the company's website can directly experience this infusing and blurring of tea and the "T" by using the text input tool. The corporate design thus adopts significant characteristics of tea and turns them into a distinctive and highly aesthetic design.

Statement by the jury

»This brand identity stands out in particular because it merges two essential aspects into one: on the one hand, it represents a very beautiful and consistently designed graphical implementation of the brand; on the other hand, it is informed by the essence of tea, turning it into a visualisation that people can relate to and understand easily beyond words.«

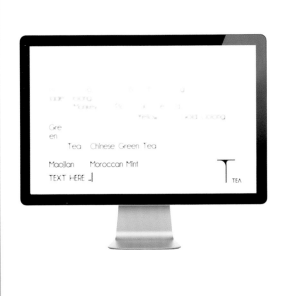

university
University of Seoul

supervising professor
Prof. Sangkeun Jeong,
Prof. Minha Yang

design
So Yeon Yu,
Seoul

→ designer portrait: p. 466

Formation GG – Eine visuelle Reise durch das Deutsche Grundgesetz
Formation GG – A Visual Guide to the Basic Law of Germany
[Book]

The Basic Law for Germany (Grundgesetz, abbr.: GG) is the most important document of Germany's democratic society. However, its significance is not fully appreciated amongst German people. The visual guide book "Formation GG" aims to build a bridge for interested citizens and non-citizens and enhances the understanding of and the interest in the constitutional law. Divided into four chapters, it illustrates the structure, formation and development of the Basic Law from its beginning in the year 1949 via historic reformations to its present state. By explaining the constitution through content analysis and information graphics "Formation GG" is highly comprehensible in particular for non-professional readers. The "visual journey" combines contemporary data graphics with retro fonts and colours into a compelling piece of didactic information design.

Statement by the jury

»The book "Formation GG" manages to convey the complex facts of the German constitution to outstanding effect, inspiring readers to further look into the subject matter. With various information graphics and typefaces, it visualises the content in an intelligent way. The work furthermore convinced the jury with the quality of its manufacture.«

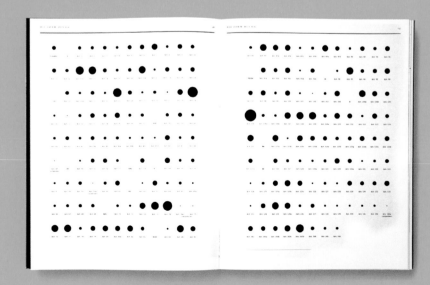

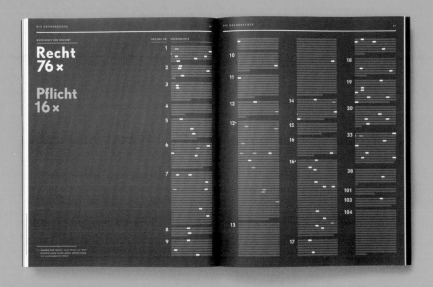

university
Schule für Gestaltung
Ravensburg /
School of Design
Ravensburg

supervising professor
Georg Engels,
Ulm

design
Mike Hofmaier,
Ravensburg

→ designer portrait: p. 451

red dot: best of the best

Ein Reisender
A Traveller

[Book]

This book is based on the original travel journal of the missionary F. Petrick, who travelled from China to South Africa in 1892. The design connects three levels that are interwoven in terms of form and content and together present a diversified amount of information. In the form of a small-sized notebook, the original text in Kurrent, the old German script, on brownish paper was stapled between the pages, on which readers find the transliteration as well as additional information. Complemented by vivid illustrations, technical drawings and graphics – all in a reduced colour palette – the book describes an exciting image of a journey that was made more than hundred years ago. The topics travel, religion, history, the missionaries' work and the fate of F. Petrick are visualised with interwoven formats, cross references between the texts as well as a grid, which identifies time and space of the events, turning the book into an impressive and engaging reading experience.

Statement by the jury

»The design of this comprehensive travel report successfully leads readers into the time of the missionary around the year 1892 with original facsimile documents and light colour tones, where the light blue echoes the colour of the ocean. Moreover, the layout is characterised by a clearly laid out typography and the inspiring presentation of the many details.«

university
IN.D Institute of Design
Düsseldorf

design
Anna Radowski,
Haan

→ designer portrait: p. 461

NORTE #2 – Werden & Sein
NORTE #2 – Becoming & Being

[Stereo-Thematic Student Magazine]

Each issue of the NORTE magazine explores two terms or concepts, which are closely related, as for example "Becoming & Being" in the current issue. Accordingly, all articles revolve around this topic, discussing questions such as: "What does the development process contribute to the finalised work?" and "Are fixed definitions, identities and conditions just tools for the construction of our reality?". The format reflects this topic in the form of a more than 12 metres long, fan-fold paper web. It allows "endless" reading from the beginning to the end and vice versa from the end to the beginning, thus illustrating the convergence of becoming and being. Also the layout is no longer bound to classic page margins, but features large-scale image series spreading over several pages and visualises the content in a diversified and exciting manner, for example with a variable type area and a wide range of different styles and illustrations.

Statement by the jury

»The special achievement of this magazine is that it translates content and concept into an appropriate formal solution. The fan-fold format is used as a dramaturgical element that counteracts the usual reading direction. Each single page presents a surprising new design and underlines the exemplary nature of this work.«

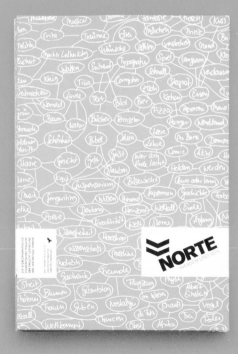

university
Hochschule Wismar / University
of Applied Sciences Wismar

supervising professor
Prof. Dr. Achim Trebess,
Prof. Hanka Polkehn

design
NORTE Redaktion, Hochschule
Wismar / University of Applied
Sciences Wismar

creative direction
Mirko Leyh

art direction
Stefanie Bolduan,
Christoph Meyer

graphic design
Simone Lehmann,
Franziska Krüger

→ designer portrait: p. 460

red dot: best of the best

Was hat Venedig zu verstecken?
What does Venice have to hide?
[Poster Series]

This poster series deals with the enormous environmental pollution in Venice during the last century, using information graphics to visualise the facts and results of research conducted on this issue. The presentation of these facts relies upon a highly variegated and creative implementation: be it the impending submersion of the city due to the rising sea level, conveyed through abstract waves demonstrating the rise in recent years, or the pollution of the industrial city of Porto Marghera, symbolised by colourful mountain peaks, the respective heights of which suggest the threat, facts and numbers merge with the graphic illustration into a meaningful and aesthetic unity that attracts attention and sparks interest. The main emphasis of the series lies on showing the causes of this pollution. However, it also depicts concepts and strategies for the future, considerations on giving nature back its original space and repairing existing damage.

Statement by the jury

»In order to present the plethora of real information, this poster series opts for an approach that strikes a balance between clarity and reduction as well as attractiveness and sensibility. The message is thus conveyed in a highly appealing manner without running the risk of the content becoming uninspiring.«

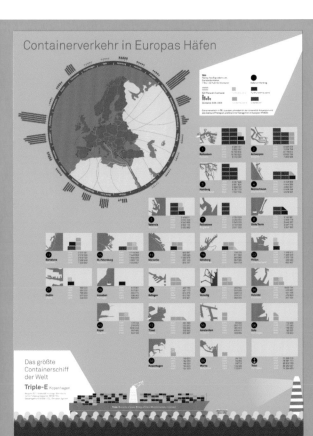

Containerverkehr in Europas Häfen

Das größte
Containerschiff
der Welt

Triple-E Kopenhagen

1'877,54 km²
Abflussgebiet

539,56 km²
Lagune von Venedig

2'515 km
Gewässer

136'000 Km²
die Adria

university
Hochschule für Gestaltung
Offenbach / Academy of Art
and Design Offenbach

supervising professor
Prof. Klaus Hesse

design
Kim Angie Cicuttin

text
Meike Langer,
Tatjana Pummer,
Lisa Adriana Kelso

printing
Berthold Druck GmbH

→ designer portrait: p. 448

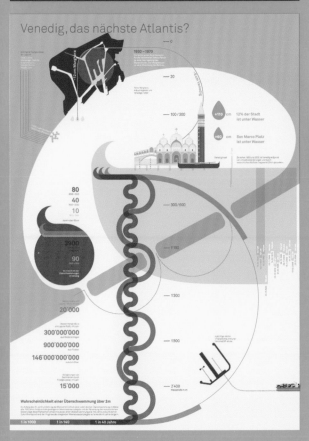

Venedig, das nächste Atlantis?

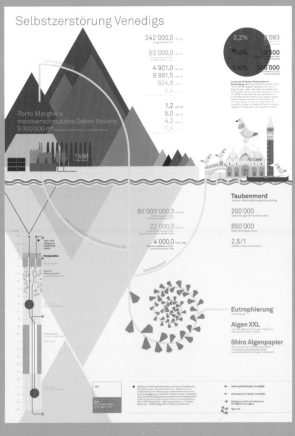

Selbstzerstörung Venedigs

Porto Marghera
meistverschmutztes Gebiet Italiens
5'000'000 m²

Taubenmord

Eutrophierung

Algen XXL

Shiro Algenpapier

red dot: best of the best

Tweens Generation
[Poster Series]

This poster series deals with the phenomenon of the Tweens Generation – that is, children aged 10 to 13 – who are characterised by the fact that their thinking shifts like the colour of a chameleon, that millions of them follow the same flow in the blink of an eye, and that the Internet and media present to them the possibilities of sudden fame. The design of three levels, R, G and B, begins with the silhouette of a person, which is converted to a symbol and then transformed back into a living creature with the aim of resolving peoples' doubts about the Tweens and convincing them that everything has a meaning. Translating the hypertense nature of these Tweens into a visually telling image, the three motif levels were superimposed to the effect that beholders are irritated at first, almost as clueless as the Tweens, and unable to make much sense of the image. The finely crafted illustration layers in red, yellow and blue actually require beholders to wear one of three special 3D glasses in order to optically decode and perceive them as individual images.

Statement by the jury

»The designs of this poster series present a highly enticing and innovative approach to visual representation. By rendering the motifs and levels in different colours, so that they can be deciphered only through special glasses, beholders are invited to experience a journey into the hidden deeper levels shown in these posters.«

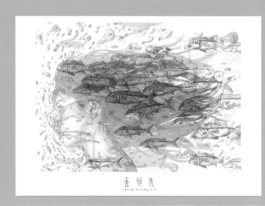

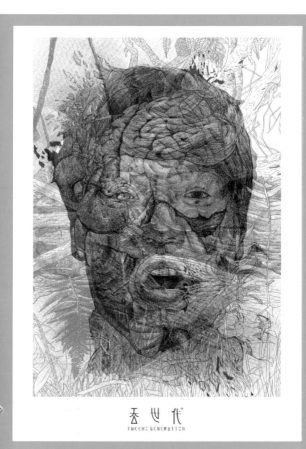

university
Da-Yeh University,
Keelung City

design
Yu-Shing Lin,
Ching Chen,
Yi-Chieh Kuo,
Hsuan-Fang Wang,
Chen-Chia Chiang

→ designer portrait: p. 456

red dot: best of the best

101 Days of Drawing
[Illustration Diary]

The book "101 Days of Drawing" deals with the topic of daily creativity and analyses
what impact daily routines have on illustrators who are obliged to meet their professional duties. As being a professional means working on things you enjoy even on days
you do not feel like doing them, the designer conducted the following experiment:
over a period of 101 days, he searched for new topics to illustrate each day. The results
were compiled for an "illustration diary", which covers a wide variety of topics including media culture, doubt, creativity, love and hatred, but also more mundane topics
such as the weather. The individual drawings present themselves with a wide variety
of approaches, visualising a topic either through a single full-page motif or through
many details that are superimposed and thus tell a story. The illustrations, which this
book combines and presents with additional information on the left side, have been
realised as independent posters.

Statement by the jury

»The illustrations in this book impress by the idea of having to deal with a different topic
every day as a challenge to one's own creativity on the one hand, and by their fresh and
consistent realisation on the other hand. Stylistically, they display a high variance and
thus make the book a pleasure to leaf through.«

design
Björn Steinmetzler,
Hückeswagen

→ designer portrait: p. 464

Yawar Fiesta

[Experimental Illustration]

The "Yawar Fiesta" is an annual festival and bloody ritual performed by the Inca for centuries in the desolate Peruvian villages in the Andes. In a subtle, controversial manner, it symbolises the vendetta against the Spanish conquerors. The work communicates this cruel ritual in a series of illustrations, mediating its drama and intensity: a wild condor is caught and given alcohol to make it drunk; in a kind of bullfight, it is then tied to the back of a bull and, in its efforts to free itself, the condor fights with the bull. The highly expressive appeal of the illustrations unfolds on double-pages, in A3 oversize book format. Showing mainly close-ups of the condor or the Indians further enhances the desired effect of dramatic intensity. The background to this bloody fight is provided briefly in the lower margin of the page. However, the illustrations are visually predominant. They build up an enormous tension, unfolding over 88 pages, and, at the same time, evoke a socio-critical approach with this controversial matter.

Statement by the jury

»On the one hand this work impresses by its consistently aesthetic visualisation of a fascinating story and on the other hand by the way it uses the materials. Its heavy paper and pastose painting style underline the strong expressive appeal of the illustrations by lending them an almost tactile quality.«

university
Ruhrakademie,
Schwerte

design
Marc Schultes,
Iserlohn

→ designer portrait: p. 463

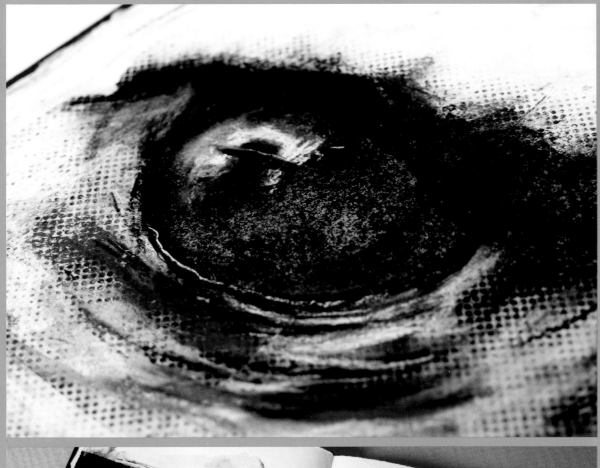

Guerilla Gardening Set

[Packaging Design]

The packaging design of this set was developed with the aim of calling attention to Guerilla Gardening and thus to encourage people to actively shape their environment. Following the idea of civil disobedience, the set is an invitation to practise secret gardening with the aim of embellishing drab concrete and urban asphalt landscapes and turning them into blooming mini-gardens. The individual items of this original and clearly designed set follow the idea of sustainability and were made from environmentally friendly materials such as paper, cardboard, cotton and wood. The set contains pop-up maps, seeds and bulbs, garden gloves and little garden tools as well as a canvas bag, a booklet and a wheel-shaped growth guide. With a logo which combines typography and illustration, the reduced visual identity incorporates graphically plain and understandable solutions in order to illustrate the characteristics of both the bulbs and the plants. Packaged in a small cardboard box, the set is intended for immediate use.

Statement by the jury

»The "Guerilla Gardening Set" impresses with the professional implementation of its design concept and its product design. The underlying idea, which also has social implications, has been realised to brilliant effect in packaging and visual identity, and presents a direct appeal to immediately become active in gardening.«

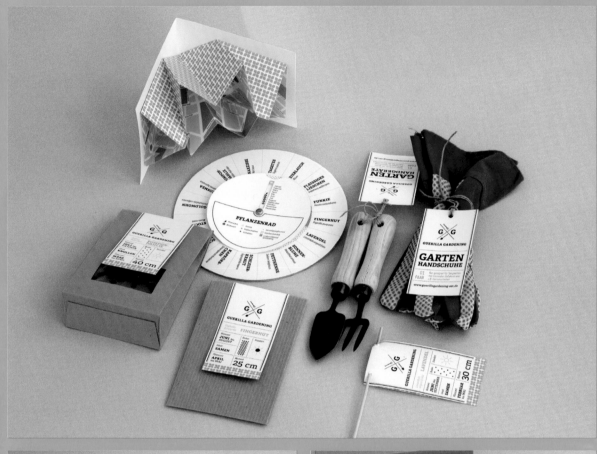

university
Fachhochschule Bielefeld /
University of Applied Sciences
Bielefeld

design
Jessica Götte,
Berlin

→ designer portrait: p. 450

Fukushima
Restricted Area

[Corporate Design]

Since the nuclear power plant accident in 2011, the area around Fukushima has been radioactively contaminated. Nevertheless, there are people who are exposing themselves to the radiation, thus suffering permanent damage. These corporate design materials illustrate this problem with a sunburst pattern around a red circle, which is reminiscent of the Japanese flag. At the same time, the pattern resembles the "sunburst" rays on the old Japanese military flag – a symbol of the kamikaze commandos during the Second World War – and thus represents human aggression and self-destruction.

university
IN.D Institute of Design
Düsseldorf

design
Jessica Kruft,
Wuppertal

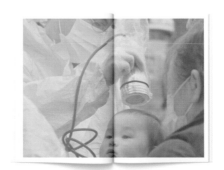
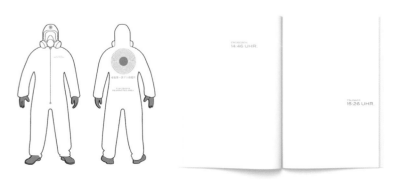

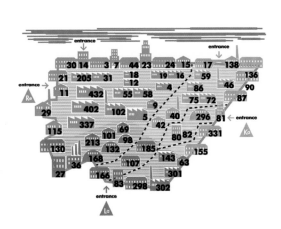

Loft Project Triangle
[Visual Identity]

Taking a holistic and flexible approach, the visual identity of the Loft Project Triangle cultural centre in St. Petersburg reflects its special architecture and history. The centre is being built on a 32-hectare former industrial area, where Russia's largest factory for rubber products, Krasnyi Treugolnik (Red Triangle), operated until the mid-1990s. The corporate design integrates elements of Russian Constructivism from the 1920s and reinterprets them in the light of contemporary design trends.

client
Loft Project Triangle,
St. Petersburg

university
Moscow Institute of Industrial
and Applied Arts

supervising professor
Prof. Alexander Panin

design
Irina Goryacheva,
Moscow

Moderne Identität der alten Institution Ehe
Modern identity for the old institution of marriage
[Corporate Design]

What would an appropriate visual identity for marriage look like if viewed from a corporate design perspective? The book at hand set out to explore this question. Initially, the characteristics of the legal partnership were analysed professionally, its historical development examined and its current meaning explored. Based on these insights, the visual identity presents itself as a tailor-made package, including a corporate image folder and brochure, business stationery and a range of further advertising materials.

university
HAWK Hochschule für angewandte Wissenschaft und Kunst / University of Applied Sciences and Arts, Hildesheim

supervising professor
Prof. Nicole Simon,
Carolin Taebel

design
Jennifer Dobslaff,
Hamburg

Elegant Querulant

[Corporate Design]

Created for a design collective comprised of eight designers from four different disciplines, this corporate design plays with the contrasts contained in the company name. The "elegant" concept is reflected by the logo's classical Antiqua font and the clearly structured Grotesque font for the running text. The word "querulant" (German for "troublemaker") is a synonym for a rebellious, unconventional thinker and is illustrated in the design through an interruption of the elegant typography with the stamped caricatures of the individual designers.

client
Elegant Querulant,
Basel

university
FHNW, Hochschule für Gestaltung und Kunst, Masterstudio Design, Basel / Academy of Art and Design, Masterstudio Design, Basel

supervising professor
Prof. Heinz Wagner

design
Susanne Hartmann,
André Konrad

illustration
Judith Dobler

photography
Martin Däster

Bright
Summit Science

[Corporate Identity System]

university
Lanzhou University

design
OKIN, Shanghai
Zhang Yangsheng

→ designer portrait: p. 467

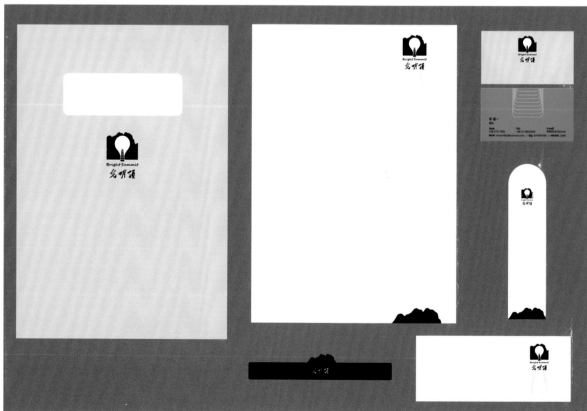

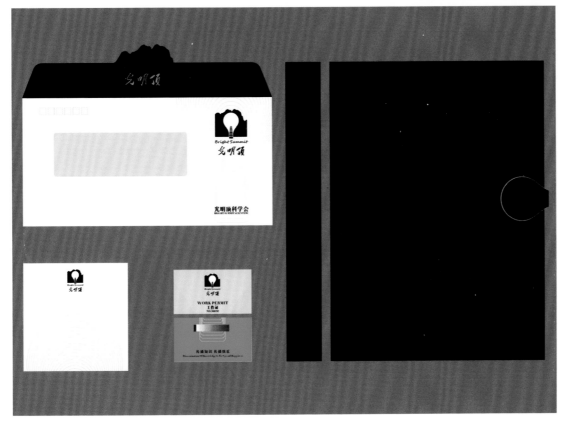

Bright Summit Science (BSS) is a Chinese institution that pursues various objectives, such as educating schoolchildren, in order to disseminate the natural sciences among the public. The institute's corporate design makes use of a silhouette of Bright Summit Peak, the second highest peak in the Huangshan Mountains, which is famous for its panoramic view. The key graphic symbol for BSS is a light bulb, symbolically bringing light to the darkness of ignorance, with stylised stairs representing the progress of civilisation. Implementing typography reminiscent of handwriting, the logo communicates that science – like the famous mountain – is to be discovered and scaled by the individual.

Inform, but score

[Poster, Card Series]

This three-part work provides material for the party of a detective story club. The first "clue" for the party is a postcard series with letters on the reverse side of the postcards. They can be arranged like an alphabet puzzle and are then turned over to decipher the invitation text. The second part of the work is a large-scale poster for outdoor use, the numerical code of which can also be deciphered as an event announcement. The person who, at the party venue, finally discovers the small hidden print on an indoor sign, which is the third part of the work, will receive a gift.

client
Young Hee Kim,
Gyeongsangnam-do

design
Eun Sil Jang,
Seoul

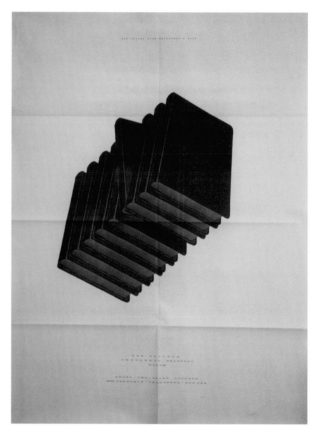

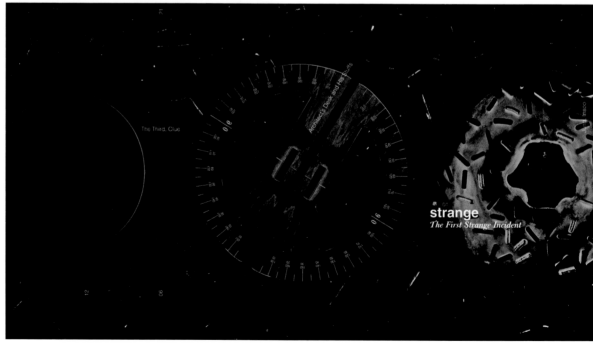

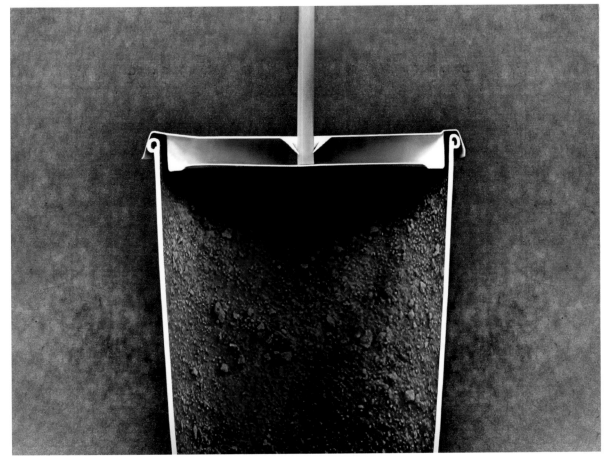

UNCOMFORTABLE CUP

[Promotion]

Scarce or contaminated water is an urgent topic for a consistently growing number of people around the world. This paper cup, which is to be handed out by Unicef and Evian during a public awareness campaign, conveys an idea of what this experience is like. The straw accompanying the cup turns out to be useless, for the cup is completely sealed in spite of what appear to be several straw holes in the lid. When the thirsty campaign participants finally succeed in removing the lid completely, they have most likely made many attempts at getting to the water – just like those people around the world suffering from thirst. A corresponding message is found on the bottom of the cup.

university
Gachon University/Main

design/head of advertising
Da Woon Jung

creative direction
Ju Ho Han

art direction
Yeo Kyu Kim

photography
Kyung Chan Ahn

→ designer portrait: p. 452

kosmo logo morph – von Sprachfamilien, häufigen Buchstaben und deutschen Wörterwanderungen
kosmo logo morph – about language families, frequent letters and the migration of German words
[Book]

The kosmo logo morph book project examines the German language in an international context and highlights its significance as well as its connections to other languages. The first chapter provides an overview of "The Languages of the World" and then goes on to compare the German language with English and Spanish in the second chapter. A third section is dedicated to the particular idiosyncrasies of the German language. An unbiased, objective presentation sensitises the reader to the linguistic topic, while the content is clearly visualised by the illustrations.

university
Fachhochschule Düsseldorf /
University of Applied Sciences
Düsseldorf

supervising professor
Stv. Prof. Irmgard Sonnen,
Mariko Takagi

design
Maren Schwitalla,
Krefeld-Uerdingen

Lufthansa + Graphic Design – Visuelle Geschichte einer Fluggesellschaft
Lufthansa + Graphic Design – Visual History of an Airline

[Book]

With its high information content and balanced, effective design, this publication shows how Lufthansa's visual identity has developed since the 1920s. The decisive step was taken at the beginning of the 1960s, when the company's communication department commissioned Otl Aicher and some of his students to conduct a study on the redesign of the corporate identity. To date, essential parts of the concept have been implemented, and it ranks among the pioneering corporate design solutions of the twentieth century.

university
Fachhochschule Düsseldorf /
University of Applied Sciences
Düsseldorf

design
optik – Kommunikation
und Gestaltung, Düsseldorf
Jens Müller,
Karen Weiland

concept
Jens Müller,
Karen Weiland

research/editorial staff/layout
Marvin Hüttermann,
Patrick Mariathasan,
Pascal Tedjagutomo,
Benjamin Welke

Als das Licht
laufen lernte
How light
learned to walk
[Non-Fiction Book]

university
Staatliche Hochschule
für Gestaltung Karlsruhe /
University of Arts
and Design Karlsruhe

supervising professor
Prof. Sven Voelker,
Prof. Urs Lehni,
Prof. Dr. Harald Lesch

design
Daniela Leitner,
Helmbrechts

→ designer portrait: p. 455

Staging light as a physical phenomenon on more than 1,000 pages is this nine-part book series. The author humorously explains relevant topics, using the course of a day in her flat as an example, starting backwards from going to bed at night (quantum mechanics) to getting up in the morning (the Big Bang). The so-called "red shift" of light serves as a visual, connecting theme. This effect makes light appear redder the further away its emanation source is located. Correspondingly, the colours of the chapter pages and several illustrations gradually change from purple to red. The project was inspired by a television science programme and the responsible astrophysicist, who also supervised this dissertation.

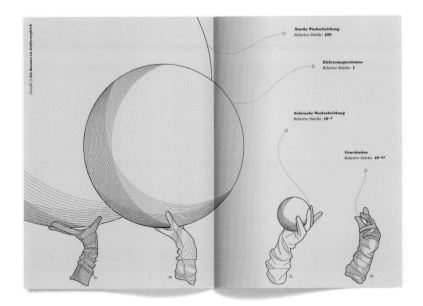

Hobbikon – Das Hobby-Lexikon
Hobbikon – the hobby lexicon

[Book]

This inspiring compendium documents a variety of hobbies that, for many people, may even constitute the meaning of life. The book's visual concept is based on the idea of introducing hobbies to the reader by using everyday objects. For example, under the topic "bird watching" a kettle stands for a bird, or a cauliflower represents a planet under the topic "astronomy". A "hobby generator" in the front cover, illustrated interviews and, last but not least, the confident design, featuring an exposed thread binding, all allow the reader to experience the subject's great variety.

university
IN.D Institute of Design Düsseldorf

supervising professor
Andrea Krause

design
Simon Haase, Remscheid

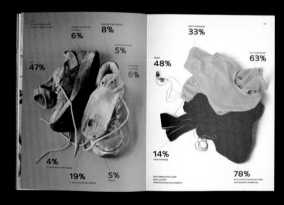

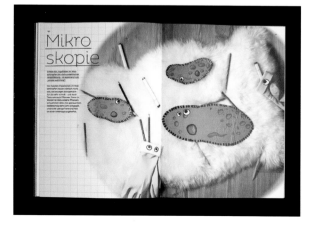

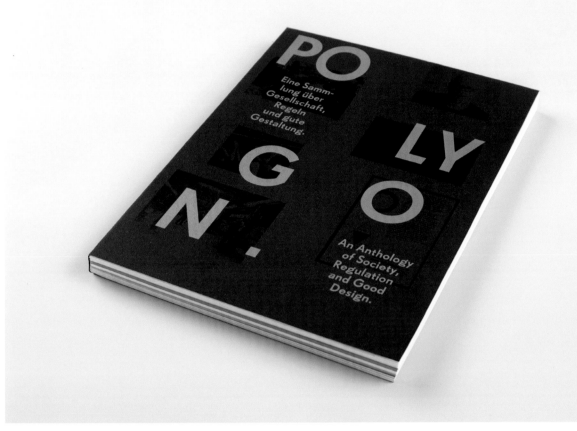

Polygon

[Book]

Examining the approach currently characteristic of our society and its graphic design, this publication offers a bilingual collection of essays, interviews and background information. The authors analyse current layout schemes in an illustrative way. Moreover, they present different views as to what defines good design. The design of the book itself presents some elements of the discussed zeitgeist trends and has incorporated them, developing a layout that is both exciting and sustainable.

university
Fachhochschule Mainz /
University of Applied Sciences
Mainz

design
Nico Bats, Ludwigshafen;
Fabian Bremer, Wiesbaden

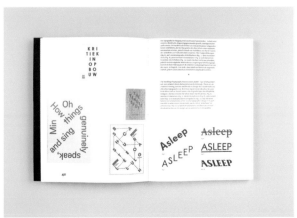

Als die Schrift laufen lernte
German
Running Hand
[Book]

The classic Kurrent script (or German running hand) was the standard writing style in the German-speaking world until banned by the National Socialists in 1941. Today, the information it conveys is becoming increasingly inaccessible, because we can no longer decipher the cursive lettering. In view of this regrettable development, the book is dedicated to the history of the Kurrent script. It explains the advantages of the almost forgotten style and demonstrates how it may easily be (re-)learned. To achieve this, the book presents selected and lovingly designed exercises as well as recipes from grandmother's recipe book.

university
FH JOANNEUM –
University of Applied Sciences,
Graz

design
Julia Kerschbaum,
Hamburg

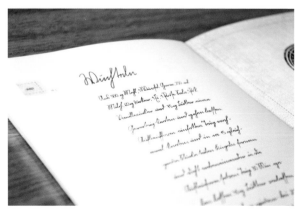

Welcome to Lungshan Temple

[Communication Design, Graphic Design, Service Design]

Situated in Taipei's busy Bangka district, the Lungshan Temple is an outstanding architectural sight. Over 200 years old, it is a place of traditional praying ceremonies and old Chinese prophecy instruments. In a user-friendly manner, the media and brochures used here have now put this temple into the focus of international tourism. The handbook provides orientation within the religious cosmos of the country. The design of the corporate identity references the aesthetics characteristic of this country, thus highlighting the spiritual centre's uniqueness.

client
Lungshan Temple,
Taipei

design
Callme Design,
Taipei
I-Chen Huang,
Hsiu-Chuan Tien

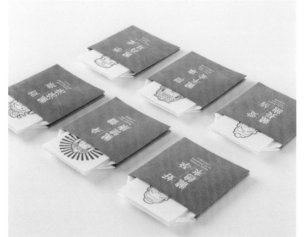

Frozen

[Conceptual Book and Calendars]

university
School of the Art
Institute of Chicago

design
Sung Suh,
New York

Doomsday	Universal Children's Day	Halloween Day	World Water Day	World No-Tobacco Day	April Fools' Day
Memorial Day	New Year's Day	International Mother Earth Day	Valentine Day	Thanksgiving Day	Columbus Day
World Population Day	Christmas Eve	World Blood Donor Day	International Day of Cooperatives	Summer Vacation Days	International Day of Peace
Labor Day	International Youth Day	New Year's Day	World Cancer Day	World Poetry Day	World Environment Day

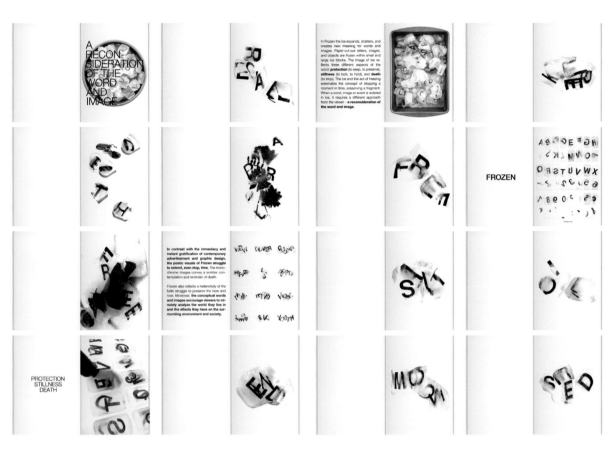

For the "Frozen" project, letters on paper and image clippings were frozen in ice cubes. The words "preserved" in ice prompt the viewer to pause and consciously engage with the monochrome objects. The piece thus fosters a contemplative attitude, thanks to which viewers perceive the surrounding world more accurately and consider their own role within it. The poetry and memento mori presented here are shown as contrasting concepts to the quick satisfaction of needs in current advertising and graphic design.

BLEEP

[Magazine]

university
Georg-Simon-Ohm-Hochschule
Nürnberg / Georg Simon Ohm
University of Applied Sciences
Nuremberg

design
Stefanie Landvogt,
Benjamin Probst,
Berlin

concept
Stefanie Landvogt,
Benjamin Probst

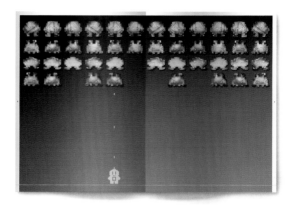

BLEEP magazine presents articles on ecology and sustainability in a fresh format. The design intentionally dismantles the conventional eco-style – hence the dominating colour is not a stuffy green, but a crisp yellow. Thanks to the eye-catching corporate identity and a humorous use of images, the young target group can easily identify with the subjects. The magazine contains articles and interviews with new visionaries, specifically written for the magazine. Furthermore, it presents lifestyle trends in photo series and illustrations. Thus, in keeping with the modern lifestyle, a brand has been created that stands out thanks to its cheeky visual identity, while motivating the readers and fostering awareness of ecological issues.

Début

[Magazine]

university
IN.D Institute of Design
Düsseldorf

design
Yasemin Gedek,
Duisburg

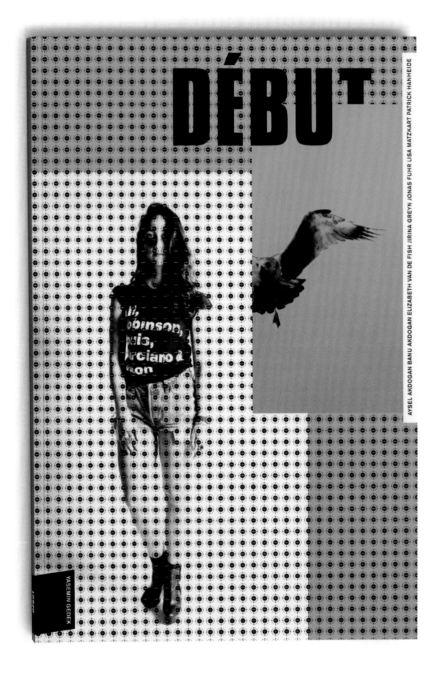

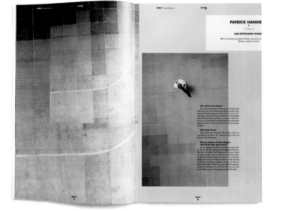

This magazine has been conceived as a stage for budding fashion designers. It presents their collections and contains numerous interviews. Analogous to the training and creation process of those profiled, the magazine's design works with process-oriented graphics, such as crop marks, crop patterns and colour matches. The clipped typography moreover reflects the process of tailoring in fashion design. On the whole, the main techniques used in the layout are layering and text-image superimposition, which elegantly represent the essence of clothing.

God is watching from above

[Poster]

university
National Taiwan
University of Arts,
Taipei County

design
Misa Design Co., Ltd.,
Taoyuan County
Wei-Chen Yao

→ designer portrait: p. 459

A Chinese proverb says, "God is watching from three feet above". This project takes the idea and develops it further: if we look up from what we do, we will perceive the divine. The visual idea for the poster is based on the combination of a raised vantage point with religious symbols – in this case a Christian cross or a Buddhist-Hindu left-facing swastika. Invoking dramatic light-dark contrasts, the design creates a graphically simplified and contemporary interpretation of the message.

Rise Above

[Poster]

Created for a design competition, this poster represents design as a path that forms through the searching for and unearthing of ideas. Corresponding to this concept, segments of the poster are coated with a silvery substance which can be scratched off; the layer underneath reveals further details about the structure of the design exhibition. The poster offers a contemporary interpretation of elements found in traditional Chinese landscapes, such as mountains, forests and a sea of clouds. An overlapping of lines at the mountain summits symbolises special achievements in design.

university
Shu-Te University,
Kaohsiung City

supervising professor
Jheng-Jhang Chen

design
Bo-Hao Syu,
Ming-Xian Lin,
Bo-Kai Wen,
Shao-Cian Jheng

→ designer portrait: p. 465

NO FUR! NO KILL!

[Poster]

Tibetan antelopes have the warmest and finest wool coat in the world. Roughly 20,000 of these animals are killed annually by poachers; hence, the species is now threatened by extinction. Minks, foxes, rabbits and even leopards are likewise hunted excessively or exploited by the animal-fur industry to meet the demands of fashion trends. The poster lashes out at these reckless practices by employing an emotionally appealing visual motif: the enormous, painted shadows of animals on the catwalk make it unmistakably clear to the onlooker where fur fashion originates.

design
Li-Hua Liu,
Taipei

→ designer portrait: p. 457

Warum Design?
Why Design?

[Poster]

With humour and self-deprecation, this poster presents the motto of a lecture in the area of communication theory. In order to depict the varied requirements placed on design, underpants are used as a leitmotif. On the one hand, they illustrate that design is a fundamental building block of human culture, while on the other they explore the significance of design. The wide range of creative ideas is reflected in the arrangement of the typography, their individual elements held together by a uniform design language.

university
Folkwang Universität der Künste /
Folkwang University of the Arts,
Campus Wuppertal

text
Dr. Bernhard Uske

design
Andreas Golde,
Thomas Kühnen,
Wuppertal

concept
Andreas Golde,
Thomas Kühnen

printing
Siebdruck-Atelier der Folkwang
Universität der Künste / Screen
Printing Studio of the Folkwang
University of the Arts,
Thomas Kühnen

Seminar im Sommersemester 2011
Studiengang Kommunikationsdesign
Lehrgebiet Kommunikationswissenschaften
Dozent: Dr. Bernhard Uske
Mittwochs 10 – 12 Uhr, ab 20. April 2011
Folkwang UdK, Campus Wuppertal
Fuhlrottstraße 10, Gebäude I, Hörsaal 30

Care Warming

[Poster]

This poster draws attention to the fact that the relationships between humans and objects around us should never be cold. When we touch or hold something in our hands, a temperature exchange between hand and object ensues and thus fosters interaction. The poster illustrates this relationship using thermochromic ink: the graphics and the patterns change colour when the poster is touched, because the surface becomes warmer. When the surface cools, the colour changes again.

university
National Taiwan University of Science and Technology, Taipei

supervising professor
Lin Pin-Chang

design
Lai Chia-Wei, New Taipei City

→ designer portrait: p. 454

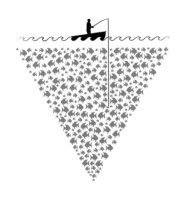

By Nuclear Energy

[Poster]

university
Asia University,
Taichung

design
Ching-Ping Yang,
Taichung

This ambitious artistic project was triggered by the large earthquake in Japan in 2011, which caused a series of catastrophic accidents and explosions in the Fukushima nuclear power plant. As a result, large amounts of radioactive waste with perilous long-term effects are circulating in the global eco-system. This poster draws attention to the dangers of nuclear energy by portraying people who have died of radiation exposure as blurred ghosts with halos in the shape of the sign for radioactivity. Thus the poster also sarcastically expresses its "appreciation" for those contemporaries who have promoted nuclear energy like a doctrine of salvation without paying any attention to its risks.

we are open
[Typographical Short Film]

client
meat for the beast,
Fürth

design
meat for the beast,
Fürth

art direction/concept
Verena Hennig

graphic design
Verena Hennig

film production
Claus Winter

film direction
Tobias Binder

music/sound design
Georg Stanka

→ designer portrait: p. 458
→ digital presentation: DVD

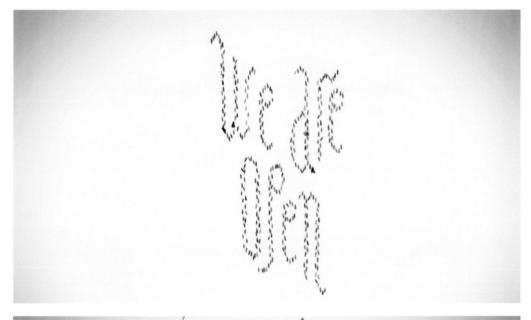

This typographic short film was created for the opening of a design office in Fürth near Nuremberg. The main actors are more than 500 larvae of the native but rare butterfly species Little Fox, obtained from a breeder in Switzerland. The cocooned caterpillars were carefully prepared and arranged on a wall to form the slightly offset sentence "we are open". The film shows the words coming to life: the butterflies hatch and flutter away, embarking on their first flight. Thus the film not only effectively announces the "birth" of the studio but also subtly translates into moving images the design studio's philosophy: the transformation of something gossamer and nondescript into something new and graceful.

**Wie Schrift entsteht
» Schriftgestaltung.
info**
How are typefaces
created
» Schriftgestaltung.
info

[Book]

university
Hochschule für Gestaltung
Schwäbisch Gmünd /
University of Applied Sciences
Schwäbisch Gmünd

supervising professor
Prof. Michael Götte,
Prof. Ulrich Schendzielorz

design
Mariella Felicia Molter,
René Ulrich,
Ebersbach

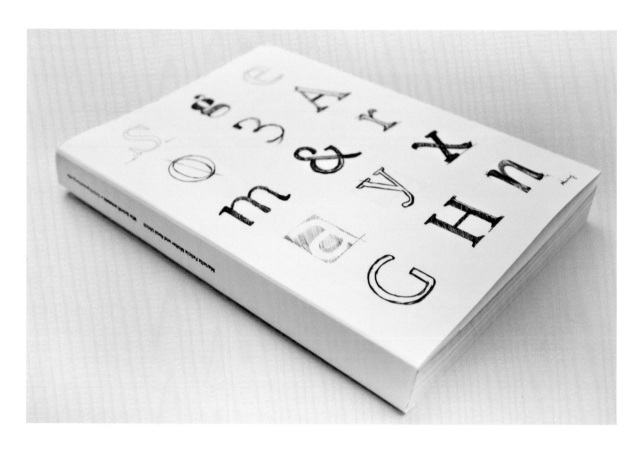

Antiquaschrift

SIGNALA

♛ Blühendes Barock

Château de Valençay

£ 1093.42 for a return ticket

Cappuccino ☕

Castillo de Torresaviñán

Ritterspiele

Sonnenkönig LUDWIG XIV.

← Exit

Queen and King

How are typefaces created that are suited to effectively communicating visual identities? The present book explores this question. In five chapters, it comprehensively depicts the whole process of designing a typeface, while also providing information on working techniques and food for thought from experienced designers. The book is supplemented with a case study, which illustrates the process of designing a serif typeface for orientation systems. In addition, it contains sketches, an overview of visual principles, and also background information on typeface programming.

Adventures of the visual difference

[Picture Book]

university
Asia University,
Taichung

design
Ya Han Huang, Taichung;
Sih Ting Mei, Keelung;
Dai Ling Yeh, Kaohsiung

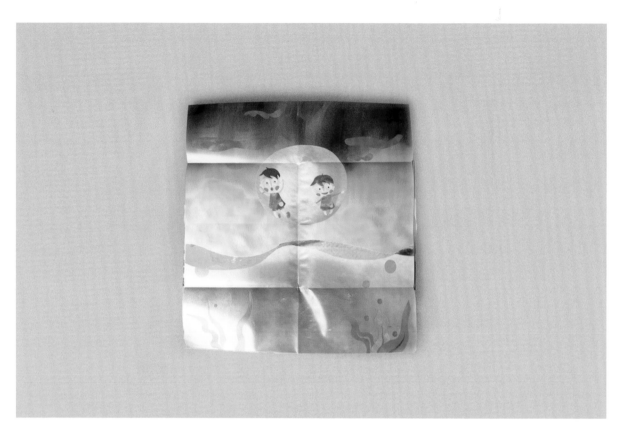

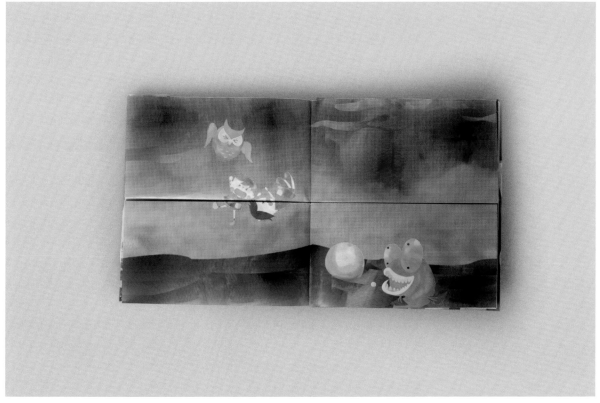

This innovative educational picture book supports children from the ages of five to eight in their exploration of the world around them. The book's general purpose is to encourage parents, teachers and, most importantly, children to come up with creative solutions. The conveyance of scientific knowledge has thus been combined with an original artistic concept. Familiar animals serve as a didactic bridge to draw attention to scientific phenomena. In this way children learn, for instance, how the world, which we believe to be perceiving objectively, is experienced entirely differently by other creatures. The book additionally features interactive tools that make the reading experience even more enjoyable.

Marriage

[Illustration]

This illustrated book thematically
explores marital relationships
in a relaxed and humorous way.
In six chapters – Prologue,
Chores, Diet, Money, Sex and
Epilogue – the book outlines the
course of modern marriages,
ranging from wedding vows to
periods of conflict, to eventually
living together happily in old age.
In terms of form, the illustrations
evince high quality thanks to
the particularly fine, detailed
lines and the aptly portrayed
figures. Furthermore, multi-
layered backgrounds lend the
drawings spatial depth.

university
Shu-Te University,
Kaohsiung City

supervising professor
Ti-Wan Kung,
Chia-Hung Yeh

design
Yi-Hsin Lu,
Sian-Shuo Chen,
Ting-Yi Huang,
Shiang-Yin Su

concept
Sian-Shuo Chen,
Ting-Yi Huang

illustration
Yi-Hsin Lu,
Shiang-Yin Su

→ designer portrait: p. 446

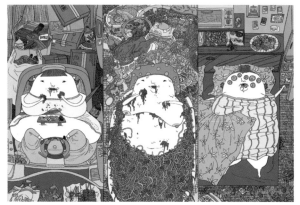

Defeater – Lost Ground

[Illustrations]

In their self-titled concept album, the US band Defeater tells the story of an African-American who fights as a soldier for his country in World War II. Yet upon returning home, he is discriminated against due to his skin colour and finally ends up living on the streets of New York as a homeless street musician. In collages set against a background of historical newspaper articles, these illustrations depict the dark plot in a graphically convincing way. The numerous typographical elements appear like fragments of song lyrics or handwritten notes by the protagonist.

university
Fachhochschule Dortmund /
University of Applied Sciences
and Arts Dortmund

design
Léon Howahr,
Essen

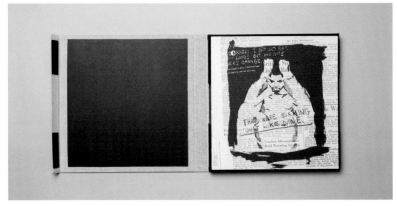

Thriller 25
[Packaging Design]

university
Handong Global University,
Pohang

design
Jiye Kim,
Sang-Ok Ha,
Sung-Hee Jung

→ designer portrait: p. 453

Commemorating the release of Michael Jackson's cult album "Thriller" a quarter of a century ago, an anniversary edition containing a CD and a DVD was created. Matching the mysterious and energetic mood of the music, the cover features a simple black-and-white design with clear typography. When users pull out the inner casing containing the CD and the DVD, an animation on the outside cover is triggered: in the foreground, a Michael Jackson figure dances the "moon walk", which was Jackson's trademark move at his performances, so that users can almost see the music before they start listening. At the same time, the anniversary number 25 appears on the back of the cover. The diamond pattern on both booklet and the CD/DVD symbolises the value of Michael Jackson's work as a "jewel of pop music".

Fusion of Era

[Packaging Design]

Sources of inspiration for this
soap set's design were both the
art of Chinese packaging and
the attentive spirit of traditional
Chinese medicine. The hand-
made bars of soap each contain
a Chinese medicine, while the
packaging design harmoniously
unites moisture-proof, untreated
bamboo with modern magnetic
elements. The series contains
a bowl with four bars of soap, a
hanging box with two bars and
a hanging soap holder, the form
of which is inspired by the
weighing dishes commonly
used in Chinese pharmacies.

university
Ming Chi University
of Technology,
New Taipei City

design
Bao-Fa Yang,
Pei-Zhen Wu

concept
Bao-Fa Yang

graphic design
Yi-Pei Lu,
Hung-Yu Chen

project management
Pei-Zhen Wu,
Hung-Yu Chen

illustration
Yi-Pei Lu,
Zhang-Rui Chen

printing
Bao-Fa Yang,
Pei-Zhen Wu

structure development
Zhang-Rui Chen

→ designer portrait: p. 447

Movie POPcorn Man

[Popcorn Packaging]

Conceived to make the simultaneous enjoyment of popcorn and a drink at the cinema easier, this packaging solution endeavours to prevent the usual mishaps with sticky foods in the dark. The answer is a design providing popcorn container and cup holder in one, which can be easily held in one hand. The witty graphic design shows a male or female figure "holding" the cup, boasting a blond afro partially consisting of real popcorn.

design
Seungkwan Kang,
Yeehyun Chung,
Jihye Bang

concept
Seungkwan Kang

graphic design
Yeehyun Chung

illustration
Jihye Bang

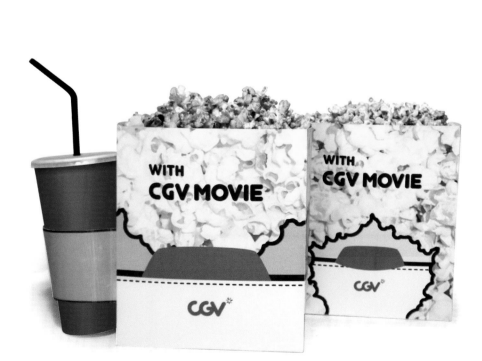

The Artist's Workshop

[Exhibition Booth]

university
Temasek Polytechnic,
School of Design,
Singapore

design
Jeremy Lin,
Singapore

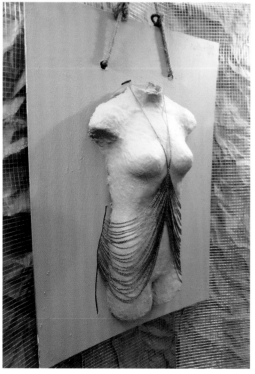

Inspired by the ideation process of constructing a product, The Artist's Workshop showcases a conceptual brand selling fashion garments and jewellery. It aims at ennobling the ignoble to communicate the intangible as well as the beauty of turning improbable dreams into reality. Using discarded materials from the collection, the pillars idealise the statement that through design and innovation even the unwanted can be given a new lease of life. Captivated by the dress forms used by the jewellery designer to drape prototypes, embossed dress forms were created using a cement and paper-mâché blend to display the product as the creator envisioned. The exhibition space invigorates the expression that the spirit of creation is not limited by technology or materials but rather engendered by one's imagination.

Ausschildern, Kennzeichnen, Markieren
Signposting, Labelling, Marking

[Orientation System]

university
Fachhochschule Düsseldorf /
University of Applied Sciences
Düsseldorf

supervising professor
Prof. Andreas Uebele,
Prof. Diane Ziegler

design
Benjamin Brinkmann,
Düsseldorf

photography
Teresa Siebein,
Düsseldorf

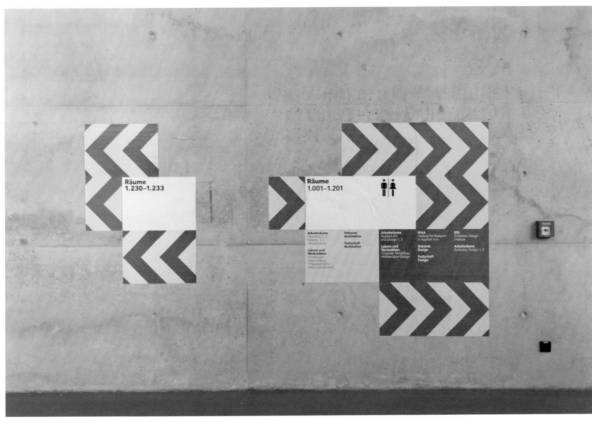

The common paper chaos that inevitably occurs on a university's wall served as the concept's inspirational approach. Similar to an advertising pillar, the components of the orientation system are primarily printed on paper and then attached to the wall. The individual parts are easily pasted over as and when required. Since the system comes with a modular construction aligned to DIN standards, users can flexibly react to different architectural situations and volumes of information. The murals therefor transmit strong messages adding a distinct identity to the place.

UNICATO –
On-Air Design 2012
[Animation Mix]

university
Bauhaus Film-Institut,
Weimar

design
Patrick Richter,
Erfurt

music/sound design
Stephanie Elizabeth Krah,
Florian Füger

→ designer portrait: p. 462
→ digital presentation: DVD

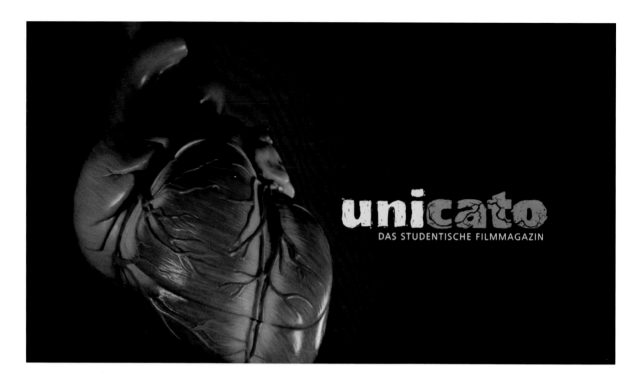

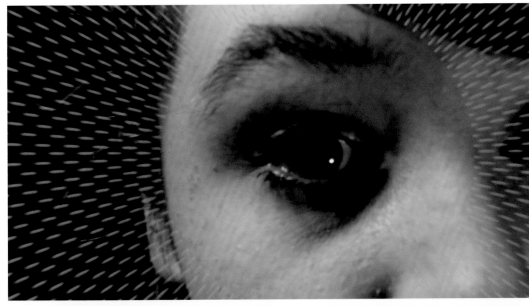

"Unicato" is a Central German Broadcasting (MDR) television programme that regularly screens films by students attending eastern German universities. The on-air design for this programme uses a collage of moving images, stop motion and digitally adapted effects from historical educational films. Shots of doll's houses and decommissioned human anatomical models from the former GDR create an exotic world of their own. The visual design thus successfully reflects the film magazine's character with its experimental, artistic productions.

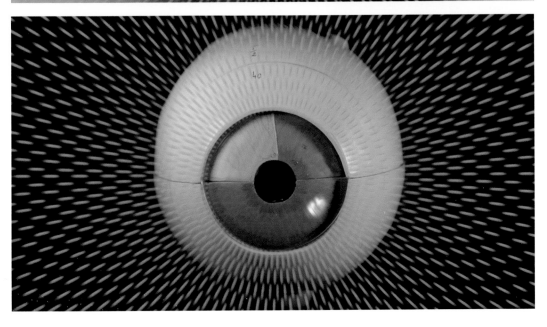

iListen

[App]

Designed for people with hearing impairment, this smartphone application helps users communicate with other people using text-to-speech and speech-recognition functionality, as well as supporting them when travelling. In addition, the app is able to recognise certain sounds, such as doorbells and sirens, and can react with vibrational or visual signals. If users end up in an emergency situation, the programme is designed to send out calls for help. On the whole, the user interface exhibits a very clear design, thereby ensuring effective and safe use.

university
National Taiwan University of Science and Technology, Taipei

design
National Taiwan University of Science and Technology, Taipei

creative direction/concept
Kai-Ting Lin, Hsien-Hui Tang, National Taiwan University of Science and Technology

graphic design/text
Kai-Ting Lin, Hsien-Hui Tang, National Taiwan University of Science and Technology

project management
Hsien-Hui Tang, National Taiwan University of Science and Technology; Chao-Hsuan Hsueh, ATEN International Co., Ltd.

programming
Li-Jen Chang, Li-Ying Wang, Kuei-Hua Chen, ATEN International Co., Ltd. Tai-Hsuan Ho, Cyberon Corporation

iCan

[Interactive Software]

iCan is an interactive communication aid for autistic children. Created for use on a tablet PC, this program provides a user-friendly alternative to conventional flash cards, which are often heavy and cumbersome. The sounds, images and words integrated into the program help children learn to understand words and body language, as well as how to pronounce words correctly. Furthermore, each child can create his or her own database with examples. The clearly structured interface facilitates intuitive operation.

university
National Taiwan University of Science and Technology, Taipei

design
National Taiwan University of Science and Technology, Taipei

creative direction/concept
Cyun-Meng Jheng,
Hsien-Hui Tang,
National Taiwan University of Science and Technology

graphic design/text
Cyun-Meng Jheng,
Hsien-Hui Tang,
National Taiwan University of Science and Technology

project management
Hsien-Hui Tang,
National Taiwan University of Science and Technology;
Jian-Ciang Peng,
Sabuz Technology Co.

programming
Jian-Ciang Peng,
Yu-Wei Wang,
Sabuz Technology Co.

Grandpa's and Grandma's Age

[Online Educational App]

university
Ming Chuan University,
Department of Digital Media
Design, Taoyuan

design
Pei-Yu Chen,
Ting-Chen Liu,
Meng-Yuan Liu,
Yu-Chun Lin,
Yu-Chien Chiu,
Pei-Jiun Liau

→ designer portrait: p. 445
→ digital presentation: DVD

With a digital archive and interactive applications, this project aims to spark the interest of different age groups in old Taiwanese children's games. Modern web technologies, such as the combination of 2D and 3D animation and interactive learning aids, are used to teach users the rules and movement sequences of the traditional games. This digital approach manages to create an entertaining historical atmosphere – which gives it the best chance of keeping Taiwan's cultural heritage alive.

Designer Portraits

+AKITIPE STUDIOS
— Welcome to the dark side.

Work awarded with a red dot
Discovery Science Human Element
[Channel Ident → p. 224-225]

Founded in 2007, +AKITIPE STUDIOS is a team with talented, skilled artists who create high-end moving pictures from motion graphics to VFX. The team specialises in services related to CG, including commercials, channel identities, TV programme openings, film VFX, as well as the full range of digital production processes ranging from concept design to post-production. Merging art and technology in their work with passion and creativity, the team is devoted to providing fresh and fascinating visual expressions and visual experiences. The studio's name is derived from the word "archetype", a concept of the structuralism advanced by Carl Gustav Jung early in the 20th century.

Where and how do you gather information on trends?
If you pay attention to the details and occurrences of everyday life, it is not hard to discover attitudes and a sense of humour in the world. We try to seek out a design logic that fits closely with the zeitgeist rather than repeatedly producing similar topics with a particular type of expression and style that happens to be trendy at the time.

What developments do you currently see in your industry?
Graphics creation formats like motion graphics are growing and spreading at an astonishing speed. People are starting to realise their unique qualities, which include the potential to have simultaneously both artistic value and commercial viability.

ALT GROUP
BEN CORBAN,
DEAN POOLE
— Do disturb.

**Work awarded with a
red dot: best of the best**
The Social Kitchen
[Event Design → p. 116-117]

Alt Group is a multidisciplinary design company based in Auckland, New Zealand. Founded in 2000 by Ben Corban and Dean Poole, the company has a core team of 20 people with a rich diversity of design, business backgrounds and experience working in brand strategy, communication design, interactive design and new product development. The company has been recognised in numerous international awards, including ADC, AGDA, AIGA, Cannes Lions, Clios, One Show, red dot, TDC and Webby Awards.

Where and how do you gather information on trends?
We look for weak signals in the market, and try and catch the trend before it breaks. Other times we ignore what's in vogue and do the opposite. Both have equal value.

What developments do you currently see in your industry?
Design is shifting from the traditional broadcasting method that has dominated visual culture to a process that enables other people to be creative within.

How do you approach new projects?
With obsession and gusto.

What are the qualities a successful communication designer must have?
The ability to write your thoughts down, then design with them.

What do you understand by good communication design?
Simplicity.

ARTIFICIALDUCK STUDIOS
DIRK HOFFMANN
— We consider ourselves
to be a digital manufactory.

Work awarded with a red dot
The Flower – Poetic Short
Messaging System
[Games & Electronic Art → p. 315]

Dirk Hoffmann was born in Münster, Germany, in 1966. He studied illustration at the Münster University of Applied Sciences from 1987 to 1989 and subsequently at the Hamburg University of Applied Sciences, where he received his degree in design in 1994. From 1995 to 2001, he studied free painting and later worked as art director at ID-Media AG in Hamburg. In 2002, he was one of the founders of Artificialduck Studios, of which, since then, he has been the director. In addition, Dirk Hoffmann is lecturer in painting and digital design at the Hamburg University of Applied Sciences.

How do you approach new projects?
We are a team of specialists. Half of them have a purely aesthetic, visual background, the other half works with the programming. We always work as dual teams so that the concepts evolve from an exactly balance of design and technology.

What else would you like to learn?
I always try to create a work process that I am not already familiar with, so that I can learn how to make it work. The central feature of our work is to include the unexpected as a starting point for new processes.

What inspires you?
Life and its cultural products from both the past and present.

YADEGAR ASISI
— Design serves life, not itself.

Work awarded with a red dot
Pergamon – Panorama der antiken Metropole /
Pergamon – Panorama of the Ancient City
[Temporary Exhibition → p. 139]

Yadegar Asisi was born in Vienna in 1955, but grew up in Leipzig. He studied architecture in Dresden from 1973 to 1978 and subsequently fine arts in Berlin. He founded the Atelier für Architekturgrafik in Berlin and the Brandt-Asi-si-Böttcher architectural practice, won numerous awards, for example the Mies van der Rohe Award 1988 and cooperated with, among others, the architects Hans Kollhoff, Josef P. Kleihues and Daniel Libeskind. Asisi realised major perspective-anamorphic projects at, for example, the IBA Berlin 1984, the Triennale di Milano 1986 and the Expo Sevilla 1992, as well as numerous stage sets. From 1996 to 2009, he was professor for free design in Berlin.

Where and how do you gather information on trends?
Wherever I go, I keep my eyes open. I walk a lot anyway, because that way I see things more consciously. I always tell people if you walked to work more, things would work more.

What developments do you currently see in your industry?
We're living in a time of upheaval and rethinking.

What are the qualities a successful communication designer must have?
He must be able to get information across in such a way that it is not only rationally, but also emotionally intelligible for the recipient.

What inspires you?
Appetite comes with eating, ideas with working.

BBDO PROXIMITY BERLIN / ANR BBDO STOCKHOLM

DANIEL SCHWEINZER,
DAVID MOUSLY,
FREDRIC ANTONSSON,
JAN HARBECK,
LUKAS LISKE,
JENS RINGENA,
MARIA SANDBERG,
SEBASTIAN FORSMAN,
TON HOLLANDER

**Work awarded with a
red dot: best of best**
smart EBALL
[Game Event → p. 118-119]

Lukas Liske (text) and Daniel Schweinzer (art) have worked together as a creative team since 2009. In 2011, they moved from Ogilvy & Mather (Frankfurt) to BBDO Proximity. In the last three years they have won seven Cannes Lions among other awards. Maria Sandberg (creative planner), Fredric Antonsson (copywriter) and Sebastian Forsman (art director) have been working together as a creative team at ANR BBDO Stockholm since 2011. They are all graduates from Berghs School of Communication in Stockholm. They have all won international awards individually and, as a team, have been awarded several Cannes Lions for the "smart EBALL" (Daimler).

What developments do you currently see in your industry?
The best advertising is that which does not feel like advertising: good communication entertains, involves and touches. Our creative playing field grows every year through technological development. This leads to ideas that entirely break up previous categories – such as a test drive that turns into a computer game.

How do you approach new projects?
With a lot of curiosity and as few preconceptions as possible.

What are the qualities a successful communication designer must have?
A good idea can get lost in a poorly executed design. As a designer you need to have a great deal of artistic talent, passion and the confidence to trust your intuition.

BBDO PROXIMITY DÜSSELDORF
ANNE KATRIN HÜSKEN,
ANTJE SCHNOTTALE
— Remain true to yourself.

**Work awarded with a
red dot: grand prix**
Progress
[TV/Cinema Commercial → p. 214-215]

The copywriters Anne Katrin Hüsken and Antje Schnottale studied in the same department at the Ruhr University Bochum – though at different times. They met ten years later at BBDO Düsseldorf, where they worked for brands including Dr. Oetker, Penaten and Mars Petcare. For six years now they have been developing the successful as well as emotional yearly campaigns for Caritas.

Which of your projects has been the biggest challenge for you so far?
The red dot awarded Caritas project. Shooting it was a real challenge. Very exciting. And perhaps a little dangerous as well. It was our first shot where we had to wear masks!

How do you approach new projects?
Depending on the task, mainly from the heart or mainly from the brain. But always a mix of both.

What do you understand by good communication design?
That it works.

With whom would you like to work together? Why?
With Ryan Gosling. To just look at him ...
And with a smart donkey.

BEL EPOK
SEBASTIAN FISCHENICH, TOBIAS MÜKSCH
— Ideas are founded in inspiration, truth is found in the process.

Work awarded with a red dot
HUMIECKI & GRAEF
[Packaging, Limited Porcelain Edition → p. 28-29]

BEL EPOK is a design and communication agency founded by Tobias Müksch in 2001. Previously, he had studied fashion design at the Chambre Syndicale de la Haute Couture Française as well as the Studio Berçot in Paris and worked as designer, among others, for Nina Ricci, Adeline André and Loro Piana. Tobias Müksch and Sebastian Fischenich, who studied fashion and product design in Utrecht and at the Berlin University of the Arts and later lectured at the latter, are the creative heads of the agency. BEL EPOK's work for such customers as Fogal, Swarovski, Shiseido, Montblanc and Dolce & Gabbana is characterised by a knowledge of the culture of the design-oriented luxury sector.

What inspires you?
Everything can be an inspiration. What is exciting is to create unexpected analogies, for example questions such as: What is the formal similarity between a backcombed hair creation of a girl from Neukölln, in Berlin, and Marie Antoinette's wig?

What does the future of communication design look like?
Object centred. We are of the opinion that communication design is becoming ever more three-dimensional and that the borders between the design disciplines will become blurred.

With whom would you like to work together? Why?
With Charles and Ray Eames. All their products and concepts are extremely considered. They exude sensuousness and retain the lightness and sheer joy of designing.

DAUM COMMUNICATIONS
BAEK SEUNG WAN,
BAE SOO HYUN,
LEE JUNE HYEONG
— Everything has a soul.

Work awarded with a red dot
Space Dot One
[Information Design → p. 190-191]

Baek Seung Wan worked for a web design agency for several years and now manages identity design projects at Daum Communications. Bae Soo Hyun, applying previous experience she gained by working on the design of a fashion brand's own label, is in charge of off-line space and project design for Daum Communications as an illustrator as well as a designer. Lee June Hyeong worked at numerous design studios where he was involved in the fields of graphic design, illustration, motion graphics and interface work, and, since 2008, he has been employed at Daum Communications as their brand design executive. In 2010, he was awarded the red dot.

What developments do you currently see in your industry?
In the case of South Korea, there are some social conflicts arising from monetary arrogance.

How do you approach new projects?
We strive to see the essence, closely examining who benefits from it and how a social relations cycle is generated from it. Ultimately, we aim to be modest about our outcomes.

What do you understand by good communication design?
A form that truly blends intuition and discernment, and not one that achieves this only from time to time.

What does the future of communication design look like?
Traditional communication design methods and processes will become an extravagance for only a few designers.

ETUDE CORPORATION
JUNG MI JUNG,
YU YEON JEONG,
SUL SE MI
— Enjoy life.

**Work awarded with a
red dot: best of best**
milk talk
[Body Wash Packaging → p. 22-23]

Works awarded with a red dot
Hands Up Deodorant/Depilatory
[Packaging → p. 24]
Missing You Honey Bee Hand Cream
[Packaging → p. 25]

Jung Mi Jung, Yu Yeon Jeong and Sul Se Mi are working
at Etude, a brand targeting 16 to 18 year-old girls. Jung
Mi Jung is a design team manager, Yu Yeon Jeong is a
marketer and Sul Se Mi is a designer. Their works have
garnered a number of international awards including Good
Design Award, iF packaging design award, Pentawards and
red dot design award.

How do you approach new projects?
We approach new projects with the question: What would
be an interesting idea? Ideas can often suggest themselves
suddenly, but for those that are interesting, the process
of application is usually very complicated and sometimes
demanding. We try to apply this process to our ideas to the
best of our abilities.

What do you understand by good communication design?
Delivering a message that can be understood at a glance.

**Is there a special time of day
when you are exceedingly creative?**
After sharing a laugh with team members.

What does the future of communication design look like?
New communication channels will continue to arise.

HEIDI FLEIG-GOLKS
— To love yourself is the secret.

Work awarded with a red dot
heidelberger naturkosmetik
[Packaging → p. 26]

Heidi Fleig-Golks studied design at the Freie Hochschule in Freiburg, Germany. Subsequently, she worked as art director for a number of advertising agencies. Since 2008, she has worked as a freelance designer for advertising agencies and companies. Her focus is the conception and creation of advertising campaigns (both off- and online) and packaging design for companies in a wide range of sectors and institutions. Heidi Fleig-Golks has won numerous awards including iF packaging design award 2012, 100 beste Plakate and New York Festivals.

What are the qualities a successful communication designer must have?
A good designer must be able to see when simplicity, beauty and user-friendliness are identical.

What does the future of communication design look like?
In a nutshell, design is growing gaining significance, because it provides structure for the increasing complexity of information in today's world. This applies to product design, advertising, off- and online information as much as to the management system of a hospital, an underground railway or an airport.

Why did you become a communication designer?
When I was two years old, I could recognise the colour ochre and even pronounce the word – maybe that's why?

FONTSHOP
JÜRGEN SIEBERT,
ANDREAS PIEPER,
JAN RIKUS HILLMANN,
MAI-LINH TRUONG
— Well begun is half done.

**Work awarded with a
red dot: grand prix**
FontBook App
[App → p. 274-275]

Jürgen Siebert studied physics, became a published author and co-founded the design magazine PAGE in 1986. He then moved to FontShop in Berlin, where he has been a member of the board since 2001. Andreas Pieper studied information technology and worked first at MetaDesign and later at FontShop International. For over ten years, he has also been one of the partners at null2 in Berlin. Jan Rikus Hillmann works in user interface and editorial design. He is co-editor and creative director of the magazine De:Bug and has been running his own design studio called burningbluesoul as a freelancer since 2003. Mai-Linh Truong is a musician and font expert. She is responsible for project management and database administration at the publisher FontShop International.

What developments do you currently see in your industry?
Mobility and mobile computing. People want to have up-to-the-minute access to reliable data, bookmarks and photos no matter whether they are sitting at their desks or on the go.

How do you approach new projects?
We place strong emphasis on individual and interdisciplinary thought. We begin with intensive team discussions to spark the kind of inspiration that can only come from a debate between diverse minds.

What are the qualities a successful communication designer must have?
He must be able to put himself in the shoes of an ordinary user, but at the same time, he needs to be able to listen to new input and evaluate all ideas with an open mind.

GRAFIK FACTORY
JONG YEOL BAIK
— Keep sketching.

**Work awarded with a
red dot: grand prix**
grafik:plastic
[Glasses/Sunglasses Case → p. 18-19]

Jong Yeol Baik started his design career at "doff'n company", Seoul, in 1993. He then moved on to an advertisiung agency called "the papergraphisfirm". In 2004, he was appointed TV commercial director and founded "617 production", working as its CEO and chief director. In 2011, he founded the company GRAFIK FACTORY, and launched the eyewear brand "grafik:plastic", for which he designed both the eyewear itself and the packaging.

**Which of your projects has been
the biggest challenge for you so far?**
The launch of grafik:plastic.

**Is there a special time of day
when you are exceedingly creative?**
Mostly in the morning before my staff come in for work.

What does the future of communication design look like?
Communication designs taking a stereotypical approach and appearance have already fallen behind. Design that suits the new media will excel.

**Which role does communication design
play in our everyday life?**
Delivering information accurately and effectively, from the most basic purpose and the very first thought, to the creator's own design philosophy. Not forcing itself onto anyone, but making people curious and observant so that the information that is being communicated becomes cherished.

GRET APES
NIKO SIPILÄ
— Great Finnish digital design
and development.

Work awarded with a red dot
Sports Tracker
[GPS-Based Workout Tracker → p. 293]

Niko Sipilä began his career as a GFX artist in the non-profit organisation demoscene and was graphic designer and co-founder of Eightball Media in 1996. From 2000 to 2003, he worked as a designer at kliQue plus, part of the BBDO Worldwide Network, and subsequently co-founded The Uncles, where he worked as an art director. From 2006 to 2008, he was art director and team leader at Satama Interactive before co-founding the agency Great Apes in Helsinki, Finland, where he currently acts as the art director.

What are the qualities a successful communication designer must have?
Naturally you need a certain skill set, but one of the most important things is to have empathy. To be able to always view what you are working on with fresh eyes and from the perspective of the end user and the target group.

What inspires you?
I don't consider myself an ad man, but George Lois kind of nailed it when he talked about getting excited about selling a new kind of pen and how you can get excited about almost anything. So, when working with commissioned projects, you try to find projects that have the possibility to really excite you, and that's where you'll find most of your inspiration.

GRECO DESIGN
GUSTAVO GRECO
— Designers are forever restless and always in search of new formats.

**Work awarded with a
red dot: grand prix**
Dauro Oliveira Orthodontics Clinic
[Signage System → p. 180-181]

Gustavo Greco is the owner and creative director of Greco Design in Brazil. As a professor at the design school at FUMEC University, he also teaches the brand management course in the post-graduate programme at IEC – PUC MG. He is the head of a team of 23 professionals running graphic design projects focused on visual identity, editorial projects, signage and promotional material.

Gustavo Greco is also the director of ABEDESIGN in the region of Minas Gerais. Under his leadership Greco Design has participated in the latest editions of the Brazilian Graphic Design Biennial. The company has received many awards and was introduced in national and international publications.

**Which of your projects has been
the biggest challenge for you so far?**
Each project is a new universe to be explored, with varied factors that lead us along different paths in the quest for visual solutions. But the most challenging project for me is Greco Design itself. I have never managed a company this size and knowing how to deal with everything that is happening requires continuous attention and learning.

What do you understand by good communication design?
In my opinion, good design is the ability to solve problems well. It must ally knowledge, imagination and innovation, thus producing an adequate solution to the problem that is pertinent to the reality of those who will be receiving the message.

GTDI
HENRY HO
— From 5 to 6. Five senses
for a general designer,
a sixth sense for a good designer.

Work awarded with a red dot
Rice Magic Sake Japan
[Sparkling Sake Packaging → p. 80-81]

Henry Ho graduated from the School of Design at the Hong Kong Polytechnic University. He started his career with GTDI in Tokyo in 1996, where today he is president and creative director. He has designed many successful brand image and packaging designs for clients in Japan, Hong Kong, Taiwan and China, including Shiseido, Kao, Kraft Foods Japan, Coca-Cola, Otsuka Pharmaceutical, Ajinomoto and Hong Kong Maxim's Group. He also established an original children's brand called "Born to Create" which has been sold all over the world. In 2011, Henry Ho published books about Japanese packaging design. Currently, he is a part-time lecturer in media design at Keio University, Japan.

What developments do you currently see in your industry?
Local mission, global vision.

What inspires you?
Pressure – both from the client and the consumer.

What do you understand by good communication design?
I don't really want to understand it. Sometimes, excessive understanding of a thing leads to a dead end in creativity. It's better to look at it as a mystery.

What does the future of communication design look like?
As information seems to abound today, creative direction needs to go back to basics and become simpler – it's the best way to stand out in our current mass of media.

ROLF HERING
— Gravity turns
the right angle into law.

Work awarded with a red dot
IdHAIR Hair Care Product Line
[Plastic Bottles → p. 33]

Rolf Hering studied product design at the University of Applied Sciences in Darmstadt, obtaining his degree in 1984. After graduation, he entered the central design department of Siemens AG, where he worked together with Prof. Tönis Käo in the in-house design studio on projects for consumer and investment goods in the field of medical, communication and lighting engineering. In 1989, Rolf Hering founded his own design office, Hering's Büro, in Kronach, and thanks to the proximity of the glass and plastics industry in Upper Franconia, quickly got into the field of packaging design, especially for cosmetics. The office provides the entire range of services for modern packaging design in glass, plastic and cardboard.

What are the qualities a successful communication designer must have?
Every designer should have a basic talent for communication in general, no matter whether in words, images or other media. If he has this, he can communicate for others.

What inspires you?
The unbelievable and endless diversity of reducing. There is nothing that you could not do better.

What do you understand by good communication design?
The striking quality of good design is that it is intuitively understood by a clear majority of users.

With whom would you like to work together? Why?
With Freedom Of Creation. They caused an immense stir to old patterns of thought.

HUMAN INTERFACE DESIGN
— Inspiring interaction.

Work awarded with a red dot
Busch-ComfortTouch App
[App → p. 297]

Human Interface Design is a design office that specialises in human-centred design for the usability of technical products, software systems and interactive media. As an experienced team of specialists in design and usability, we make technology understandable for users and easy to use. Together with clients such as ABB, BSH, Busch-Jaeger, Dräger, Gaggenau, Sartorius and the German press agency dpa, the office develops products that convince through their functionality and are emotionally appealing.

What developments do you currently see in your industry?
In interaction design, we see a trend of designing the disappearance of "computer operation" in our daily lives.

How do you approach new projects?
With curiosity! Basically, we start as a multidisciplinary team in a "workshop creative brief" together with the client.

What do you understand by good communication design?
Good interface design convinces on two levels: it fascinates on an aesthetic level and rewards on a second level through good usability.

What else would you like to learn?
How to have a lasting positive influence on political decisions through design.

INPIX
GYEONGYEON KIM
— Commitment to thinking hard!

Work awarded with a red dot
A plain convergence with INPIX
[Online Communication → p. 241]

In around 2000, Gyeongyeon Kim was one of a few highly motivated young designers who launched their own studios, where they turned their creative ideas into online products and released those items on the market. She later joined the global company Yahoo Korea as the product manager in charge of platform services. As the nature of these services required taking usability and functionality into account over visual design, she analysed user experience to reflect their demands on the design. Based on this experience, at her own company INPIX, she now engages in developing and visualising user interfaces optimised for diverse environments and devices based on online media.

Where and how do you gather information on trends?
I usually acquire basic information through research or subscriptions, but I use communities such as social networks to gain more sensitive and subjective information.

What developments do you currently see in your industry?
Overarching corporate trends have started to settle and third parties like us, who can take advantage of this new ecosystem, will play bigger roles.

How do you approach new projects?
I try to understand the experience of the customers of my clients, prior to finding out what my clients want.

JNS COMMUNICATIONS
YONG-TAE SHIN,
MAN-HEE JANG
— In good designs, people may experience and share sensitivity.

**Work awarded with a
red dot: best of best**
Kia Rio
[iPad App → p. 278-279]

Yong-Tae Shin is the CEO and Man-Hee Jang the creative director at JNS Communications, a design company founded in 1995. The company has produced new and challenging creative work for the last 18 years, striving for perfect functionality, taking into consideration sophisti-cated strategy and the characteristics of each medium to further perfect the aesthetic purpose of the designs. Communication design demands new values and out-comes by the fusion of new and constantly evolving high technology. JNS aims to render its active and intuitive efforts to provide customers with their most-needed service earlier than others in any circumstances.

How do you approach new projects?
By thinking it over in a free atmosphere.

**What are the qualities a successful
communication designer must have?**
The ability to grasp the core of things, motivation and a creative mind.

What does the future of communication design look like?
A harmony of technology and human sensibility.

**Which role does communication design
play in our everyday life?**
It offers convenient and easy access to purposes and objects, makes people understand easily and objects look beautiful.

Dörte Spengler-Ahrens

Jan Rexhausen

Armin Jochum

Florian Paul

Michael Kittel

Henning Mueller-Dannhausen

Alexander Norvilas

JUNG VON MATT
JVM/FLEET
— What is special about WWF is that it is a product, PR campaign and nature conservation initiative all rolled into one.

**Work awarded with a
red dot: best of best**
Save as WWF, Save a Tree
[Online Advertising → p. 232-233]

Works awarded with a red dot
Online Stolpersteine / Stones Telling Stories –
Online Holocaust Memorial
[Online Advertising → p. 260]
Online Straßenmusiker / Online Street Musicians
[Online Advertising → p. 261]

JvM/Fleet sees itself as the most colourful member of the Jung von Matt group of agencies. The 40-strong team is an intentionally international melting pot of talent from across the world set up to deliver fresh impulses and innovative, creative solutions to national and international customers with high creative expectations such as Zalando, WWF, Sixt, Mercedes and DER SPIEGEL. Their offering ranges from classical campaigns to integrated brand communication across all media.

Dörte Spengler-Ahrens started her career as a junior art director in 1992. In 2000, as CCO, she opened up the Jung von Matt/Spree office in Berlin. Today, she is CCO of JvM/Fleet and is one of the most awarded German creatives.

Where and how do you gather information on trends?
Online, offline, on the road – by keeping my eyes wide open and listening to people, in particular to my nine-year-old son.

What developments do you currently see in your industry?
A great need for "authenticity". This need is so strong that it brings everything down onto the same level and will trigger "staging" as the next trend.

How do you approach new projects?
With my antennas on "receive", in a relaxed state of aggregation and with switched-on guts.

What are the qualities a successful communication designer must have?
Common sense. He or she must, truly, understand people.

LEAGAS DELANEY HAMBURG
— The brand in one second.

**Work awarded with a
red dot: best of best**
Followfish. Good Catch.
[Film → p. 198-199, 216-217]

Leagas Delaney Hamburg is part of an international creative family with agencies in London, Milan, Rome, Hamburg, Prague, Tokyo and Shanghai. The office works for international clients including Škoda, Wempe and Parship.de, and in Germany also for Motor Presse Stuttgart, Advocard, Patek Philippe, Maxi, Followfish, ALNO, Greenpeace Energy, the Elbphilharmonie Foundation and the Hamburg Theatre. The agency is directed by Hermann Waterkamp, Stefan Zschaler and Tjarko Horstmann.

What developments do you currently see in your industry?
The diversity of formats that need to be designed for is constantly increasing – and thus also the demands on designers. We think this is good, since this way we all stay fresh.

How do you approach new projects?
Before we start designing something, we approach the task very strategically and look at the entire brand and the respective target groups. Only when the direction for the content is set and everyone is attuned to the client we do start with the design process.

Which role does communication design play in our everyday life?
You can't actually get around it.

LOEWE
EDMUND ENGLICH,
MARC JOSCHKO,
JASMIN KASTNER

**Work awarded with a
red dot: best of best**
Loewe Assist Media
[iPad App → p. 276-277]

Edmund Englich, born in 1962, studied industrial design in Hannover, Germany, and at Brunel University, England. He worked with .molldesign, before moving to Loewe in 1998, where he has headed the design department since 2001. Marc Joschko studied product design at the University of Applied Sciences in Potsdam and worked in the Siemens FutureLab, among other things, before he moved to Loewe in 2008, helping to develop the user interface design department. Jasmin Kastner studied product design at the University of Applied Sciences in Coburg and after working with Marcel Wanders, among others, has been a freelance designer in the area of user interfaces with Loewe since 2010. Together with Marc Joschko, in summer 2012, she founded the agency zwei21.

What developments do you currently see in your industry?
A continuous "de-materialisation of TV sets" changing in utility from a classic TV set into a multimedia system.

What inspires you?
Simple solutions without straining after effects are highly inspiring: reduced to the essential. Quiet, not loud. Orderly arranged, not confusing. Modern, not fashionable.

Which role does communication design play in our everyday life?
Communication design is an essential point of intersection in the dialogue between people and their environment. Good communication design creates orientation and assurance and thus lasting added value for people.

MARTIN ET KARCZINSKI
BJÖRN MATTHES,
ULRIKE GOTTSCHILD,
SIMON MAIER-RAHMER
— The brightest stars shine the furthest.

**Work awarded with a
red dot: best of best**
Occhio App
[Interfaces & Apps → p. 280-281]

Ulrike Gottschild, Björn Matthes and Simon Maier-Rahmer work for the Martin et Karczinski agency. Ulrike Gottschild is a screen designer and the head of multimedia, Björn Matthes the motion interactive designer and Simon Maier-Rahmer the manager of the Occhio design unit. The agency combines communication strategies with design quality at a high level and understands corporate identity as an important steering instrument throughout a company. Thus, since 2000, the agency has contributed to the success of such customers as Alape, Audi, Daikin Europe, McDonald's Kinderhilfe, Occhio, Parador and Siemens Gigaset. Martin et Karczinski is number six in the current PAGE rating of leading German CI/CD agencies. Furthermore, it was Upcomer of the Year as early as 2007.

Where and how do you gather information on trends?
We keep our eyes wide open – every second of every day.

What developments do you currently see in your industry?
The bad news is price dumping, creative arbitrariness and arrogance. The good news is that it can only get better!

What are the qualities a successful communication designer must have?
The ability to listen – more of an art than a characteristic trait.

What do you understand by good communication design?
Aplomb and implicitness.

MPREIS
JOHANNA MÖLK,
SIMONE HÖLLBACHER
— We cannot not change the world.

Work awarded with a red dot
Liebensmittelei – Food for Soul
[Food Packaging, Gift Box → p. 64-65]

Johanna Mölk, born in 1983 in Austria, studied at the Academy of Advertising and Design in Innsbruck, Austria, and at the Academy of Art and Design in Basel, Switzerland, from 2007 to 2010, graduating with a Bachelor of Arts. Since 2010, after working freelance, she has been working for the supermarket chain MPREIS in Innsbruck. Simone Höllbacher, born in 1982 in Austria, first studied psychology at the University of Innsbruck, and subsequently, from 2003 to 2007, design at the Vorarlberg University of Applied Sciences, graduating with an MA in Arts and Design. After internships for various companies including the communication agency Plantage Berlin, since 2008, she has been a graphic designer with MPREIS.

Where and how do you gather information on trends?
It is important to keep your eyes open, to remain attentive and develop your own thoughts. We believe more in perceiving trends that are "in the air" than in gathering information from market research centres or trend bureaus. We are more interested in things that happen in the alternative art scene, in our environment, for instance.

What do you understand by good communication design?
Good communication design is responsible. We must keep in mind that what we do has an ecological and social impact. Graphic design is very powerful because it influences our attitude towards things. Therefore, it should be used cautiously and consciously.

NATIONAL MUSEUM OF CONTEMPORARY ART, KOREA – DESIGN TEAM
— Creating resonance.

Work awarded with a red dot
Dansaekhwa – Korean Monochrome Painting
[Exhibition → p. 166-167]

The design team of the National Museum of Contemporary Art, Korea, consists of specialists in all design areas, including space, graphic and product design.

They are charged with design-related works for exhibitions and audience services. For exhibition design projects, the specialists of the team create overall images in accordance with the theme of an exhibition, and make a title graphic for the exhibition, space structure, graphic design and other promotional materials for communication with audiences using visual language. In addition, the design team is charged with designs for advertising, events and cultural products.

How do you approach new projects?
First we imagine how the viewers would be touched by the outcome of the project and what they would experience through the project.

What are the qualities a successful communication designer must have?
You should be able to project feelings from the point of view of an inanimate object and not miss the purpose of design.

What kind of project would you like to realise someday?
We would like to do a project that creates a new feeling in terms of synaesthetic experience beyond visual experience – with a dynamic design that makes viewers appreciate the work from a new point of view, using all five senses.

MORIYUKI OCHIAI
— Create works of vivacious beauty!

Work awarded with a red dot
ARKHE Beauty Salon
[Interior Design → p. 146-147]

Moriyuki Ochiai, born in Tokyo in 1973, is an architect and designer. He established his own studio Moriyuki Ochiai Architects / Twoplus-A in 2008, specialising in different design fields such as architecture as well as landscape, interior, furniture and industrial design. The studio's aim is to create works that fulfil people's dreams, become the energy for their lives and which move on to a deeper dimension that exceeds life itself.

The studio received numerous awards including the iF design award (Gold), Germany; the Interior Design Best of Year Award (Grand Prix), USA; the German Design Award; the SBID International Design Award, UK; the Design for Asia Award, Hong Kong; the Japanese Society of Commercial Space Designers Award; the Japan Display Design Association Award, and the Japan Sign Design Association Award.

Where and how do you gather information on trends?
I travel to many different countries and observe the lives of people to gather information.

How do you approach new projects?
By developing a new sense of values.

What are the qualities a successful communication designer must have?
One must be able to create works that fascinate people and make them dream or make them find those works astonishing.

What do you understand by good communication design?
A design that resonates deeply, addressing all five senses.

PHOCUS BRAND CONTACT
SUSANNE KREBS
— The idea as the highest form of energy.

Work awarded with a red dot
Black Box – Mercedes-Benz
at Commercial Vehicle Fair RAI,
Amsterdam
[Installation → p. 127]

The communication design agency PHOCUS BRAND CONTACT was founded in 1998 and aims to provide brand experiences. It creates an appropriate frame, in terms of aesthetics and content, for the diverse requirements of its clients and fills it with concise, innovative forms of representation. The solutions for this are developed by inter-disciplinary teams and continuously checked for whether they perfectly meet the assigned task.

The human being and its specific demands are put centre stage by the conceptual work, which has been awarded several red dot awards. Susanne Krebs is the managing director and is responsible for design and creation.

What developments do you currently see in your industry?
Sustainability through interdisciplinary teamwork: the idea that people with different backgrounds work together and in this way generate better solutions is getting increasingly important.

How do you approach new projects?
By intensively exploring all relevant related topics in order to find innovative communicative solutions. That is design thinking: to understand, observe, find ideas, refine, apply and learn.

What are the qualities a successful communication designer must have?
He must be an explorer, be open to new ideas and always find new things, even in the well known.

PIXELBUTIK BY DELI PICTURES
MICHAEL REISSINGER
— Yes, exactly! However, …

**Work awarded with a
red dot: grand prix**
The first mark
[Recruitment Film → p. 196-197]

Michael Reissinger was born in Erding, Germany, in 1969, but has lived in Hamburg since 1992, where he works in graphic design, typography and illustration. In 2006, he began working for Deli Pictures and is the managing partner responsible for the creation department. In 2009, the Deli label Pixelbutik, a small studio for motion design and the direction of digital moving images, was set up. Michael Reissinger is, among others, a member of ADC, D&AD and the international Bitfilm Club. As recently as last year, he won a "red dot: best of best" for his film "Hail of criticism" for Leagas Delaney and the Hamburg Theatre.

What developments do you currently see in your industry?
The fragmentation of the creative offering will continue. Distinct key design categories such as web, print, product, film and installation are increasingly disappearing to be replaced by emerging new professional areas of expertise.

What are the qualities a successful communication designer must have?
Humbleness, endurance and inquisitiveness.

What else would you like to learn?
Oil painting in the style of the Old Masters, for example, or flying a helicopter, cooking really tasty fish, how to use all the animation programs and speaking intelligible Spanish and Italian.

SCHMIDHUBER /
KMS BLACKSPACE
— We make brands tangible.

**Work awarded with a
red dot: grand prix**
The Audi Ring –
Brand Pavilion IAA 2011
[Event Design → p. 112-113]

Michael Ostertag-Henning studied architecture and developed a passion for the connection of marketing and architecture early in his career. After studying by Daniel Libeskind and Graft Architects, he has supported the work of SCHMIDHUBER since 2005. Since 2008, he has been managing partner and has had a major impact on the spatial appearance of the Audi brand.

KMS BLACKSPACE specialises in the activation of brands in the fields of spatial communication design, motion design and customer experience design. Together with KMS TEAM and KMS MINDSHIFT, it is Germany's biggest owner-managed brand agency with more than 100 employees. Marc Ziegler is managing partner at KMS BLACKSPACE.

What developments do you currently see in your industry?
Michael Ostertag-Henning: Brands are increasingly staged in a vibrant, innovative spatial communication that is particularly tailored to the requirements of the target group. Quality plays a more important role than it used to, and equally so does sustainability.
Marc Ziegler: A brand experience that you can touch and feel becomes increasingly significant, while the information content remains important too, and interdisciplinary constellations are more frequently applied.

What do you understand by good communication design?
Marc Ziegler: Good communication design is that which develops from the synergy of design, space, media and the communication of information.

SCHOLZ & FRIENDS
JÜRGEN KRUGSPERGER,
OLIVIER NOWAK
— You need to fight for a good idea.

**Work awarded with a
red dot: best of best**
Amnesty International
Light Sculpture
[Installation → p. 182-183]

Jürgen Krugsperger was born in Ingolstadt in 1973. He studied product design in Pforzheim and at the University of Illinois in Chicago, and then subsequently worked for Vogt+Weizenegger. Since 2003 he has been at Scholz & Friends Berlin, where he is responsible for product design and public design as senior art director. Olivier Nowak was born in Paris in 1977. He studied in Passau and Munich, and began working at Jung von Matt afterwards in Hamburg in 2004. Since 2007, he has been at Scholz & Friends Berlin, where he is senior art director. Jürgen Krugsperger's and Olivier Nowak's work has won awards from many bodies and at various ceremonies, including the ADC, DDC, D&AD, Clio Awards, New York Festivals, iF design award, Cannes Lions and the red dot design award.

Where and how do you gather information on trends?
The question is rather how to filter the flood.

What developments do you currently see in your industry?
More brands, more opinions, more media.

How do you approach new projects?
Start by being open minded and unprejudiced and then really delve into the subject.

What inspires you?
Art and the everyday.

What do you understand by good communication design?
When you would have liked to have done it yourself.

431

SKIN CONCEPT
WOLFGANG MAYER
— One must still have chaos
in oneself to be able
to give birth to a dancing star.

Friedrich Nietzsche

Work awarded with a red dot
VETIA FLORIS
[Packaging → p. 30-31]

Wolfgang Mayer, chief operating officer of Medena AG, spearheaded the company's entry into branded cosmetic and cosmeceutical products under the Skin Concept banner. He joined Medena in 2005, with more than 20 years of experience in diagnostic and pharmaceutical business sectors, most recently as CEO of Vitest AG in Zurich, where he was instrumental in the rapid start-up of in-vitro home testing and other medical devices. Prior to that, he occupied senior marketing and product development positions with several German companies, including DPC Biermann GmbH, Sanofi Diagnostics Pasteur GmbH and Pasteur Diagnostika GmbH.

How do you approach new projects?
By courageously rejecting limits. We start each project from scratch with a blank piece of paper and discuss ideas as a team. We rely on short decision-making processes and the courage to take risks.

What does the future of communication design look like?
In a globalised world it is ever more important to communicate beyond the limits of language on a universal level. That is why communication design will play a key role in the future.

With whom would you like to work together? Why?
Pedro Almodóvar. I would like to be part in the creative process for one of his films. He is a true master of communicating the fate and stories of people with absolute immediacy.

SPOT°ENTWICKLUNG
MARC BÖTTLER
— Enjoy the little things.

Work awarded with a red dot
The story of the fisherman
[Computer-Animated Spot → p. 203]

Marc Böttler was born in Stuttgart. He trained in television and then moved to animation, which combines all his interests (illustration, music, storytelling). Since 2007, he worked as a motion designer, taking on projects such as cinema advertising for the Deutsche Stiftung Denkmalschutz (the German foundation for protected buildings), an animated stage set for the Deutscher Zukunftspreis (the German award for technical innovation) and other short films. Marc Böttler studied communication design at the Karlsruhe University of Arts and Design and, together with the musician Udosson, created the live audio-visual show "Nachtstück" in 2009. He has been art director for the agency spot°entwicklung in Tübingen since 2012.

What developments do you currently see in your industry?
Motion design is increasing in popularity and the software is becoming easier to work with. Graphic animation is omnipresent. As a result a good idea, when combined with professional realisation, increases in value.

How do you approach new projects?
In an ideal world, with pencil and paper in a place as quiet as possible. Once I have sketched out my first thought and ideas, I look for the right person to "ping-pong" ideas. The best ideas come from brainstorming between two people.

Which role does communication design play in our everyday life?
Designers should not take themselves too seriously, but at the same time should not underestimate the effect that their work has.

MARIO STOCKHAUSEN
— Ideas are rocket ships
for business.

Work awarded with a red dot
Lightweight.info
[Corporate Website → p. 248]

Mario Stockhausen was born in Neuwied, Germany, in
1977. He studied to be a technical design assistant and
subsequently worked at BBDO Interactive, Publicis,
Zenithmedia and Euro RSCG in Düsseldorf. He founded
Stockhausen GmbH in 2001 and serviced customers in
the automobile and fashion sectors. At the beginning of
2007, he was named head of design at LBi Germany. At the
end of 2008, he moved to Ludwigsburg, where he became
a unit leader of design for Bassier, Bergmann & Kindler
and was responsible for the digital brand management of
Porsche and the HUGO BOSS University, among others.
In 2012, he broke free again, and since then has built the
creative agency "bölb" with a team of six people.

Which of your projects has been
the biggest challenge for you so far?
Projects whose structure is based on established processes. It is always an exciting challenge to question such
processes and to persuade the customer to think them
over so that you can break them down. There is nothing
better than seeing the reworked process unfolding its
positive effect in the end.

What are the qualities a successful
communication designer must have?
A good communicator is an actor and stage director in one.
He must be able to take on a role and tell an exciting story.
Both of these help us to deal constructively with customer
feedback in order to do things even better.

STUDIO 38

— People will forget
what you said, people will forget
what you did, but people will
never forget how you made them feel.

Maya Angelou

Work awarded with a red dot
MINI Pop-Up Store London Westfield
[Temporary Store → p. 144-145]

The team at studio 38 comprises communication, product and fashion designers, as well as interior architects, account managers, project managers and programmers. The members team up according to the requirements of each individual project to combine their interdisciplinary expertise and time and again realise innovative and successful solutions in communication design. For studio 38, design is convincing when it is based on a strong idea that beholders can relate to emotionally. The projects created by the studio merge accurate and efficient project management including production with the joy of aesthetically sophisticated, intelligent and surprising communication.

What developments do you currently see in your industry?
Despite all the rapidly advancing possibilities in virtual interaction between brands and customers, it is holistically staged and tangible brand experiences that gain ever more in significance, in particular when they manifest an emotional quality and communicate it in an authentic way.

Which of your projects has been the biggest challenge for you so far?
The MINI Pop-Up Store in London was one of our biggest challenges for sure, not just because of the relatively confined floor space of only 180 square metres available for staging this multi-layered brand, but also because we had to realise the entire project within a three-month deadline for the opening of the shop.

STUDIO NOVO
— Design is never arbitrary.

Work awarded with a red dot
Caffè Gemelli –
L'espresso di elevata qualità
[Packaging → p. 49]

Studio Novo was founded in 2005 by Nik Pelzl and focuses on industrial and communication design. The agency works in trustworthy, passionate and long-term collaboration with its customers and analyses their history and strategic direction, target markets and groups, technical restrictions and financial possibilities as well as their competitors. This allows it to determine content, range of functions, distinguishing features and, in the end, the design vocabulary that serve as starting points for design implementation. The result is good design as the outcome of a comprehensive phase of research and analysis.

What developments do you currently see in your industry?
The return of many companies to their core competencies. That has a direct effect on the demands made of a communication design concept, as it requires a long-term, strategic orientation that also takes account of the content. Coupled with an increased awareness of quality in the industry, this results in innovative communication initiatives that are tailored to the organisation, but may occasionally also be controversial.

What do you understand by good communication design?
The content is clear, as is the target audience. It is the logic result of these two parameters and resists the need to please everybody.

PIER TAYLOR
— To use communication design to create orientation.

**Work awarded with a
red dot: best of best**
A50 Motorway Information Graphic
[information design / public space → p. 184-185]

Pier Taylor, born in 1979, graduated in graphic design from the Hogeschool voor de Kunsten in Arnhem, Netherlands. Subsequently, he worked as a graphic designer at the design studio MINT in Arnhem, which he co-founded. He has worked freelance on a wide variety of design projects, based in Amsterdam. His client work revolves around topics such as cultural identities, mobility and living environments. He taught editorial design at the art academy in Arnhem and recently obtained a Master of Advanced Studies in Design Culture at the Design2context Institute of Zurich University of the Arts (ZHdK), Switzerland.

What developments do you currently see in your industry?
There is a lack of site-specific engagement in corporate culture when it comes to communication design.

How do you approach new projects?
There is nothing static about identity design. To avoid being led too much by preconceptions, to start fresh, I ask myself in what way a design project can become a receptacle for identity and how it invites identification.

What inspires you?
When going for walks I tend to look for the gap between planned intentions and realised design solutions in the urban and rural environment. I derive a strange sense of consolation from this kind of reality check as well as encouragement to do better.

THEODENT
ARMAN SADEGHPOUR
— Don't try to explain the ineffable –
just trust your vision.

Work awarded with a red dot
Theodent Toothpaste
[Packaging → p. 36-37]

Arman Sadeghpour is the president and CEO of Theodent. He received a BA in French, a BS in psychology as well as a master's degree in computer science and a PhD in bioinformatics from Tulane University in New Orleans, Louisiana, where he currently resides. His doctoral thesis work on a revolutionary new extract from chocolate, which will ultimately replace fluoride in toothpaste, has been featured in INC magazine, Men's Health, Business Week, Los Angeles Times, the New York Times, and Forbes. Arman Sadeghpour is dedicated to helping rebuild the New Orleans economy, post-Katrina, by stimulating the biotechnology sector of New Orleans and creating new quality jobs.

Which of your projects has been the biggest challenge for you so far?
Theodent's high-end luxury feel was a big challenge for us. We needed the toothpaste to evoke the look and feel of chocolate but in the classiest way.

What do you understand by good communication design?
Good communication design evokes a strong feeling from the viewer.

How do you approach new projects?
New projects always start with music. Every project needs a soundtrack. Theodent has a lot of Goldfrapp in there.

What are the qualities a successful communication designer must have?
An open mind to new ideas, but grounded in good decision making tempered with a complete disregard for the "rules".

TRIAD BERLIN
HARALD LIPKEN
— Team Play! Uninhibited.
Strategic. Creative.

**Work awarded with a
red dot: best of best**
Nord Stream – The Arrival
[Corporate Event → p. 114-115]

Harald Lipken studied architecture at the Berlin University of the Arts and worked in the communication and design departments of the Töchter + Söhne communication agency in Berlin from 1998 to 1999.

Since 2000, he has been the creative director for Triad Berlin, except for periods when he worked as lecturer at the University of the Arts in Bremen and creative director at av communication (Berlin, Ludwigsburg, Munich). He has been running the event unit at Triad Berlin together with Sabine Kahlenberg since 2011, standing in for Nora Penadés, who is on maternity leave.

How do you approach new projects?
I am interested by the people behind the brands, products and services and not just the shape. In order really to get to know their sometimes subconscious desires in depth and find out what motivates them, one needs to ask questions and above all be able to listen.

**What are the qualities a successful
communication designer must have?**
Discontent, team play, endurance and enthusiasm.

What inspires you?
People who continually manage to stretch their own limits.

What do you understand by good communication design?
As much content as possible, as much form as necessary.

VBAT
JOHN COMITIS,
EUGENE BAY
— Building refreshing brands.

Work awarded with a red dot
SOL Bottle and Outer Box –
Portal to the sun
[Packaging → p. 86-87]

Founded in 1984, VBAT is an award-winning branding and design agency, experienced in a broad range of branding issues from fast-moving consumer goods, customer services, and business-to-business communications on a local and global scale. Working closely with its clients, including D.E Master Blenders 1753 (formerly Sara Lee Corp.), Heineken International, PostNL, Vattenfall, Makro and Gamma, the agency constantly strives to deliver valuable and fresh thinking to unlock the full potential of their brands. VBAT, based in a former bicycle factory in Amsterdam, consists of a team of around 60 experts and is part of WPP, the world's biggest marketing communication network.

What developments do you currently see in your industry?
The ability to create solutions quicker than ever before without compromising on quality.

What are the qualities a successful communication designer must have?
An open mind and the ability to be self-critical.

What inspires you?
Being awake. Being alive. Constantly searching. Never resting.

What else would you like to learn?
To be naive again. Getting rid of the mechanism of right and wrong. Not just going with the flow but enjoying the journey you take.

VICTOR BRANDING DESIGN CORP.
B. B. SHEE,
FRED WANG,
CHUNG YUAN KUO
— Victor Branding Design Corp. has long adhered to the "Your Design Partners" service concept.

Work awarded with a red dot: best of best
kiyutaro weather station
[Packaging → p. 20-21]

Work awarded with a red dot
Formosa Ecology Tea Gift Set
[Packaging → p. 52-53]

Victor Branding Design Corp. was founded in 1988 and, since then, has set up the mission "Your Design Partners" by gathering talent with a commitment to branding, visual design, role shaping, packaging design and advertisement from relevant fields. Based on many years of accumulating expert design knowledge, the company has developed the concept of "Brand Engineer". This was achieved by focusing on the spirit and performance of all team members and divisions and establishing outstanding synergy in the creation of brands. The company plays the role of "Brand Housekeeper" as part of its services to long-term clients.

What developments do you currently see in your industry?
An increasing number of Taiwanese companies understand the value of design in terms of products and brand marketing. This will lead to better overall design in Taiwan.

What do you understand by good communication design?
Good communication design has the power always to attract attention and appeal to people. It makes us understand product characteristics and branding at the same time, both perceptions which are frequently generated within few seconds.

What kind of project would you like to realise someday?
Taiwan was once the main centre for toy manufacture, but has rarely launched domestic brands. Because of our passion for toys, we would, if possible, like to produce our own toy brand and packaging.

FENG YAN
— Time is fleeting,
but art remains.

Work awarded with a red dot
Chinese Traditional Furniture
[App → p. 300-301]

Prof. Feng Yan, born in 1978 in Beijing, China, has been devoted to experimental art with expanded media, UI and UE design, as well as design education. He received a BA degree from the Academy of Arts and Design at Tsinghua University, Beijing, in 2000, and later MFA degrees from Birmingham Institute of Art and Design, Birmingham, United Kingdom, and from the Academy of Art University, San Francisco, USA. He worked as a project manager for Dialogue Space, the Forbidden City Concert Hall, and at the Art Museum of China Millennium Monument. Currently he is a professor at China Central Academy of Fine Arts. Feng Yan received numerous international awards and is a member of many professional associations.

What does the future of communication design look like?
I believe that communication design will be more inclusive, covering various subjects that are highly interdisciplinary. Unlike design in the past, which laid emphasis on extending vertically, it will look more to the combination of both vertical and horizontal extension, meaning, interdisciplinary integration.

What inspires you?
I am deeply in love with traditional Chinese culture and I believe it is my responsibility to spread it further. At the same time, I adore Chinese handicrafts. Using new technologies a fascinating and enjoyable way of showcasing those traditional and pristine handicrafts has emerged.

ZEROS+ONES
LUCA CAPELLETTI
— Carpe diem!

Work awarded with a red dot
"pass on your passion" initiative
[Microsite → p. 252-253]

Luca Capelletti, born in 1963 in Cesena, Italy, worked as technical draughtsman after graduating from high school in 1983 and went on a trip around the world in 1986. Subsequently, he worked in the field of computer-aided design, took part in international trade shows and moved to Germany in 1990, having spent all of his savings on a Macintosh IIci and catapulting himself right into a completely new life. From 1990 to 1993, he worked for publishing houses in Munich, both as a freelancer and employee, before founding zeros+ones together with Torsten Green, Michael Teltscher and Dietrich Hueck. Since then, he has been working on projects for clients such as Audi, BMW, BR, Deutsche Bank, E.ON and the ZDF.

What inspires you?
The sliding apart of thunder and lightning.

What kind of project would you like to realise someday?
I am fascinated by cycles and repetitions, because repetition does not create replicas or duplicates but something unique. I have documented these phenomena for ten years with pictures from the same, daily train route. I would love to make them publicly available and publish them.

What does the future of communication design look like?
The flow of information is immense and will increase in the future. This is why communication design needs to focus even more on clarity. On being transparent. Invisible. Becoming a "superconductor".

Junior Designer

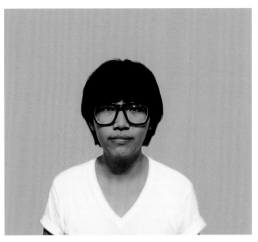

PEI-YU CHEN, TING-CHEN LIU, PEI-JIUN LIAU, YU-CHUN LIN, MENG-YUAN LIU, YU-CHIEN CHIU

— I know nothing except the fact of my ignorance.

Socrates

Work awarded with a red dot
Grandpa's and Grandma's Age
[Online Educational App → p. 398-399]

Pei-Yu Chen, Ting-Chen Liu, Pei-Jiun Liau, Yu-Chun Lin, Meng-Yuan and Liu Yu-Chien Chiu are all senior students from the Department of Digital Media Design at the School of Design, Ming Chuan University, Taiwan. From 2011 to 2012, it took them a year and a half from the initial project development, using modern information technology skills, to create the Taiwanese classical atmosphere and, eventually, introduce the online educational app in Taiwan. The design process required a great deal of effort by many designers, comparing and discussing a great number of visual effects and different concepts.

What developments do you currently see in your industry?
Digital design plays an important role for the advancement of design in general. In addition, communication design is the key to digital design. Some designers ignore the fact that the basic design should be considered first. The important design value should be constructed at the first design stage. Our basic idea is to emphasise the value of Taiwanese culture for the individual.

What are the qualities a successful communication designer must have?
A successful communication designer should have several abilities. The first ability for us is intensive observation. Thus a designer can see what other people cannot see.

SIAN-SHUO CHEN, YI-HSIN LU, TING-YI HUANG, SHIANG-YIN SU

Work awarded with a red dot
Marriage
[Illustration → p. 384]

Sian-Shuo Chen, Yi-Hsin Lu, Ting-Yi Huang and Shiang-Yin Su are students of the Department of Visual Communication Design at Shu-Te University in Kaohsiung City, Taiwan. They each originate from a different city in Taiwan and became classmates and design partners. "Marriage" is part of their graduate project and the first illustrated book they designed.

What are the qualities a successful communication designer must have?
He or she needs to be curious about everything and be able to embrace new things.

What do you understand by good communication design?
Good communication design can convey the concepts hidden behind it and spark sympathetic responses from others.

Why did you become a communication designer?
We wanted to express our opinions on different social phenomena.

Which role does communication design play in our everyday life?
It can either communicate the relationships between people or between manufacturers and consumers and thus make our world more interesting.

ZHANG-RUI CHEN, PEI-ZHEN WU, YI-PEI LU, HUNG-YU CHEN, BAO-FA YANG

— Be brave enough to live the moment.

Work awarded with a red dot
Fusion of Era
[Packaging → p. 388]

Zhang-Rui Chen, Pei-Zhen Wu, Yi-Pei Lu, Hung-Yu Chen and Bao-Fa Yang all studied in the Department of Visual Communication Design at the Ming Chi University of Technology in Taiwan. They are experts in different areas including the creation of spatial concepts as well as strategic and administrative matters. As a team, they bring together different points of views and design approaches into integrative solutions.

Where and how do you gather information on trends?
From life and people.

What developments do you currently see in your industry?
Most developments are confused yet unified.

Which of your projects has been
the biggest challenge for you so far?
Our graduation project.

How do you approach new projects?
With a positive attitude and through learning.

What are the qualities a successful
communication designer must have?
He or she needs to have a feeling for beauty, simplicity
and clarity.

What does the future of communication design look like?
It will be about how effectively to convey messages across
different cultures.

KIM ANGIE CICUTTIN
— Curiosity and utopia
bring the best ideas.

**Work awarded with a
red dot: best of the best**
Was hat Venedig zu verstecken? /
What does Venice have to hide?
[Poster Series → p. 338-339]

Kim Angie Cicuttin was born in Udine, Italy, in 1983. She
initially studied product design and graphics at ISIA in
Florence and graduated with a bachelor in 2005. She then
undertook a second-degree course at the visual communication department of the Academy of Art and Design
Offenbach, Germany. She majored in typography, graphic
design and illustration, as well as the design of infograph-
ics. She qualified as a designer in 2011. For several years,
she has been working together with a variety of companies
and agencies in the field of corporate identity, editorial
design and illustration.

What developments do you currently see in your industry?
It is not only the outward appearance that counts, but also
good concepts and content. The trend is away from large,
expensive agencies to small, creative studios.

**What are the qualities a successful
communication designer must have?**
He or she must be able to dream and be inquisitive.

What does the future of communication design look like?
Design is considered holistically; the isolation of the individual disciplines will disappear.

Why did you become a communication designer?
I adore delving into unknown subjects and then visualising
them.

STEPHEN ERCKMANN, DAMON AVAL, JENS KINDLER
— Good communication design plausibly conveys its uniqueness.

**Work awarded with a
red dot: junior prize**
Hochschule Niederrhein /
University of Applied Sciences
[Image Film → p. 326-327]

Stephen Erckmann, Damon Aval and Jens Kindler studied design at Niederrhein University of Applied Sciences. Stephen Erckmann, born in 1987, worked for Ogilvy Düsseldorf during his studies and, since 2011, has been a student trainee at Scholz & Friends Düsseldorf.

Damon Aval, born in 1985, became, after traineeships at Scholz & Friends Düsseldorf, a junior art director at Scholz & Friends OPC and, today, is an art director at BBDO Proximity Berlin.

Jens Kindler, born in 1986, continued to expand on his expertise in motion design and 2D/3D computer animation as an apprentice at the agency lostview.

What developments do you currently see in your industry?
The presentation of brands is converting more and more from a monologue to a dialogue. Social media offers an easy opportunity to address customers. The challenge here lies in distinguishing oneself from the masses.

**Which of your projects has been
the biggest challenge for you so far?**
Every single one, because at the outset it is not clear where the journey will lead and which problems will have to be faced and overcome.

**What are the qualities a successful
communication designer must have?**
They must have a strong interest in society, be able to understand complex emotions and processes, have a keen sense for the novel and unseen, and manage to surprise with their work.

JESSICA GÖTTE
— Keep it simple and straight.

**Work awarded with a
red dot: best of the best**
Guerilla Gardening Set
[Packaging → p. 346-347]

Jessica Goette was born in Rheda-Wiedenbrück, Germany, in 1985. She graduated in graphic design from the University of Applied Sciences in Bielefeld at the beginning of 2012. The subject of her diploma thesis was Guerilla Gardening. During her studies, she gained her first practical experience during a three-month work placement at a small design agency. After finishing her studies, she undertook a six-month work placement at the DDB Tribal advertising agency in Berlin.

What are the qualities a successful communication designer must have?
Above all, in my opinion, a successful communication designer should have passion, but also patience, self-confidence, flexibility and a healthy portion of inquisitiveness. He or she must be able to filter information and not lose sight of what is important.

What do you understand by good communication design?
As design is part of our everyday life and is present in every basic commodity, good design should demonstrate reality and get the essentials across in an innovative and honest way. Good design affects us emotionally, is full of life, different and compelling.

MIKE HOFMAIER
— There is arguing about taste, not about quality.

**Work awarded with a
red dot: best of the best**
Formation GG – Eine visuelle Reise durch
das Deutsche Grundgesetz / Formation GG –
A Visual Guide to the Basic Law of Germany
[Book → p. 332-333]

Mike Hofmaier studied communication design at the
School of Design in Ravensburg, Germany, and worked
as an intern at 2einhalb in Biberach, a communication
office directed by Simon Gallus. He did his internship term
at Braun Engels Gestaltung in Ulm, where he worked on
projects for industry customers, such as LMT and roba-
therm, as well as on the design for the permanent exhibition
"Topography of Terror" in Berlin.

His diploma project "Formation GG" about the German
Basic Law has won several awards, including "Best in
Show" and "Best in Show Student" at the TDC New York
in 2012. In September of the same year, Mike Hofmaier
enrolled at the graduate course "Masterstudio" at the
Academy of Art and Design in Basel.

How do you approach new projects?
First, I clarify my design quality goals. Then I start
unselfconsciously with a broad research on appropriate
contents and off-topic design solutions.

**What are the qualities a successful
communication designer must have?**
Amazement and critical faculty.

Why did you become a communication designer?
Because this occupational field combines geometrical
clarity, artistic expression, technical know-how, psycho-
logical sensitivity and commercial application. You also
have the possibility to constantly engage with topics from
highly diverse areas.

DA WOON JUNG,
JU HO HAN,
YEO KYU KIM,
KYUNG CHAN AHN
— Effort brings success.

Work awarded with a red dot
UNCOMFORTABLE CUP
[Promotion → p. 355]

Da Woon Jung, Ju Ho Han, Yeo Kyu Kim and Kyung Chan Ahn all studied at Gachon University, Korea. Together they won a series of national and international awards, including at the 31st Cheil Worldwide Awards, 47th Korea Design Exhibition, 41st Creativity International Awards Student, iF communication design award, AD STARS Awards and the Chip Shop Awards.

Where and how do you gather information on trends?
We observe people's behaviour whenever and wherever possible because trends start from the individual. If we pay attention to the ordinary happenings around us, like in the subway, in a restaurant, on the street or even when listening to the radio, we are able to notice the trends of the present time.

What are the qualities a successful communication designer must have?
The most important one is hunger for a "big idea". People walk through changes every day thanks to the diversification of media. In this situation, a "big idea" that is accepted by all types of media can be a great advantage.

JIYE KIM
— Those who want to wear
the crown, bear the crown.

Work awarded with a red dot
Thriller 25
[Packaging → p. 386-387]

Jiye Kim, born in 1990 in South Korea, is studying visual design and product design at the Global University in Handong. She is planning to go to the University of Cincinnati to learn more about communication design. Over the years, she has built up many interesting design projects and experiences.

How do you approach new projects?
Whenever a fun idea comes to me I note it down, and put it into practice when I get time.

What do you understand by good communication design?
Good communication design is literally a design that communicates effectively to people.

What kind of project would you like to realise someday?
I want to create my autobiography in the form of a pop-up book.

**Is there a special time of day
when you are exceedingly creative?**
Actually, I prefer night-time. At night, the atmosphere of calm and restfulness helps me to focus my thoughts on something creative.

LAI CHIA-WEI
— Keep dreaming, keep rocking!

Work awarded with a red dot
Care Warming
[Poster → p. 375]

Lai Chia-Wei is currently doing an MA programme in industrial and commercial design at National Taiwan University of Science and Technology. He worked as a design assistant in Shout Studio and is currently a freelance designer. His work has received the iF concept design award and recently has been nominated at the 23rd Golden Melody Awards 2012 (Best Album Design).

What developments do you currently see in your industry?
I believe that graphic design in Taiwan is gradually getting better, even though the average Taiwanese generally has a limited understanding of it. To be honest, I think graphic design in Taiwan hasn't yet found its own cultural style.

How do you approach new projects?
I usually approach new projects with an enthusiastic attitude and curiosity.

What are the qualities a successful communication designer must have?
He should get into the habit of observing all sorts of things and people.

What inspires you?
The idea that I can use my own design work to change the look of the world a bit.

DANIELA LEITNER
— Design meets science.

Work awarded with a red dot
Als das Licht laufen lernte /
How light learned to walk
[Non-Fiction Book → p. 358-359]

Daniela Leitner, born in 1985 in Naila, Upper Franconia, graduated with distinction in communication design from the Karlsruhe University of Arts and Design at the beginning of 2012. Her work has already won several awards, among them the ADC Junior Award. Since 2006, she has worked as a freelance designer, specialising in scientific themes, which she communicates in a humorous and unconventional manner in both text and design.

With her talent to link the world of science with the world of design, she works as a freelance designer for the publishing house Spektrum der Wissenschaft in Heidelberg.

What do you understand by good communication design?
When it is not just a fancy accessory, but possesses and fulfils a true purpose. You recognise good communication design when the meaning of a project reveals itself only in its design or when it surprises users in a way that would not have been possible without the design.

**Is there a special time of day
when you are exceedingly creative?**
In the morning, right after waking up, when the brain cells are still nicely fresh. I often still think about a project in the evening, and then the next morning, possible solutions suddenly come into my mind. As if my brain prefers to work in the background, when I myself don't notice it.

YU-SHING LIN,
CHING CHEN,
YI-CHIEH KUO,
HSUAN-FANG WANG,
CHEN-CHIA CHIANG
— You never know what
you can do until you try.

**Work awarded with a
red dot: best of the best**
Tweens Generation
[Poster Series → p. 340-341]

Yu-Shing Lin, Ching Chen, Yi-Chieh Kuo, Hsuan-Fang Wang
and Chen-Chia Chiang are five very different personalities
who fortunately happened to meet and come together to
work on design. When they unite their different ideas to
produce designs, the result is something special. They in-
tend to maintain their creative thought regardless of rapid
external and technological changes.

What developments do you currently see in your industry?
The advertising industry is trying to use graphic design
more than ever before.

**Which of your projects has been
the biggest challenge for you so far?**
Our most difficult project has been the presentation of our
project "Tweens Generation".

**What are the qualities a successful
communication designer must have?**
Simply to have fun with what he is doing, but also making sure he has studied his material beforehand. In other
words, having fun, but being careful at the same time.

**Is there a special time of day
when you are exceedingly creative?**
We love to work at night with music playing; it is such a
good time for creativity.

LI-HUA LIU
— Life is full of possibilities, if you try hard enough!

Work awarded with a red dot
NO FUR! NO KILL!
[Poster → p. 373]

Li-Hua Liu, born in 1975 in Taiwan, is a Taiwanese comic artist, a Fine Arts PhD graduate at National Taiwan Normal University, as well as a teacher of computer graphic and illustration courses at several universities in Taipei. She won the Best New Comic Artist distinction at the Taiwan Golden Comic Awards in 2011 and, in recent years, has developed a series of comic stories based on Taiwanese culture. Li-Hua Liu's studies focus on graphic design, national design policy, digital comics and the comic industry. She has published and co-published two articles, "Korea National Design Policy" and "A Study on the Global Trends and Developments in Digital Comics", in 2011.

What developments do you currently see in your industry?
The emergence of graphic designers who have become philosophers and advocates of non-violent social movement who have great influence or impact in society.

How do you approach new projects?
I do lots of research in related design cases, articles and studies. If it is a commercial project or a website, I spend a huge amount of time studying the company history, its target audience and market analysis. If it is a personal artwork project, I do brainstorming to develop a wealth of ideas or drafts in order to widen my imagination and to explore different techniques when expressing the idea of the project.

MEAT FOR THE BEAST
VERENA HENNIG
— What we play is life.

Work awarded with a red dot
we are open
[Typographical Short Film → p. 378-379]

Verena Hennig is an illustrator, graphic designer and art director. She has been studying visual communication in the class run by Felten/Girst at the Academy of Fine Arts in Nuremberg since 2007. In 2008, she set up the Chain-sawthis Idea Lab with Suvi Häring. Following internships by Sagmeister Inc. and the Süddeutsche Zeitung Magazin, she founded her own design agency: meat for the beast.

What developments do you currently see in your industry?
The blending of different creative movements such as music, video, installation, typography, art and handicraft. This "cross-over" connects a variety of people and leads to new ideas and freedoms that can create different, surprising qualities.

What are the qualities a successful communication designer must have?
Passion, intelligence, inquisitiveness, courage, reliability, empathy and a healthy portion of obstinacy.

Why did you become a communication designer?
To put my ideas into practice on my own or with others and, in the best case scenario, to be able to inspire and enthral people.

MISA DESIGN
WEI-CHEN YAO
— Design is a work that reaches others.

Work awarded with a red dot
God is watching from above
[Poster → p. 370-371]

Wei-Chen Yao was born in Taiwan. He graduated in design and is currently working on his doctorate degree. In 2009, he started a studio and was engaged to work on brand and corporate design. Realising the problems that young designers are facing, he started out to try to solve them. He loves public speaking and sharing his experiences and even wrote a book about solutions for young designers who are entering the job market. Wei-Chen Yao has an enthusiastic attitude to design and hopes proprietors and young designers will achieve more.

How do you approach new projects?
I use local elements to convey an international message.

What are the qualities a successful communication designer must have?
He needs to have a vision. As communication design is a wide field and differs between countries and industries, a communication designer has to make sure that he either knows enough already or can learn fast enough.

What inspires you?
I don't know exactly where my inspiration comes from but I can get it anytime.

What do you understand by good communication design?
It is a design that people can understand quickly, no matter what their origins are and what their profession is.

NORTE MAGAZINE
DESIGN TEAM
— Everything has its opposite.

Heraclitus

**Work awarded with a
red dot: best of the best**
NORTE #2 – Werden & Sein /
NORTE #2 – Becoming & Being
[Stereo-Thematic Student Magazine → p. 336-337]

In 2008, a group of students of the design department at Wismar University of Applied Sciences got together in order to create their own student magazine, inspired by similar initiatives at other design schools. The aim was to develop a publication based almost entirely on their own requirements, resources and ideas and thus create a platform and forum for experimentation that would showcase their own ideas, content and design tools.

After in-depth analysis, concept work, research and a lot of writing, illustrating and designing, the first edition of NORTE appeared in the summer of 2009. Its contrast topic was "Order & Chaos". In summer 2011, the present #2 appeared, on the subject of "Becoming & Being".

What developments do you currently see in your industry?
Communication design, just like the media world, is steadily getting more complex. Considered concepts that cover several media sectors and take technology into account, are gaining in importance. Structure is becoming more important than the surface; but the most important constants are still good ideas, good content and an adequate design.

What are the qualities a successful communication designer must have?
Good communication designers must want to do what they do and enjoy it. Enthusiasm, alert senses, a basic feeling for aesthetics, a healthy dose of obstinacy and debating skills are important.

ANNA RADOWSKI
— Only those who know
their destination find the way.

**Work awarded with a
red dot: best of the best**
Ein Reisender / A Traveller
[Book → p. 334-335]

Born in 1988, in the Rhineland town of Haan, Anna Radowski spent six months of her school years in Townsville
on the northeast coast of Australia. She continued to
explore other countries while studying at the IN.D Institute
of Design Düsseldorf. Over the three years of her course,
she concentrated on illustration and typography as well as
conceptual work and editorial design.

    After qualifying as a communication designer, she
undertook several work placements in various agencies
in Düsseldorf (BBDO, RAPP and Jahns & Friends) and at
the DuMont publishing house in Cologne. She is currently
working for a national newspaper.

What developments do you currently see in your industry?
At times, communication design no longer corresponds to
people's needs. I think it is important that we get back to
what is really needed.

**Which of your projects has been
the biggest challenge for you so far?**
Always the next one.

How do you approach new projects?
Any task is feasible when it is broken down into small
steps. An overview of the various segments of a project is
the most vital.

What inspires you?
I'm inspired by travel and dancing the tango. The spark for
new ideas always comes from people, colours, smells and
music.

PATRICK RICHTER
— Inspiration is created by the situation.

Work awarded with a red dot
UNICATO – On-Air Design 2012
[Animation Mix → p. 394-395]

Patrick Richter was born in Erfurt, Germany, in 1985. Initially, he studied to be a media designer, but in 2009 moved to studying media art at the Bauhaus University in Weimar. His documentary "Bettina's Job" won a number of awards including Film of the Year 2011 (FiSH, Rostock) and Unicato Award 2011, Best Documentary Film (MDR). It was also shown at important festivals such as the 27th Kassel Documentary Film and Video Festival, the 24th European Media Art Festival (Osnabrück) and video_dumbo 2011 (New York). Patrick Richter received the Bauhaus Scholarship in 2011 and the Bauhaus Graduation Scholarship in 2012. Among others, he has worked for media artist Julian Rosefeldt and the documentary film producer Christiane Büchner.

What are the qualities a successful communication designer must have?
A lot of ambition, enthusiasm and self-confidence. What you demand of yourself drives your ambition and success naturally builds confidence.

What do you understand by good communication design?
In my opinion, at first glance, good design always poses a question and, when you look again, subsequently answers it. Good design manages to awake sustainable emotion in me.

What does the future of communication design look like?
White, pure, light and dirty, used and black. There is constant interplay between dreams and reality. In my opinion, reality will win.

MARC SCHULTES
— Well done is better than well said.

Benjamin Franklin

**Work awarded with a
red dot: best of the best**
Yawar Fiesta
[Experimental Illustration → p. 344-345]

Marc Schultes grew up in the Ruhr area and trained as media designer in Iserlohn, Germany. A year later, he obtained his general qualification for university entrance. In 2005, he began studying both communication design and liberal arts at the Ruhrakademie der Künste in Schwerte, Germany. He qualified as communication designer and independent artist with the work "Yawar Fiesta" in 2011.

Throughout his training and studies, he undertook a number of work placements in the areas of desktop publishing and digital production. Marc Schultes has been running his own advertising agency in Iserlohn/Menden since 2004.

Which of your projects has been the biggest challenge for you so far?
My diploma project and the gamble of self-employment.

How do you approach new projects?
Basically, I always start with an open mind; then work meticulously and frequently too much as a perfectionist.

What are the qualities a successful communication designer must have?
Having an eye for the essential and recognising the right way to communicate.

Why did you become a communication designer?
Even as a child I was always taking photos and making films. I took part in my first Photoshop workshop when I was 12. From then on it was clear that this was the road I wanted to take.

BJÖRN STEINMETZLER
— Illustration = Fantasy

**Work awarded with a
red dot: best of the best**
101 Days of Drawing
[Illustration Diary → p. 342-343]

Björn Steinmetzler studied communication design at the IN.D Institute of Design Düsseldorf. He qualified at the end of 2011 and graduated with the highest grade. In the same year, the Art Directors Club Deutschland singled out his illustrations with an award. Since 2012, he has been freelancing as an illustrator and communication designer for a range of customers.

What inspires you?
I get my inspiration from many things. That could be an article in a magazine, the news, a conversation with a friend or just my imagination.

How do you approach new projects?
Firstly, I familiarise myself with the subject and make a few sketches in my sketchbook. This gives me sufficient material to complete an illustration on the Mac.

Why did you become a communication designer?
My passion is to translate stories, quotes, thoughts and especially feelings into very imaginative images.

BO-HAO SYU,
BO-KAI WEN,
MING-XIAN LIN,
SHAO-CIAN JHENG
— The way to good design is
a road we find after searching.

Work awarded with a red dot
Rise Above
[Poster → p. 372]

Bo-Hao Syu, Bo-Kai Wen, Ming-Xian Lin and Shao-Cian Jheng are students of the Department of Visual Communication Design at Shu-Te University in Kaohsiung City, Taiwan. Beginning with the concept of the work, "The way to good design is a road we find after searching", they developed a serial of visual recognition systems for their work, including posters, special booklets, peripheral products, motion graphics and the exhibition design of the event venue.

Where and how do you gather information on trends?
We obtain information on trends from the yearbooks published by different international award competitions as well as websites on design.

With whom would you like to work together? Why?
We would like to work with Pentagram, because it is one of the most prestigious design companies. It would be very exciting to do so.

How do you approach new projects?
Stay passionate and apply whatever you learn to the next project.

What do you understand by good communication design?
Good communication design needs to please its audience and the work should convey the intended message.

SO YEON YU
— Simplicity is the best way.

**Work awarded with a
red dot: best of the best**
T
[Corporate Design → p. 330-331]

So Yeon Yu, born in 1987 in Seoul, Korea, graduated in visual communication design from the University of Seoul in 2012 and continues to work on various types of design.

**Which of your projects has been
the biggest challenge for you so far?**
My diploma thesis. It was a challenge for me to express these various kinds of work such as programming, font design and brand identity in a single project.

How do you approach new projects?
I usually collect information and try to find an easier and clearer way to fulfil the designated function.

What inspires you?
Most of my inspiration stems from my feelings.

What do you understand by good communication design?
Good communication design does not require much explanation. The content that the designer wants to express should be clear and easy to understand immediately.

ZHANG YANGSHENG
— Design is born to communicate.

Work awarded with a red dot
Bright Summit Science
[Corporate Identity System → p. 352-353]

Zhang Yangsheng was born in 1978 in Guixi, China, and started his studies at Lanzhou University in 2011. He has always been interested in art and design and he obtained his first degree from Jiangxi Normal University in 2000. Subsequently, he worked for ten years in the clothing industry.

In 2003, he co-founded DOCARE Clothing Co., Ltd. in Shanghai and, in 2005, founded OKIN Culture Communication Co., Ltd., a company engaged primarily in public welfare activities. Unable to accept the company's philosophy change, he left in October 2011 and began a commercial design- and brand planning business. In August 2012, he set up lovewell textile technology Co., LTD. in Shanghai, a company for brand design textiles. He has been awarded the National Outstanding Brand Management Division Prize.

What developments do you currently see in your industry?
Thanks to the revolution of information dissemination and communication triggered by the Internet, Chinese designers have begun to adhere to international educational and innovation practices. As a result, their creative design has risen to a high level.

What kind of project would you like to realise someday?
I would like to create some public projects about people and the urban environment, because the urban development, environment, transport, etc. of many Chinese cities have fallen behind the changes in society. Cities should make the lives of people better, not make them feel ever more confused.

Jury Portraits

01

PROF. MICHEL DE BOER
NETHERLANDS

01   **The puzzle of life
     and its religions**
     An illustration for the month
     September of the Ahn Graphics
     calendar.

02   **Introduction poster of the
     "Arita Sans" typeface**
     A new corporate typeface for
     Amorepacific, a cosmetic company
     in South Korea and other Asian
     countries, owning more than 30
     brands. It connects the various
     brands by an endorsed typographic
     design system.

Prof. Michel de Boer, born in 1954, studied at the Academy of Fine Arts and Higher Technologies in Rotterdam. In 1989, he became creative managing partner at Studio Dumbar, where he was responsible for the creative output up till 2010. From 2011, he started his independent design company: MdB Associates with liaising offices in Germany, Korea, Hong Kong and Malaysia. With more than 25 years of experience in corporate design, brand identity and graphic design, Michel de Boer has worked for clients around the world such as Apple, Allianz, Shell, Nike, Randstad, General Motors China, TNT, Woongjin as well as the Dutch and the South Korean government.

He has won numerous awards, takes part in international design conferences as well as in the jury of international design competitions. In 2005, Michel de Boer became professor at the Istituto Universitario di Architettura in Venice, Italy. From 2011, he has run a design course, Comunicazione d'Impresa (corporate image), at ISIA in Urbino, Italy.

Next to this, he has been working to set up a design educational programme in China, to be started in 2013. He is a member of several professional organisations, and he is the co-initiator of the start-up of a new design joint venture in Shanghai.

02

— THE MARKET IS DESPERATE FOR TALENTED DESIGNERS WITH A GENUINE INDIVIDUAL APPROACH.

What do you watch out for while evaluating works?
The criteria are a series of mind facts. First for the conceptual idea, then the visual execution, then the communicative values and finally I try to imagine if it works for this particular client/market.

What does being a juror for the "red dot award: communication design" mean to you?
It is always an honour to be asked. Next to that, it is nice to work with fellow designers and friends from all over the world and last but not least, to be confronted with good designs.

A designer can stand out with an idealistic idea or go with the flow of the client's wishes. How do you see yourself in this situation?
Design is always a struggle. To be uncertain in the beginning is part of the game. But finally, you need to make decisions by finding the best creative solution which should actually work for a certain market, thus for a client. To present this in a convincing manner is crucial.

What special advice would you give to a talented young designer entering this field?
To stay close to themselves; but with an understanding of the crowd. The market is desperate for talented designers with a genuine approach who are conceptually strong and have the power to visualise it uniquely: connecting design to the business – I guess that's it.

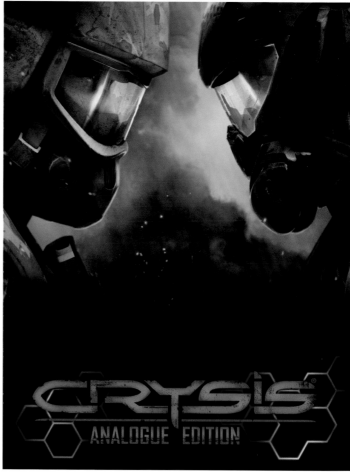

01

PROF. DR.
LINDA BREITLAUCH
GERMANY

01   **Crysis Analogue Edition**
Board game, 2012

02   **First Ade**
Prototype of a serious game
for kids and teenagers with
type 1 diabetes, 2010
[content4med GmbH,
King Baudouin Foundation,
Ion Games]

Prof. Dr. Linda Breitlauch initially studied business economics before she graduated in film and television scriptwriting from the Film & Television Academy (HFF) in Babelsberg, Germany. In 2008, she completed her PhD on dramatic composition in computer games. In addition to working as a project manager in the export and publishing sectors, she has been the creative producer of several film projects, has written film scripts and game concepts as well as scientific and expert articles, among other things.

In 2007, Linda Breitlauch was appointed Europe's first female professor of game design at the Mediadesign University of Applied Sciences in Düsseldorf, Germany. There, she teaches and researches with a special focus on serious/applied games and dramatic composition.

Furthermore, she works as an evaluator and is a consultant in the areas of media didactics and interactive storytelling. In 2011, she was nominated for the European Women in Games Hall of Fame award.

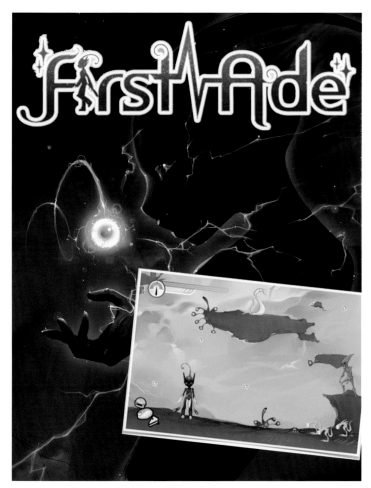

02

How did you experience this year's jury process?

First of all, it was an opportunity to see fantastic submissions and great design. The adjudication process this year was marked by stimulating discussions and a creative exchange with colleagues from many different creative fields. It is exciting to bring the focus of game design into the discussion on the possibilities of cross-media staging and thus be able to contribute to an intensive exchange on innovative ideas. The diversity of the submissions together with the venue of the adjudication, the red dot design museum, is always inspirational.

What do you watch out for while evaluating works?

The basic criteria in evaluating a design is creativity of the idea, the quality of craftsmanship and realisation, and, last but not least, functionality. Concerning the different project requirements, many aspects have to be taken into consideration, e.g. the budget, demands toward the project or the different media used in the different categories. This year we saw several submissions addressing topics relevant to society.

What does being a juror for the "red dot award: communication design" mean to you?

It is an honour to adjudicate excellent design. Many works, including those of up-and-coming designers, are inspiring and remarkable in many respects. The red dot design award is a distinction that honours excellent (game) design independent of the genre, rather than being an industry prize. It thus also acknowledges the cultural and social significance of computer games.

A designer can stand out with an idealistic idea or go with the flow of the client's wishes. How do you see yourself in this situation?

It is important to serve the project and designers can do this best if they have a vision. In the end, the product has to work for its target group. This means that the designer must be able to strike a good balance between typical expectations and visionary innovation. In game development, for example, and in particular in the area of the so-called "serious games", which is my research focus, clients usually need not only a specialist for the particular theme but also the expert knowledge of both a game designer and an educator. It is very important to know and understand the target group and the needs it has. However, there is more to a good and effective game: visionary approaches, extraordinary ideas and outstanding game design are all essential.

What special advice would you give to a talented young designer entering this field?

In the area of game design, education and craftsmanship are particularly important. However, it is even more important to be critical of one's own talent, yet, at the same time, always believe in oneself. To sharpen one's perception, build up one's own profile, be a good team player. To observe and understand the world in all its facets. And most importantly: think everything even if it seems impossible. Creativity knows no limits – only budget does.

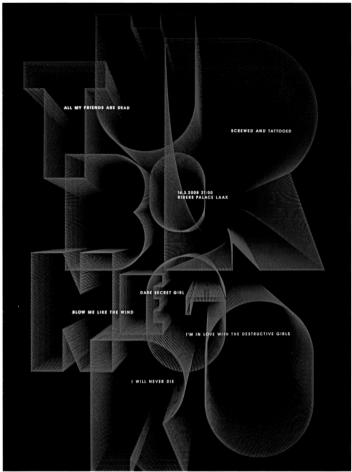

01

REMO CAMINADA
SWITZERLAND

01 **Turbo Negro**
Three-colour silkscreen printing
by Serigraphie Uldry,
for Riders Palace, Laax, Switzerland
[120 x 170 cm, 2008]

02 **Businesscard for a dentist**
Three-colour offset printing for Anita
Wehrle-Lechmann, Switzerland
[2008]

Remo Caminada was born in Vrin, Switzerland, in 1974.
After becoming a trained architectural draughtsman and
five years of being trained as a primary school teacher,
he started studying interaction design at the Zurich University of the Arts in 2001.

In 2002, he switched to visual design and graduated in
2006. While being a student he worked at Sean Perkins's
design company North and James Goggin's design studio
Practise, both of which are located in London.

Later, he founded his own design offices based in
Swiss Sagogn, in Amsterdam and in Zurich. Remo Caminada has received many renowned international awards.

— SWIMMING AGAINST THE TIDE IS HARD WORK BUT IT BUILDS MUSCLES.

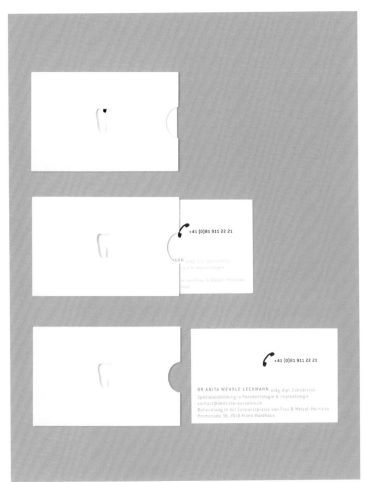

02

How did you experience this year's jury process?

As is the case every year, the decision-making process was very well prepared by red dot. This gave the jury a quick, good overview of all submissions which made the decisions very fair and transparent. There are always some good and very good submissions, but in the end "only" a handful are outstanding. With a few exceptions, we were of one mind when it came to selecting the awards that were given.

What do you watch out for while evaluating works?

I don't really mind by what means a submission awakens my interest. The main thing is that it does so. I welcome work that is fresh and new. Good craftsmanship is required to do a good job but it is not enough for a top award. Personally, I like it when a project has a strong conceptual approach and is realised in an appropriate visual style. This gives the project an independent character, prevents it from being inconsistent and may perhaps even make it appear rather irritating or provocative. I also like it when poetry and humour are used in the implementation.

What does being a juror for the "red dot award: communication design" mean to you?

It is an honour for me to be invited to join such a renowned international jury to make a statement about developments in design. Of course, opinion is not truth, but an opinion can help by providing an additional point of view to people's existing personal one. Just as every work should be unique, I should also try to look at and judge each submission individually.

A designer can stand out with an idealistic idea or go with the flow of the client's wishes. How do you see yourself in this situation?

Swimming against the tide is hard work but it builds muscles. I don't think that a designer today should be someone who just implements a project; in my opinion he should rather be the creative force behind a design project. The combined energy of a strong designer and a good customer who is prepared to stick his neck out can result in something outstanding. The phrase "the customer always comes first" has little place in a design process. Rather, an idea or a project should itself be considered to come first so that both the customer and the designer will serve it.

Is there a special time of day when you are exceedingly creative?

I'm creative around the clock. I let thoughts mature over days and weeks without processing or assessing them. As soon as they have come together in focused creative energy, I put the ideas down on paper. Sometimes this happens easily and quickly, sometimes not at all. Failure must be part of developing something new.

What special advice would you give to a talented young designer entering this field?

Be distinctive, be bold and, if needed, be irksome and insistent. Try to push through your own ideas and visions because this automatically allows you to contribute to the development of design. What is scorned today will be loved tomorrow. Finally, be yourself and the result will be superb work.

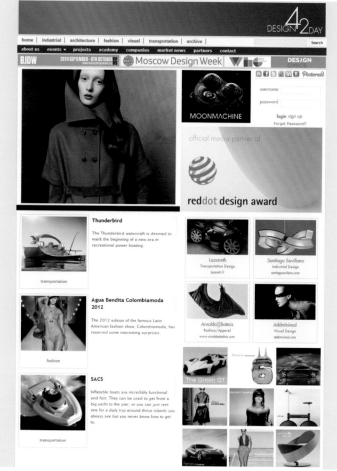

01

RICCARDO CAPUZZO
ITALY

01   **Design42Day website**
The simple layout works as
a frame to expose the selection.

Riccardo Capuzzo studied visual and web design at the
Scuola Politecnica di Design in Milan. In 2004, he moved
to Chicago for two years working for a company as a visual
designer. Afterwards, he wanted to change the environment around him and started working in Istanbul as a
freelancer. From 2006 to 2008, he was commuting between Milan and Istanbul as he used to have some clients
in Milan as well.

In 2008, Capuzzo started a blog as he did not like any
available magazines. He wanted to show the real good
design of today. What was actually meant to be a hobby
turned into a proper web magazine in 2010. The same
year, Patrick Abbattista, one of his mates in kindergarten,
joined the project. Within two years, the magazine became
one of the most prestigious voices of the design world and
a partner of Beijing Design Week, Moscow Design Week,
International Talent Support, Istituto Europeo di Design,
red dot design award, agIdeas, Adobe Design Achievement
Awards, Electrolux Design Lab and many others.

How did you experience your premiere as a juror
for the "red dot award: communication design"?
Overall, I can say that three things stood out: good design,
good people and good food. It was wonderfully entertaining. And assessing approximately 200 projects in two days
with highly praised professionals is an opportunity to fully
immerse yourself in the world of design, which exceeds
many experiences in graduate school.

What do you watch out for while evaluating works?
I would say that the first visual impact is very important
for any communication project. It is easy to categorise a
project as "good" or "bad" in a couple of seconds. After
this initial "coup d'œil", I try to understand the train of
thoughts and the motivations that made the designer
finalise the project the way it is presented before me.

What does being a juror for the
"red dot award: communication design" mean to you?
It is like getting a chance to play for the team you have
always cheered for. It is a great honour to be able to make
a contribution to such a prestigious award and it is a
remarkable reference for both my clients and business
partners.

A designer can stand out with an idealistic idea
or go with the flow of the client's wishes.
How do you see yourself in this situation?
It depends on the client's know-how on the subject of the
project. If the client knows what they are talking about,
they can give precious, perhaps even unique, advice to the
designer, who, in turn, can reach a level that would otherwise be out of reach, without the clients' initial input. If
this is not the case, the designer must use all of his or her
persuasive skills to mould the client's opinion. Metaphorically speaking: I would not tell a surgeon where to operate
and, in some circumstances, neither should the designer's
clients when discussing the details of finalising projects.

Is there a special time of day
when you are exceedingly creative?
Nighttime is surely the best time to think without any
distractions. I must say that lots of good ideas come to me
when I am in a boring or vapid situation that I can't get out
of so I'm somewhat obliged to start thinking. This is where
the creative wheels start rolling.

What special advice would you give to
a talented young designer entering this field?
Don't fossilise in your own field if you are a visual designer.
Watch fashion shows, go to motor shows or fairs to get a
wider view of what design is. This is because we all speak
the same language with colours, shapes, cuts, shades and
so forth.

01

LIZÁ DEFOSSEZ RAMALHO
PORTUGAL

Lizá Defossez Ramalho has a BA Honours degree from the Faculty of Fine Arts of the University of Porto and a master's degree in design research from the Faculty of Fine Arts of the University of Barcelona, where she is currently doing her doctorate with a scholarship from the Foundation for Science and Technology.

In 1995, in partnership with designer Artur Rebelo, she founded R2, a Porto-based design studio specialising in visual communication design. At R2, she has worked for a wide range of cultural organisations, artists and architects. She has been lecturing in graphic design since 1999 and is currently teaching in the design and multimedia course at the University of Coimbra. Lizá Defossez Ramalho is a member of the Alliance Graphique Internationale.

01 **Go with God**
Typographic installation in a chapel in Lisbon. The texts, with expressions that refer to God, look as if they are coming out from the chapel's wall.

02 **House of Tales**
Typographic intervention in concrete in the ceilings of an art residence in Porto.

— DESIGNERS HAVE TO DEVELOP NEW APPROACHES, AND TRY TO DO THINGS DIFFERENTLY.

02

How did you experience your premiere as a juror for the "red dot award: communication design"?

Being a juror for the first time was a great experience! It was a very intense process, with a lot of interesting discussion with the other jury members. The whole process was very enriching due to the exchange of knowledge and perspectives. It was a chance to experience, analyse and discuss a lot of design projects inside the sublime red dot design museum.

What do you watch out for while evaluating works?

I especially look at the conceptual approach, adequacy, innovation, typography, coherence and formal quality.

What does being a juror for the "red dot award: communication design" mean to you?

I was very pleased with this invitation. As a participant in the past editions, it was very interesting to get to know the other side of this competition, the discussion process and criteria for evaluating design.

A designer can stand out with an idealistic idea or go with the flow of the client's wishes. How do you see yourself in this situation?

We must stand out. Designers have to develop new approaches, and try to do things differently. In the studio I run with Artur Rebelo, we have done this right from the beginning; and back then, our proposals were systematically rejected. But then, one day, a project was accepted and it made up for all the rest. More recently, we have had the opportunity to work with people who gave us a great degree of freedom. We'd taken many risks developing proposals that sometimes went beyond the client's initial request, pursuing lines of enquiry in which we believed but we were almost certain would result in rejection. Nonetheless, we continued to face some rejections. We are also not utopian. We have learned how to strike the right balance.

Is there a special time of day when you are exceedingly creative?

It can happen anytime, anywhere. But I had several great flashes of inspiration very early in the morning. No interruptions.

What special advice would you give to a talented young designer entering this field?

The search for new concepts, new approaches, debate and collaboration with other fields of knowledge are all essential for those who want to work in this field.

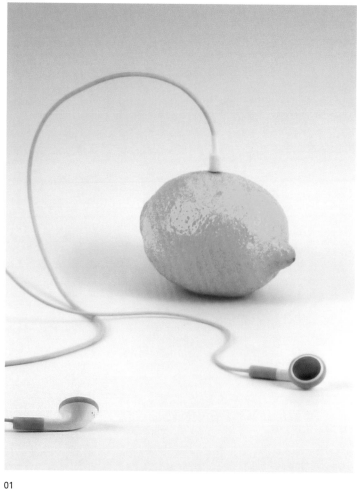

01

RAINER HIRT
GERMANY

01 **Sound of Citrus**
/02 What does a flavour sound like?
A sound design study for
Symrise AG.

Rainer Hirt, born in 1979, studied communication design at the University of Applied Sciences in Constance. After graduating, he founded "audity" together with Michael Hoppe and Markus Reiner, an agency that specialises in audio branding, audio interaction and audio experience.

Back in 2003, he had already founded the corporate sound Internet platform audio-branding.de, a well-known expert resource on the topic of sound branding. Rainer Hirt is, among other things, the author and co-editor of the compendium "Audio-Branding".

He is in charge of research projects at various universities and, in 2009, founded the first independent institution for acoustic brand communication, the "Audio Branding Academy", together with Kai Bronner and Cornelius Ringe.

02

— I PAY CLOSE ATTENTION TO STRATEGIC AIMS AND BRAND POSITIONING THROUGH DESIGN.

How did you experience this year's jury process?
The whole collegial decision-making process was highly professional and the jury's deliberations were held in a friendly atmosphere.

What do you watch out for while evaluating works?
I try to put myself in the position of the recipients and to look at the work and judge it from their point of view.

What does being a juror for the "red dot award: communication design" mean to you?
It is an honour for me that the joint decisions I took with my colleagues on the jury and our selection lend a small but precise impetus to the quality of design.

A designer can stand out with an idealistic idea or go with the flow of the client's wishes. How do you see yourself in this situation?
In my opinion, design must send a clear message. Design moulds and transforms content into something which can be perceived by a multitude of senses. In my work, I therefore pay close attention to strategic aims and brand positioning through design. I therefore tend to focus on customers and users.

What special advice would you give to a talented young designer entering this field?
A healthy mixture of naivety, the urge to explore new frontiers and not taking myself too seriously.

01

PROF. LAURENT LACOUR
GERMANY

01 **Corporate design for the magazine "form – The Making of Design"**
The design of the magazine and website combines contemporary elements with the austerity typical of "form".

02 **New corporate design for the Museum of Modern Art in Frankfurt/Main**
It is based on the triangular shape of the building and the design of the interior rooms.

03 **Siemens stand for home**
/04 **appliances at the IFA Berlin with Franken\Architekten**
Design and architecture with the focus on branding, product communication and the design of interactive exhibits.

Laurent Lacour studied visual communication and art at the Academy of Art and Design Offenbach, Germany. He is an associate of the design studio hauser lacour, based in Frankfurt/Main. hauser lacour carries out extensive, award-winning corporate design projects.

He developed corporate identity programmes and ran communication projects for the Deutsche Börse Group, Munich Re, Sony, De Gruyter, Bavarian Re and Siemens. But also in the cultural sector, i.e. the corporate design for the Museum of Modern Art in Frankfurt/Main, the Kölner Philharmonie, the Frankfurter Kunstverein, the Museum of Contemporary Art in Siegen and further institutions and companies. hauser lacour developed book- and magazine designs such as the current layout of the design magazine "form".

He taught visual communication as design research at the universities of Zurich, Basel, Karlsruhe and Darmstadt (Karlsruhe and Darmstadt as a visiting and substitute professor). Since April 2011, he has held a full professorship at the University of Applied Sciences in Düsseldorf, Germany.

02

03 / 04

How did you experience this year's jury process?
The work was great this year. We could see a definite increase in quantity and quality in the digital sector. The members of the jury worked together very harmoniously. As we were able to take clear-cut decisions very quickly and efficiently, we had enough time to relish the brilliant ideas of some projects.

What do you watch out for while evaluating works?
In the digital sector, the focus is on holism. In order to take clear decisions, it is necessary to explore the complexity of the medium in a virtual manner and to try to detect latent potential. After all, the many and various possibilities to be found in the linking of the themes means that good ideas are not immediately obvious.

**What does being a juror for the
"red dot award: communication design" mean to you?**
It is simply a great privilege. I learn a lot and can actually see what standards prevail on the market, where visionary work is being done, and who is producing great stuff and why. That information is very helpful in two respects. I can use it in my teaching and keep my students up to date on the hottest trends, and, as constant benchmarking, to influence the work of my agency. What could be better?

**A designer can stand out with an idealistic idea
or go with the flow of the client's wishes.
How do you see yourself in this situation?**
Like many of my colleagues, I feel that the era of the designer who works alone is over. Individualists may possibly find niches, but they no longer have a substantial impact on innovation. Today, innovation means teamwork with customers and various other people from a wide range of lines of business. Effective cooperation with the customer is what I like best. Of course, that doesn't mean that I am an opportunist who is prepared to do just anything and to sacrifice quality.

**Is there a special time of day
when you are exceedingly creative?**
Sometimes, when I wake up in the middle of the night, I think, "wow, what a stroke of genius". I write the idea down, only to realise the next morning that it wasn't that great. But I'm certain that one day a mega idea will come along and it will change everything and I'll live happily ever after. Oh dear, there I go, dreaming again.

**What special advice would you give to
a talented young designer entering this field?**
To quote my colleague Prof. Holger Jacobs: "Work more – talk less". I think that says it all.

01

PROF. APEX LIN
PANG-SOONG
TAIWAN

01 **Two Sides of the Strait**
The work symbolises two brothers
who need to work hard on their own
but at the same time should still keep
a good relationship with each other.
[Poster 70 x 100 cm, 2010]

02 **My Homeland**
This work assembles the images
of the postcards Apex Lin Pang-Soong
sent from around the world since 2007 –
all in the shape of Taiwan Island
that is always in his heart, facing the
colourful world.
[Poster 70 x 100 c   2009]

Prof. Apex Lin Pang-Soong, born in Donggang, Taiwan, in
1957, received his MFA from the Graduate Institute of Fine
Arts at the National Taiwan Normal University, where he
is currently professor in the Department of Visual Design.
He established the Taiwan Image Poster Design Association in 1990, and in 1993 he was listed among the top 12 of
corporate identity designers in Asia by New DECOMAS.

In 2002, he was honoured with the Icograda Achievement Award. In 2003, he was listed among the 100 most
interesting graphic designers in the world by Phaidon. In
2004, Apex Lin Pang-Soong received the First Outstanding
Award of Commercial Creativity by the Chinese Ministry of
Economic Affairs (MOEA), and in 2005 he was awarded
the Design for Asia Award by the Hong Kong Design Centre
as commendation of his great artistic influence in Asia.

He has been an acclaimed mentor of design in Taiwan
and was the winner of the 2007 National Award for Litera-
ture and Arts. In 2011, he was honoured with the Icograda
Education Award.

02

How did you experience this year's jury process?
It was a great experience. The jury process was smooth and pleasant.

What do you watch out for while evaluating works?
I appreciate original concepts and works that express different aspects of culture and visionary ideas. I also value new ways of skills that strengthen the idea of the work.

**What does being a juror for the
"red dot award: communication design" mean to you?**
It was my great honour to be the juror of this award. I enjoyed it a lot when seeing excellent works from different parts of the world. And I was impressed by the creativity and passion of the designers who participated and also by the works with various views and deep thinking; they all made this judging process a fantastic experience!

**A designer can stand out with an idealistic idea
or go with the flow of the client's wishes.
How do you see yourself in this situation?**
It's inevitable to be asked to go with the client's wishes when you are a designer. As a result, trying to find the balance between the client's wishes and your own idealistic idea is rather important and necessary. At the earlier stage of being a designer, you have to try to find the balance and build your own idea/style at the same time so that when your style/idea is mature enough, the clients will find you and respect you because of your idea.

**Is there a special time of day
when you are exceedingly creative?**
Ever since I became a grandfather, only couple of months ago, I always feel extremely energetic and creative when being in touch with my young grandson. There is no specific creative hour for me. I tend to get inspirations from day to day life.

**What special advice would you give to
a talented young designer entering this field?**
Be open-minded: to understand and respect different culture/manner/thinking. Be concerned with the big issue: to find out the reasons and results of something important, such as global warming, political relationship between far eastern countries, EU economical crisis... etc. Be humble: it is always a valuable attitude for everyone, no matter who you are.

01

PROF. UWE LOESCH
GERMANY

01 **Myth Krupp**
Ruhr Museum, Essen
[Poster 84 x 119 cm, 2012]

02 **AGI**
Alliance Graphique Internationale –
German Members 1954–2011
[Book, published by hesign Berlin, 2011]

03 **fairy-tale: Little Red Riding Hood
and other monstrosities**
Klingspor Museum Offenbach
[Poster 84 x 119 cm, 2012]

In 1968, Uwe Loesch founded his own "studio for visual and verbal communication" in Düsseldorf. His extraordinary graphic and typographic work is published and exhibited worldwide. The Museum of Modern Art in New York has been collecting and showing his works since 1983.

He has received many awards such as, among others, the Gold Medal for Corporate Design of the Art Directors Club of Europe and the "red dot: grand prix". In 2009, he was honoured with the Gutenberg Prize of the City of Leipzig and in 2011 with the Tapani Aartomaa Prix of the International Poster Biennial in Lahti, Finland.

In 1985, he was appointed professor for multimedia at the University of Applied Sciences in Düsseldorf. From 1990 to 2008, he held a professorship for communication design at the University of Wuppertal.

Uwe Loesch is past president of the German members of the Alliance Graphique Internationale. He is a member of the Art Directors Club for Germany and the Type Directors Club New York. He was president of the juries of international biennales, e.g. in Warsaw, Lahti, Brno, Fort Collins/Colorado, Chaumont, Moscow and Hangzhou.

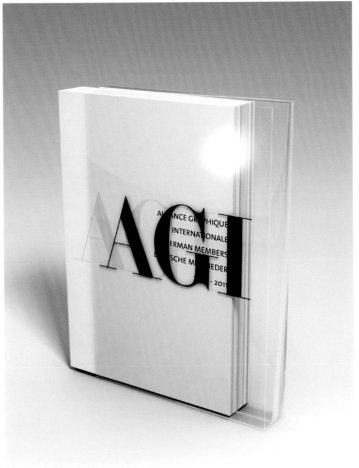

02

03

I AM ONLY ONE OF THE "12 ANGRY MEN" AND OF COURSE INCORRUPTIBLE.

How did you experience this year's jury process?
It was "The same procedure as every year!" Anyhow, I am surprised over and over again about the steadfastness and the staying power of the jury members. Jury work is a heavy work!

What do you watch out for while evaluating works?
Is it love at first sight? Or do I need a marriage broker? What you see is (not always) what you get!

What does being a juror for the "red dot award: communication design" mean to you?
I am only one of the "12 Angry Men" and, of course, incorruptible.

A designer can stand out with an idealistic idea or go with the flow of the client's wishes. How do you see yourself in this situation?
Everyone has three wishes. Every good design job is a win-win game.

Is there a special time of day when you are exceedingly creative?
At the end of the day, after work.

What special advice would you give to a talented young designer entering this field?
Don't follow me. Trust yourself.

01/02

TYRON MONTGOMERY
GERMANY

01 **Quest**
/02 Puppet animation film,
produced in cooperation
with Thomas Stellmach.

Tyron Montgomery, born in Ireland in 1967, first studied physics in Wuppertal, before changing to the School of Art and Design Kassel to study visual communication with an emphasis on film, animation and photography. In 1996, he gained international success in one fell swoop: he won the Oscar in Los Angeles and worldwide over 40 other awards for his film "Quest".

In 1997, he founded his own film production company, working, among others, in Bristol and London as director of animated commercials for TV and cinema. One year later, "Unser Garten" (Our Garden), the world's first completely digitally produced puppet animation, was created for the German Federal Environment Ministry, and he worked on the German motion picture "Die grüne Wolke" (The Green Cloud) as the VFX supervisor.

In 2000, he founded AUGENREIZ, an agency especially for Internet, multimedia and film, in Munich. Since 1996, Tyron Montgomery has been a lecturer at different universities, among them the Bavarian Academy for Television (BAF) in Unterföhring.

— THE REUNION WITH THE RED DOT TEAM
AND COLLEAGUES FROM AROUND THE WORLD,
THE LIVELY EXCHANGE WITH THE OTHER
JUDGES AND JURIES, MANY EXCITING ENTRIES
AS WELL AS THE EVER-INSPIRING EXHIBITION
IN THE RED DOT DESIGN MUSEUM – THAT IS
WHAT FOR ME THE JUDGING PROCESS OF THE
"RED DOT AWARD: COMMUNICATION DESIGN"
MAKES SO SPECIAL AND JOYFUL.

01

MALGOSIA
PAWLIK-LENIARSKA
POLAND

01   **Dulux portfolio**
     Redesign of Akzo Nobel's
     inspiring brand to repaint
     your world with.

02   **Lay's**
     New design for the product line
     of the crisps with more taste.

Malgosia Pawlik-Leniarska is managing partner of Dragon Rouge Warsaw, the first branding agency in Central and Eastern Europe she founded in 1994. She started her marketing career at Colgate-Palmolive, where she was responsible for introducing new products into the market. As a consulting director, she managed projects for major company clients in the region such as Coca-Cola, Nestlé, Danone, Kamis, Bahlsen, Hochland, Pernod Ricard, ETI and others. Committed to brand design education, she lectures at the Brand Strategy School and at the Academy of Fine Arts in Warsaw.

She is president of the Brand Design Club and board member of the epda (European Packaging Design Association), she holds an MA in cultural studies and an MBA from the International Business School and the University of Illinois.

— IT IS A GREAT HONOUR AND PRIVILEGE TO JUDGE WORKS OF THE MOST TALENTED DESIGNERS IN THE WORLD.

02

How did you experience your premiere as a juror
for the "red dot award: communication design"?
It was simply a great experience. Exchanging views with
the other jury members, understanding different points of
view and, on the other hand, discovering similarities in the
perception of design. My jury group was coming from very
different cultures: Taiwan, the Netherlands and Poland.
And surprisingly enough, our verdicts were unanimous in
most cases. When assessing works from Asia, which came in
a high number this year, I needed some explanations of the
intricacies of Chinese lettering and colour symbolism. But it
became apparent that good design is a universal language
that works everywhere regardless of cultural differences.

What do you watch out for while evaluating works?
For me, good design should be original, unique and should
have a power to involve people emotionally. It should make
them feel good, smile or think, and raise their curiosity.
It should have an influence on people, not just be simply
aesthetic. It is great when design has some social impact,
works for a good cause, considers sustainability issues;
there were some good examples of that among the works
sent to red dot this year.

What does being a juror for the
"red dot award: communication design" mean to you?
It is a great honour to judge works of the most talented
designers in the world. It is also a huge responsibility. By
awarding a work, we have influence on what will be the
new standards of the industry, the benchmarks of excellence that will inspire and drive other designers next year.

A designer can stand out with an idealistic idea
or go with the flow of the client's wishes.
How do you see yourself in this situation?
This is a big question, especially as I am managing a design
agency, not being a designer myself. I think the role of a designer is to show new solutions, new ideas to the client, not
to draw the images from the client's head. These solutions
should come from very good understanding of the client's
goals and of the people to whom the design is addressed.
If a designer is able to show this link, a smart client will
accept. I believe a designer should not give up easily. If he
really believes in the idea, he should do his best to find
strong arguments to defend it.

Is there a special time of day
when you are exceedingly creative?
There are rather specific moments than a special time of
day: talking with inspiring people, driving a car outside a
city or flying.

What special advice would you give to a
talented young designer entering this field?
Look at more: read a lot, watch films, listen to interesting
people, go to festivals, exhibitions, listen to music... Be
curious. Ask questions. Don't give up easily. Look for better.
Have fun!

01

DR. CORINNA RÖSNER
GERMANY

01 **Unplugged.**
   Mirko Borsche. Design Works!
   Die Neue Sammlung – The International
   Design Museum Munich.
   [Exhibition 13.01. – 18.03.2012]

02 **Deadly and Brutal.**
   Film posters from Ghana
   Die Neue Sammlung – The International
   Design Museum Munich.
   [Exhibition 01.04. – 26.06.2011]

Dr. Corinna Rösner, art historian, is chief curator and
deputy director of "Die Neue Sammlung – The International Design Museum Munich". She studied art history,
archaeology and ethnology at the University of Munich
and took her PhD in 1988.

As a curator, she has worked at Die Neue Sammlung
since 1990, accompanying the plannings and realisation
of the museum's new buildings in Munich and Nuremberg
until their opening in 2000 and 2002. She was involved
in the development of the concept for the permanent
exhibitions in those buildings as regards content and
exhibition design.

She has been the curator and co-organiser of numerous
temporary exhibitions of the museum as well as a co-au-
thor and author of publications and exhibition catalogues
of Die Neue Sammlung.

02

— SELECTING THE BEST WORK AFTER A DISCUSSION WITH THE JURY COLLEAGUES IS A RESPONSIBILITY.

How did you experience your premiere as a juror for the "red dot award: communication design"?
Exciting and stimulating. It is like climbing a mountain; you need stamina and concentration. The overall level was very high, even among the rising generation of designers – but I wish there had been more really cheeky works.

What do you watch out for while evaluating works?
Unusual ideas which transcend clichés; startling new solutions of a high international standard.

What does being a juror for the "red dot award: communication design" mean to you?
Selecting the best work after a discussion with the other jury members is a huge responsibility and an opportunity to take part in a truly international exchange with experts who have different cultural backgrounds.

A designer can stand out with an idealistic idea or go with the flow of the client's wishes. How do you see yourself in this situation?
Idealism is the opposite of realism; neither results in visionary products. It is the designer's job to mould a company's visions into something that is credible, acceptable and memorable.

What special advice would you give to a talented young designer entering this field?
The musician Don Henley hit the nail on the head: "Let hope inspire you, but let not idealism blind you. Don't look back, you can never look back."

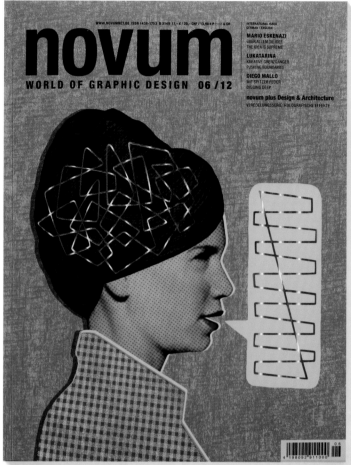

01

BETTINA SCHULZ
GERMANY

01 **novum – world of graphic design**
Cover of the magazine's issue 6, 2012.
The cover features foil stamping carried
out by Gräfe Druck & Veredelung.
[Design: Lizzie Roberts]

02 **novum – world of graphic design**
Cover of the magazine's issue 8, 2012.
The cover of this issue was finished
with daylight luminous paint
by Stainer Schriften & Siebdruck.
[Design: Duygu Ölcek]

Bettina Schulz, born in Munich, Germany, in 1974, has
been editor-in-chief of the international journal "novum –
world of graphic design" since 2001. She joined the editorial
staff of the magazine in 1994.

Bettina Schulz also works for national and international magazines and for a range of clients in different sectors
as a freelance writer and editor.

She is a co-founder of the "Creative Paper Conference"
in Munich and has already been a member of design juries
on a number of occasions, e.g. for the European Design
Awards, for the Best of Corporate Publishing award, for
the MfG competition of the German printing and media
industries federation (bvdm), the Monaco de Luxe Packaging
Award and the biannual diploma awards presentation at
the U5 design academy.

02

How did you experience this year's jury process?
I felt that the editorial design category was a very impressive demonstration of the fact that the print medium is alive and well. The increasing use of interaction between materials and finishings shows what a magnificent effect can be achieved with tactile features.

What do you watch out for while evaluating works?
As high design quality is a given, for me relevance was a priority. Does the medium suit the person for whom it is intended? Does it speak to them? The deciding factor is an innovative approach.

**What does being a juror for the
"red dot award: communication design" mean to you?**
As the editor-in-chief of an international design magazine, I am, of course, delighted to note the trends in quantity and quality that are apparent from the submissions. I often discover new studios and designers who are worth presenting. What is more, the exchange of views with my colleagues on the jury and their specialist knowledge and experience are enriching.

**A designer can stand out with an idealistic idea
or go with the flow of the client's wishes.
How do you see yourself in this situation?**
I am in the comfortable position that our customers are creative… But that does not necessarily mean that idealism and expectation exclude each other. Designers always have to walk a tightrope during a difficult economic period. It is ultimately a personal decision whether turnover or creativity takes priority. I find both completely acceptable. After all, graphic designers are not duty-bound to save the aesthetics of our world, even though they could make a big contribution to doing so.

**Is there a special time of day
when you are exceedingly creative?**
Just before I go to sleep, when thoughts are free and flying around in my head, I often get back on my feet and get stuck at the laptop.

**What special advice would you give
to a talented young designer entering this field?**
I think that nobody summed it up better than Walt Disney: If you can dream it, you can do it.

01 / 02

JENNIFER TSAI
TAIWAN

01 **Pomelo-shaped mooncake gift box**
The packaging design shows special printing techniques expressing the haptic feeling of a real citrus peel. Before opening the box, one may savour the ambience of the Mid-Autumn Festival in the prime season for pomelos.

02 **GeneHerbs**
Packaging design for the nutritional supplement "Ginseng Royal Jelly" which with the smooth paper in pure tones and meaningful graphics of traditional herbs invokes associations with lightness and health.

Jennifer Tsai has been the director of the management and the creative department of Proad Identity since 1987. She was placed among the Top Ten at the Business Excellence Awards in Taiwan, made it into the Top 100 of Outstanding Business Women in China and received the Glory of Taiwan award from the President of Taiwan in 2011.

She has more than 20 years of brand design expertise and management experience. She specialises in branding and corporate identities and has worked with many famous enterprises and brands in Asia.

Jennifer Tsai has devoted herself to present the Eastern elements in Western designs and worked on linking the international alliances and associations such as Global Design Source and European Packaging Design Association.

— I WAS INSPIRED BY A LOT OF GOOD DESIGN WORKS FROM TALENTED DESIGNERS FROM ALL OVER THE WORLD.

How did you experience this year's jury process?
It is a great experience to be a jury member of the red dot design award. I was inspired by a lot of good design works from talented designers, coming from all over the world. Even during the judging process, there were different points of view due to the fact that the jury members come from different countries. But I think that this is also one of the best parts of the jury's work because through this "differentiation", we get a strong impact on our audience.

What do you watch out for while evaluating works?
I always pay more attention to the "new idea" because, in these times of the Internet, we have too many ideas that always look too similar! And I also care about the meaning behind the design.

**What does being a juror for the
"red dot award: communication design" mean to you?**
The red dot design award has already been recognised worldwide as the most authoritative design award; thus, it is a great honour and it meant a lot to me to become a red dot juror.

**A designer can stand out with an idealistic idea
or go with the flow of the client's wishes.
How do you see yourself in this situation?**
To me, the meaning of good design does not include just a good piece of work; it also should have the capacity to create a deeper value for the client.

01

ROB VERMEULEN
NETHERLANDS

01 **Bio Bandits**
Contemporary brand and
packaging design for organic
sauces and dressings.
[Bottles, 2011]

02 **Gulpener Biologisch /
Gulpener Organic**
Creation of a new sub-brand for
the Gulpener Bierbrouwerij.
[Packaging Redesign, 2012]

Rob Vermeulen, born in 1952, studied free art at the Academy of Arts in Breda, before changing to a design degree course at the Academy of Arts in Maastricht. In 1976, he founded his own firm which had its focus on corporate and packaging design and quickly gained international recognition.

In 2005, he sold his company to Total Identity, but remained a member of the board of directors. In 2009, Rob Vermeulen finally separated from Total Identity and founded a new design agency, Vermeulen / Brand Design. In addition to his everyday work, since 1993 he is committed to the European Packaging Design Association (epda), the president of which he was from 2003 to 2006. Furthermore, he is a member of the Dutch design associations BNO and Creating Brands.

He gives presentations and works as a lecturer in the fields of communication and brand design at different institutes in Europe. Moreover, he is a member of several international expert juries.

02

— START NETWORKING, CONNECT THE SUPPLY CHAIN AND WORK IN TEAMS, IS MY ADVICE TO YOUNG DESIGNERS.

How did you experience this year's jury process?
For me, it is important to see that creativity never stops to develop itself. Even in difficult economic periods, creativity is used to diversify products and companies, even when budgets are cut. This is for me the real creative challenge.

What does being a juror for the "red dot award: communication design" mean to you?
You have to know the market, to be connected with the design community. An open mind is a must in order to climb in the concepts. It makes me feel years younger, by the way.

A designer can stand out with an idealistic idea or go with the flow of the client's wishes. How do you see yourself in this situation?
Design is no autonomic art. You always act in a reaction to a demand. It can be a client or yourself but a good design has to fulfil a wish or briefing.

Is there a special time of day when you are exceedingly creative?
It is more about the comfort zone and not the time. Nice wine, good and nice people around you, and for me, my car is my castle, where I get most of my ideas!

What special advice would you give to a talented young designer entering this field?
Start networking, connect the supply chain and work in teams as much as possible, even with people from the client side.

esign museum

Packaging Design

Event Design

Information Design /
Public Space

Corporate Films

TV, Film & Cinema

Index Clients/
Universities

0–9
100 Beste Plakate e. V.
www.100-beste-plakate.de
Vol. 2: 154

A
adidas AG
www.adidas.com
Vol. 2: 142, 188–189
Vol. 1: 144–145, 420–421

Adris Group
www.adris.hr
Vol. 2: 141

Aekyung Industry
www.aekyung.co.kr
Vol. 2: 34

Alape GmbH
www.alape.com
Vol. 2: 135
Vol. 1: 189

Amnesty International
Sektion der Bundesrepublik
Deutschland e.V.
www.amnesty.de
Vol. 2: 182–183

AMOREPACIFIC
Corporation
www.amorepacific.co.kr
Vol. 2: 35
Vol. 1: 396

Antikensammlung der
Staatlichen Museen
zu Berlin
Collection of Classical
Antiquities of the National
Museums in Berlin
www.smb.museum/smb/
sammlungen
Vol. 2: 139

Asia University
www.asia.edu.tw
Vol. 2: 376–377, 382–383

ASUSTeK Computer Inc.
www.asus.com
Vol. 2: 91, 210

AU Optronics Corporation
www.auo.com
Vol. 2: 108, 109

AUDI AG
www.audi.de
Vol. 2: 112–113, 128–129,
136, 209, 298
Vol. 1: 178, 179, 190,
278–279

B
Bauhaus Film-Institut
www.uni-weimar.de
Vol. 2: 394–395

Beauté Prestige
International
www.bpi-sa.com
Vol. 2: 27

Beauty Studio Therapy
ARKHE Beauty Salon
www.arkhe.jp
Vol. 2: 146–147

Beetroot Design Group
www.beetroot.gr
Vol. 2: 256

BFF
Bund Freischaffender
Foto-Designer e.V.
www.bff.de
Vol. 2: 92

Biblia Chora Winery
www.bibliachora.gr
Vol. 2: 84

Biologische Präparate
Dr. Groß GmbH
www.dr-gross.com
Vol. 2: 55

BKKC
Brabants Kenniscentrum
voor Kunst en Cultuur
www.bkkc.nl
Vol. 2: 184–185

BMW AG
www.bmw.com
Vol. 2: 144–145, 247,
272–273, 282, 304

Böhm Stirling-Technik e. K.
www.boehm-stirling.com
Vol. 2: 211, 236

Brunner GmbH
www.brunner-group.com
Vol. 2: 140

Busch-Jaeger Elektro
GmbH
www.busch-jaeger.de
Vol. 2: 297

C
CarbonSports GmbH
www.lightweight.info
Vol. 2: 248

Centraal Museum Utrecht
www.centraalmuseum.nl
Vol. 2: 238

China Tours Hamburg
CTH GmbH
www.chinatours.de
Vol. 2: 234

CJ Cheiljedang
www.cj.net
Vol. 2: 50

Closed GmbH
www.closed.com
Vol. 2: 98

D
Da-Yeh University
www.dyu.edu.tw
Vol. 2: 340–341

Daimler AG
www.daimler.com
www.mercedes-benz.com
Vol. 2: 10–15, 118–119, 124,
125, 127, 239, 249, 267
Vol. 1: 185, 275, 368, 416

DART
Beratende Designer GmbH
www.dartwork.de
Vol. 2: 201

Daum Communications
http://info.daum.net/
DaumEng
Vol. 2: 190–191

Dauro Oliveira
Orthodontics Clinic
dauro.bhe@gmail.com
Vol. 2: 180–181

DB Mobility Logistics AG
www.deutschebahn.com
Vol. 2: 218–219, 228–229

Gunter Demnig
www.stolpersteine-online.
com
Vol. 2: 260

Deutsche Bank AG
www.db.com
www.pass-on-your-passion.
com
Vol. 2: 252–253

Deutsche Lufthansa AG
www.lufthansa.com
Vol. 2: 132

Deutsche Telekom AG
www.telekom.com
Vol. 2: 290, 291

Deutscher Bundestag
German Bundestag
www.bundestag.de
Vol. 2: 305

Deutscher
Caritasverband e.V.
www.caritas.de
Vol. 2: 214–215

Deutsches Rotes Kreuz
German Red Cross
www.drk.de
Vol. 2: 261

Deutschlandradio
www.dradio.de
Vol. 2: 292

DIF Deutsches Filminstitut
www.deutsches-filminstitut.
de
Vol. 2: 158

Discovery Networks
Asia-Pacific
www.discoverychannelasia.
com
Vol. 2: 224–225

Drift Innovation
www.driftinnovation.com
Vol. 2: 94

DROOM /
DESIGN YOUR ROOM
DROOM GmbH & Co. KG
www.droom.de
Vol. 2: 262

Dutch Ministry of Infra-
structure and the Environment (Rijkswaterstaat)
www.rijkswaterstaat.nl
Vol. 2: 184–185

Dutch National Ballet
www.hetballet.nl
Vol. 2: 240

Dutch Province
of Noord-Brabant
www.brabant.nl
Vol. 2: 184–185

E
E-Plus Mobilfunk GmbH
www.base.de
Vol. 2: 265

EDG Entsorgung
Dortmund GmbH
www.entsorgung-dort-
mund.de
Vol. 2: 131
Vol. 1: 282

Elastique.
www.elastique.de
Vol. 2: 257

Elegant Querulant
Vol. 2: 351

Esporão S.A.
www.esporao.com
Vol. 2: 83, 85

Etude Co., LTD, Seoul
www.etude.co.kr
Vol. 2: 22–23, 24, 25

EURO-VAT spol, s r.o.
www.eurovat.sk
Vol. 2: 90

Europcar
Autovermietung GmbH
www.europcar.com
Vol. 2: 174–175

European Parliament
Parlamentarium
www.europarl.europa.eu/
visiting
Vol. 2: 160

F
Fachhochschule Bielefeld
University of Applied
Sciences Bielefeld
www.fh-bielefeld.de
Vol. 2: 346–347

Fachhochschule Dortmund
University of Applied Sciences
and Arts Dortmund
www.fh-dortmund.de
Vol. 2: 385

Fachhochschule
Düsseldorf
University of Applied
Sciences Düsseldorf
www.fh-duesseldorf.de
Vol. 2: 356, 357, 392–393

Scholz & Volkmer GmbH
www.s-v.de
Vol. 2: 243

School of the Art Institute
of Chicago
www.saic.edu
Vol. 2: 364–365

Schule für Gestaltung
Ravensburg
School of Design
Ravensburg
www.sfg-ravensburg.de
Vol. 2: 332–333

Selux AG
www.selux.com
Vol. 2: 237

Shu-Te University
www.stu.edu.tw
Vol. 2: 372, 384

simINN GmbH
www.siminn.de
Vol. 2: 171

Skin Concept AG
www.skinconcept.ch
Vol. 2: 30–31

Sports Tracking
Technologies
www.sports-tracker.com
Vol. 2: 293

Staatliche Hochschule
für Gestaltung Karlsruhe
University of Arts
and Design Karlsruhe
www.hfg-karlsruhe.de
Vol. 2: 358–359

Städel Museum
www.staedelmuseum.de
Vol. 2: 193
Vol. 1: 46

Stichting Kunst langs de
A50
Vol. 2: 184–185

SuperTrash
www.supertrash.com
Vol. 2: 263

Daniel Swarovski
Corporation AG
www.swarovski.com
Vol. 2: 150–151

SWR
Südwestrundfunk
www.swr.de
Vol. 2: 314

T
T.D.G. Vertriebs
GmbH & Co. KG
www.deli-garage.com
Vol. 2: 59, 97
Vol. 1: 34–35, 314

T.D.G. Vertriebs UG
(haftungsbeschränkt)
& Co. KG
www.deli-garage.com
Vol. 2: 68

Telefónica Germany
GmbH & Co. OHG
www.telefonica.com
Vol. 2: 254–255

Temasek Polytechnic
School of Design
www-des.tp.edu.sg
Vol. 2: 390–391

The Deli Garage
www.deli-garage.com
Vol. 2: 47
Vol. 1: 422–423

Tinti GmbH & Co. KG
www.tinti.eu
Vol. 2: 26

Tiroler Landesmuseum
Tyrolean State Museum
www.tiroler-landesmuseum.
at
Vol. 2: 159

Troi GmbH
www.troi.de
Vol. 2: 288–289

Tropenhaus Frutigen AG
www.tropenhaus-frutigen.
ch
Vol. 2: 40

Trurnit & Partner Verlag
www.trurnit-filmmedien.de
Vol. 2: 202

Tzukuan Fisheries
Association
www.eatfish.org.tw
Vol. 2: 42

U
undSchwieger
www.undschwieger.com
Vol. 2: 315

University of Seoul
www.uos.ac.kr
Vol. 2: 330–331

Uzin Utz AG
www.uzin-utz.de
Vol. 2: 155

V
Vet-Concept
GmbH & Co. KG
www.vet-concept.de
Vol. 2: 45

VS Vereinigte Spezialmöbelfabriken GmbH & Co. KG
www.vs-moebel.de
Vol. 2: 250–251

W
Wagner System GmbH
www.wagner-system.de
Vol. 2: 222

Woongjin Coway Co., Ltd.
www.coway.co.kr
Vol. 2: 285

World Excellent Products
www.fiveoliveoil.com
Vol. 2: 70

WWF Germany
www.wwf.de
Vol. 2: 232–233

X
Xue Xue Institute
www.xuexue.com.tw
Vol. 2: 66–67

Y
Yang Da Biotec Co., Ltd.
www.yangda.com.tw
Vol. 2: 74–75

Z
z zg Zentrum Zeitbasierte
Gestaltung
FH Mainz/HfG Schwäbisch
Gmünd
www.moving-types.com
Vol. 2: 162–163

Ljubo Zdjelarević
ljzdjelarevic@yahoo.com
Vol. 2: 73

Zweifel Pomy-Chips AG
www.zweifel.ch
Vol. 2: 56

red dot design award

red dot design award –
the qualification platform for the best in design and business worldwide

With more than 15,000 entries from more than 70 nations, the red dot design award is one of the largest and most prestigious design competitions in the world today. Divided into three disciplines, "red dot award: product design", "red dot award: communication design", and "red dot award: design concept", this annual competition gives designers, agencies and companies from a diverse range of industries the opportunity to have their latest works and products assessed and adjudicated by an independent expert jury.

As a qualification platform for innovations emerging worldwide in areas such as furniture, lamps, automobiles, jewellery, fashion and accessories, life science and consumer electronics as well as corporate branding, packaging, advertising, posters, book publications, event design, games, apps, sound and virtual design the red dot design award identifies the most outstanding design achievements of each year. It thus not only provides orientation in a market that is becoming increasingly complex, but also – and above all – creates differentiation: products, works and concepts that are awarded a red dot rank among the best in their field worldwide.

The sought-after quality label for design excellence allows the award-winning works to stand out from the myriad of competitors and can thus significantly contribute to a company's or a brand's success in the global market.

Proud winners

The history of the competition dates back to 1955, when the Haus Industrieform in Essen, Germany, selected products with exemplary design for an exhibition. The strict assessment criteria adopted at the time laid the foundation for today's consistent guideline to award only designs of exceptional achievement. The red dot design award has thus become one of the most important trend barometers of our time, based on an infallible strength of judgement that continues to set standards today: those who win an award in this competition belong to the international crème de la crème.

The red dot design award has developed such high international renown thanks to its initiator, the design expert Prof. Dr. Peter Zec. Under his leadership, the competition was given a new name and a new face in 1992 – the basis for a quality seal that can be communicated internationally and for which designers and companies from all around the world have competed since.

"red dot award: communication design"
the competition for outstanding and innovative design achievements

In 1993, the Wettbewerb für Produktdesign (Product Design Competition) was complemented by the Deutscher Preis für Kommunikationsdesign (German Prize for Communication Design). Known since 2001 as the "red dot award: communication design", it has become one of the major, internationally recognised competitions in the industry today, and, with this year's 21 categories, comprises all the relevant areas in current communication design.

In detail, designs were awarded in the following categories: Corporate Design, Annual Reports, Advertising, Packaging Design, Editorial, Magazines & Daily Press, Typography, Illustrations, Posters, Event Design, Information Design/Public Space, Online Communication, Online Advertising, E-Commerce Design, Games & Electronic Art, Interface Design, TV, Film & Cinema, Corporate Films, Sound Design & Sound Branding, Mobile & Apps as well as Social Media Design. The entries are selected following strict criteria. Only those that meet the high requirements with regards to innovative achievement and quality of design as well as realisation and execution receive an award. The winners are decided by an international jury that is committed to absolute impartiality and determines the award winners by democratic vote. With its high competence and sophisticated judgement it guarantees the competition's extraordinary quality and contributes to its excellent reputation.

www.red-dot.de

Since 2011, the awards ceremony of the "red dot award: communication design" has been held in the Konzerthaus Berlin. From 25–28 October 2012, the award-winning design achievements will be presented to the broad public as part of the special exhibition "Design on stage – winners red dot award: communication design 2012", held in the Alte Münze Berlin in the capital of Germany. Subsequently, all works honoured with a "red dot: grand prix" or a "red dot: best of the best" will be shown in the red dot design museum in Essen for one year. The red dot design museum houses the world's largest collection of contemporary design and attracts over 180,000 visitors each year.

red dot online –
design portal, presentation platform and research tool for a worldwide audience

One of the red dot design award's pivotal communication tools is the website www.red-dot.de. As one of the most interesting and most frequently visited industry forums in the world it presents the varied activities of the competition and presents the red dot winners to the general public in the online exhibition. Furthermore, it provides information on the latest news, trends and highlights from the international design scene and at the same time serves as a research tool and a source of inspiration.

red dot design museum –
a unique exhibition and communication forum in a fascinating ambience

With its approximately 1,500 exhibits, the red dot design museum in Essen is considered the largest exhibition of contemporary design worldwide. The products awarded a red dot are presented in the former boiler house of the Zeche Zollverein which has been redesigned by Lord Norman Foster into a unique presentation and communication forum. The crowd puller at the UNESCO World Heritage Site offers, together with the red dot design museum in Singapore, a wide range of opportunities to present the selected design innovations and to make the activities of the red dot design museum accessible to a wide audience.

red dot edition –
publisher of sophisticated design publications

The yearbooks of the red dot design award document the latest developments and trends in the industry. For many years now, they have been widely regarded as international reference works for outstanding design. The on-site publishing house, red dot edition, also publishes additional high-grade compendia and professional publications around the subject of design.

red dot design museum, Essen

Editor
Peter Zec

Project and editorial management
Dijana Milentijević

Project assistance
Sarah Hockertz
Jennifer Bürling
Theresa Falkenberg

Contributing writers
Kirsten Müller (supervision), Essen
Bettina Derksen, Simmern
Bettina Laustroer, Rosenheim
Karin Kirch, Essen
Mareike Ahlborn, Essen

contribution writer
"red dot: agency of the year"
Kristina Halilovic

contribution writer
"red dot: client of the year"
Burkhard Jacob

Editorial board
Kristina Alexandra Halilovic
Marie-Christine Sassenberg
Achim Zolke
Jörg Zumkley

Proofreading
Klaus Dimmler (supervision), Essen
Jörg Arnke, Essen
Dawn Michelle d'Atri, Kirchhundem
Karin Kirch, Essen
Regina Schier, Essen

Translation
Heike Bors, New York, USA
Stanislaw Eberlein, New York, USA
Bill Kings, Wuppertal
Cathleen Poehler, Montreal, Canada
Jan Stachel-Williamson, Christchurch,
New Zealand
Philippa Watts, Exeter, Great Britain

Photographs Jury
Peter Nierhoff, Cologne
Vol. 2, page 470-499

Photographs winning works
Die Neue Sammlung –
The International Design Museum
(Alexander Laurenzo), Munich
Vol. 2, page 492

Gewista Werbegesellschaft, Vienna
Vol. 1, page 46

Paris Mexis, Athens, Greece
Vol. 1, page 430

Präsenz Schweiz, Bern, Switzerland
Vol. 2, page 138

Steiner Sarnen Schweiz
Vol. 2, page 137

TAMSCHICK MEDIA+SPACE GmbH, Berlin
Vol. 2, page 137, 138

Rainer Viertlböck, Munich
Vol. 2, page 493

Layout
Prometheus GmbH
Verlags-, und Kommunikationsgesellschaft,
Wuppertal

Production and lithography
tarcom GmbH, Gelsenkirchen
Bernd Reinkens (Production Management)
Gregor Baals (DTP, Image Editing)
Jonas Mühlenweg (DTP, Image Editing)

Printing
Dr. Cantz'sche Druckerei Medien GmbH,
Ostfildern

Bookbindery
BELTZ Bad Langensalza GmbH,
Bad Langensalza

multimedia special (DVD)
Prometheus GmbH
Verlags-, und Kommunikationsgesellschaft,
Wuppertal

Publisher + worldwide distribution
red dot edition
Gelsenkirchener Straße 181
45309 Essen
Germany
Phone +49 201 8141-822
Fax +49 201 8141-810
woell@red-dot.de
www.red-dot.de
www.red-dot-store.de
Verkehrsnummer: 13674

ISBN: 978-3-89939-140-4

© 2012/2013 red dot GmbH & Co. KG
Printed in Germany

Bibliographic information published
by the Deutsche Nationalbibliothek
The Deutsche Nationalbibliothek
lists this publication in the Deutsche
Nationalbibliografie; detailed bibliographic data are available in the Internet
at http://dnb.ddb.de

The competition "red dot award:
communication design" is the
continuation of the "German Prize
for Communication Design". The
"international yearbook communication
design" is the continuation of the
"red dot communication design yearbook".